An Illustrated Account of

Common Chinese Characters

(Second Edition)

www.royalcollins.com

An Illustrated Account of
Common
Chinese Characters

(Second Edition)

Edited by Xie Guanghui
Complied by Xie Guanghui, Li Wenhong, Xie Aihua, Zhao Zhiqing
Illustrated by Lao Wu, Chen Zheng, Chen Rong

Books Beyond Boundaries
ROYAL COLLINS

An Illustrated Account of Common Chinese Characters (Second Edition)

Edited by Xie Guanghui

First published in 2023 by Royal Collins Publishing Group Inc.
Groupe Publication Royal Collins Inc.
BKM Royalcollins Publishers Private Limited

Headquarters: 550-555 boul. René-Lévesque O Montréal (Québec) H2Z1B1 Canada
India office: 805 Hemkunt House, 8th Floor, Rajendra Place, New Delhi 110 008

Original Edition © Peking University Press

ISBN: 978-1-4878-0923-2

To find out more about our publications, please visit www.royalcollins.com.

Notes on the Second Edition

An Illustrated Account of Common Chinese Characters specifically described the origins and the evolutions of 651 commonly used Chinese characters, listing Chinese characters' shapes from the Oracle-Bone Inscriptions to today's Inscriptions. Each character in the book has an illustration according to its sources so that the readers can easily understand the history of Chinese characters' evolution and the original meaning. This book has been widely welcomed by the readers at home and abroad since its publication in 1997.

In this revision, we did some additions and deletions. Considering the development of Chinese characters' meaning, we appropriately explained some current meanings of these characters. Now, we have the book published in eight sections according to the meaning categories of Chinese characters: human body, organ, instruments, building, animal, plant, natural, and others.

Although the book is a popular book, we insist on explaining the characters' origins in accordance with their uses in classical records. Hence, these volumes not only have some values on Chinese characters research, but also are convenient for the general readers to better understand the origins and the evolutions of Chinese characters.

Department of Chinese Language & Linguistics
Peking University Press
September, 2017

Introduction

The Chinese script is one of the oldest and most widely used writing systems in the world. It has a history of five or six thousand years, and is used by about one fourth of the total population on the earth. The creation and evolution of Chinese characters is closely interwoven with the development of Chinese culture. Chinese characters are the basic carriers of the traditional Chinese culture and as an important tool for extending, spreading and exchanging ideas, they have played a tremendous role in the long history of the Chinese nation. One may well argue that without Chinese characters there would be no such splendid Chinese culture. In the world today, Chinese characters are not only indispensable to any Chinese user but also have an ever increasing important role to play in worldwide cultural development.

Anyone learning Chinese will have to learn the characters first. How to help learners master the characters efficiently, therefore, is a major task for Chinese language workers.

The Chinese script is an ideographic writing system, in which the form is related to the meaning directly. Hence the first step toward the mastery of Chinese characters is to learn the characteristics and regularity in their composition. It is a rule every student of Chinese characters must follow to base one's judgment of the original meaning of a character on its form, and only when that relation is clear can one go on to discuss its extended and shifted meanings.

In the study of the composition of Chinese characters, there is a traditional theory known as *Liu Shu* (six writings). That is, there are six types of characters in terms of their composition: pictographs, indicatives, ideographs, phonetic compounds, mutual explanatories and phonetic loans. Strictly speaking only the first four refer to the ways to compose Chinese characters, the last two are concerned with the ways to use them. The traditional view that *Liu Shu* is a summary of the different ways of composing characters, therefore, is not very accurate. Nevertheless the theory *Liu Shu* is basically correct in revealing the general pattern in the creation and development of Chinese characters. It may help learners to better understand the composition of Chinese characters and their original meanings, and thence use them more accurately.

1. Pictographs

A pictograph is a depiction of a material object. Chinese characters mostly originaled from picture writing. In other words, most Chinese characters were originally pictures of objects. However there is a fundamental difference between pictographs and pictures: the former, usually rough sketches of objects (e.g. 日 "sun," 月 "moon," 山 "mountain," 川 "river," 人 "man," 大 "big") or consisting of a characteristic part only (e.g. 牛 "ox," 羊 "sheep"), are much simpler than the latter. More important is that pictographs are associated with definite meanings and pronunciations, and have become symbolic. And as a result of increasing simplification and abstraction, pictographs of the later ages are quite different from their originals. Compared with those in the Oracle-Bone Inscriptions, pictographs in the Regular Script are no longer picturelike. In a sense they are not really pictographic, but simply symbdic.

Pictographs are based on the external form of material objects, but the abstract concepts in language are formless, which renders it impossible to picture them. This impossibility inevitably hinders the growth of pictographs, and that is why their number is limited. However, pictography remains the most important method of composing Chinese characters. The others are only developments on this basis: indicatives are mostly formed by adding indicating signs to pictographs, ideographs are usually made up of two or more pictographs, and phonetic compounds are also composed of two pictographs (or ideographs or indicatives), except that one of them specifies the meaning while the other represents the pronunciation.

2. Indicatives

Indication refers to the way to form abstract characters with indicating signs. There are two subtypes of indicatives: one is composed of a pictograph and an indicating sign, e.g. 刃 (knife-edge), 本 (root), 末 (treetop); the other is composed purely of abstract signs, e.g. 上 (on top of), 下 (underneath), 一 (one), 二 (two) and 三 (three).

Indicatives account for the smallest percentage of Chinese characters. The reason is that for most characters there are simpler ways of composition: characters referring to material objects may be composed pictographically and those expressing abstract concepts may be composed ideographically or by way of phonetic-compounding.

3. Ideographs

Ideographs are compounds, composed of two or more than two existing characters. In terms of structure, an ideograph is the composition of two or more characters side by side or one on top of another. In terms of meaning, an ideograph is also the composition of the meanings of its component characters. For example, a single character 木 stands for a tree, two trees together (林) refers to a group of trees—forest, and the character made up of three trees (森) means a place full of trees, a thick forest. And the character 休 consists of 人 (man) and 木 (tree), signifying that a man is taking a rest against a tree.

Ideographs are made up of two or more than two pictographs, hence they differ from each other in that the former are complex while the latter simplex. Compared with pictography and indication, ideography is more adaptable. Characters of various kinds may be composed in this way, whether they refer to material objects or express abstract concepts, depict static states or describe dynamic processes. The same pictograph may be used to form different ideographs with different pictographs, or with the same pictograph by appearing in diffent positions. Thus there are more chances of existing pictographs used in the composition of new characters. As a result there are much more ideographs than pictographs or indicatives in Chinese. Ideography was the most important way of composing characters before Phonetic compounds became popular. It was only because phonetic compounds, with a phonetic component, are more convenient to use that the importance of ideographs decreased. Some ideographs were even changed into phonetic compounds, e.g. 块 (the original complicated from being 塊), and some were replaced by phonetic compounds pronounced the same, e.g. 渺.

4. Phonetic compounds

A phonetic compound consists of a radical and a Phonetic. The radical indicates its semantic field and the phonetic is pronunciation. For example, phonetic compounds with 木 (tree) as the radical like 松 (pine), 柏 (cypress), 桃 (peach) are all names of trees; those with 手 (hand) as the radical like 推 (push), 拉 (pull), 提 (lift), 按 (press) all refer to actions performed by the hand. However the radical only shows the general semantic class of the character, not its specific meaning. The specific meanings of the characters sharing the same radical are differentiated by the phonetics they each have. The phonetics in some phonetic compounds may also be semantical, e.g. the phonetic 取 in 娶 is also meaningful in the sense of "take," hence the name ideographic-phonetic compounds. But as far as the majority of phonetic compounds are concerned, the phonetic is only phonetical, not semantical. For example, the phonetics 工 and 可 in 江 and 河 respectively are only indicative of their pronunciations, and have nothing to do with their meanings.

Compared with pictography, indication and ideography, phonetic compound is more flexible. There are many objects and abstract ideas which are difficult to express through pictography or ideography. For example, 鸟 is the general term for birds, but there are tens of thousands types of birds in the world, and it is impossible to differentiate each of them by way of pictography or ideography. In contrast this is easily achieved in phonetic compounding by adding different phonetics to the radical 鸟, e.g. 鸽 (pigeon), 鹤 (crane), 鸡 (chicken) and 鹄 (swan). Thus there is an enormous number of phonetic compounds in Chinese, and this number is growing larger and larger in the modern period. Statistics show that phonetic compounds accounted for 80% of the total characters in the *Origin of Chinese Characters* (Shuo Wen Jie Zi) of the Han Dynasty, 88% in *Aspects of the Six Categories of Chinese Characters* (Liu Shu Lüe) of the Song Dynasty, and 90% in *Kangxi (K'ang-hsi) Dictionary* of the Qing Dynasty. In the modern simplified form currently in use, phonetic compounds make up an even larger percent.

5. Mutual explanatories

Mutual explanation is a most dubious concept in the theory of *Liu Shu*. Numerous definitions have been offered, but none of them is definitive. According to Xu Shen's definition in his *Origin of Chinese Characters*, mutual explanatories are those which share the same radical, mean the same and are mutually explainable. For example, the characters 老 and 考, both of the age radical (老) and meaning the same, are mutual explanatories. Thus the *Origin of Chinese Characters* says, "老 means 考" and "考 means 老."

Strictly speaking, mutual explanation is a way to explain the meaning of characters through comparison. There is no new character created in this way. Hence mutual explanation is not a way of composing new characters, but a way of using existing ones.

6. Phonetic loans

Phonetic loan is also a way of using existing characters. Xu Shen defined it as a character which is used in a new sense on account of its pronunciation. In other words, it is an internal borrowing on the basis of pronunciation: a character is used in a new meaning which is expressed by a similar sound in the spoken form. In this way an existing character has acquired a new meaning, but no new character is created. Phonetic loan, therefore, is not a way of composing Chinese characters either.

At the early stage, there were quite a few phonetic loans in the writing system. As the number of existing characters at that time was limited, many concepts had to be expressed by phonetic loans. For example, the character 自 in the Oracle-Bone Inscriptions was Originlally a pictograph and referred to the nose, but it is now used in the sense of "self" as a result of phonetic loan. The character 来 in the Oracle-Bone Inscrip·tions was also a pictograph, referring to the wheat, but is now used in the sense of "come" as a phonetic loan.

This book is entitled the *An Illustrated Account of Common Chinese Characters*. The characters in the book, 651 in total, mostly have a high frequency of use. A few characters, which are not as frequently used, are also included for the purpose of presenting a complete picture of the characters in the same series, e.g. the character 镬 in the 鼎 series. In terms of composition type, most of the characters are pictographs, indicatives and ideographs. The few phonetic compounds included are developments of earlier pictographs or ideographs.

The 651 characters are classified on the basis of their meaning into categories of the human body, implements, buildings, animals' plants, nature, etc., under which there are specific classes, again based on the meaning. The arrangement of characters in this way is intended to help readers better understand the regularity and characteristics of character creation in the early stage, that is, people modeled the characters on all kinds of things, as close as the various parts of the human body and as distant as material objects like implements and buildings. In order to compose characters more rationally, they looked closely upward at the celestial bodies in the sky and downward at the configuration of the earth's surface. They observed the movements of animals and appearances of plants.

The original meaning of a character is determined in accordance with its form in ancient writing systems and its use in classical records. The emphasis is on the revelation of the relation between the original meaning and the shape of the character, the extended and shifted meanings are mentioned in passing. To show the original meaning of the characters more vividly, there is a picture, or rather a cartoon, accompanying the text for each character.

At the beginning of each entry, the character is represented by its simplified form in the Regular Script, after which is its original complicated form in brackets, and the variant, if any, is enclosed in square brackets. The phonetic transcription given shows how the character is pronounced when it is used in its original meaning or common meaning. We also emumerate the representative forms of the character in ancient writing systems, tracing it to its source. The characters 甲, 金 and 篆 beside the ancient forms are abbreviations of 甲骨文 (the Oracle-Bone Inscriptions), 金文 (the Bronze Inscriptions) and 小篆 (the Later Seal Character). In addition, 石 is short for 石鼓文 (the Stone-Drum Inscriptions) and 玺 is short for 古玺 (Ancient Seals).

To facilitate readers' use of the book, there are two indexes in it, one is in an alphabetical order of the characters in *Pinyin* and the other is in the order of the number of strokes in a character.

Xie Guanghui
Jinan University, Guangzhou

Contents

CHAPTER 3 INSTRUMENTS 89

CHAPTER 8   OTHERS   339

CHAPTER 1

HUMAN BODY

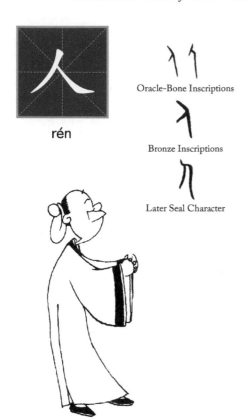

人

rén

Oracle-Bone Inscriptions

Bronze Inscriptions

Later Seal Character

There are many characters based on the shape of a human body, e.g. 大 representing the frontal view of a man on his feet, 人 the side view of a man on his feet, 尸 a man lying down, 卩 a man on his knees, 女 a woman, 长 an old man, and 儿 a child. The character 人 in ancient writing systems presents the side view of a man on his feet. It is a general term, referring to all mankind. Characters with 人 as a component are all related to the human race and their behaviour, e.g. 从 (to follow), 众 (many), 伐 (to attack), 休 (to rest), 伏 (to lie prostrate), 保 (to protect), and 介 (to interpose).

元

yuán

Oracle-Bone Inscriptions

Bronze Inscriptions

Later Seal Character

The original meaning of 元 was "the head of a man." In the early Bronze Inscriptions, 元 looks like the side view of a man on his feet, with the head especially prominent. In the Oracle-Bone Inscriptions and late Bronze Inscriptions, the part signalling the head is simply a horizontal stroke, on top of which a dot is added to indicate the position of the head in a human body. From "the head of a man" have derived its extended meanings of "the beginning" and "the first." That is why when an emperor changes his reign title, the first year is called 元年. And the first month in a year is 元月, the first day is 元旦. The beginning of an event is 元始. In addition, 元 could mean "original," though the more usual character for it now is 原.

bǐ

Oracle-Bone Inscriptions

Bronze Inscriptions

Later Seal Character

In ancient writing systems, the character 比 looks like two men standing together, one in front of the other. Its primary meaning, therefore, is "to stand side by side," "to get close to," from which have derived its extended meanings "to compare" and "to compete." And it can also mean "to gang up with," e.g. 朋比为奸 (to associate with for treasonable purposes).

cóng

Oracle-Bone Inscriptions

Bronze Inscriptions

Later Seal Character

In ancient writing systems, the character 从 looks like two men walking together, one in front of the other. Its primary meaning is "to follow," from which have derived the meanings "to heed" and "to obey." It can also mean "to be engaged in," e.g. 从军 (to join the army), 从政 (to go into politics) and 从事 (to go in for).

Oracle-Bone Inscriptions

Bronze Inscriptions

Later Seal Character

běi

In ancient writing systems, the character 北 looks like two men standing back to back, hence its original meaning "to be contrary to." When an army suffered a defeat, the soldiers all ran for their lives with their backs toward each other, so the character 北 has come to mean "to be defeated" as well. In addition, 北 is also used as a locative, meaning "the north," opposite to 南 (the south).

bìng

Oracle-Bone Inscriptions

Bronze Inscriptions

Later Seal Character

In the Oracle-Bone Inscriptions and Bronze Inscriptions, the character 并 looks like two men linked together. Its primary meaning is "to combine." But it may also be used as an adverb, meaning "all," "altogether" or "simultaneously."

zhòng

Oracle-Bone Inscriptions

Bronze Inscriptions

Later Seal Character

In the Oracle-Bone Inscriptions, the character 众 looks like a picture in which many people are tilling the soil in the scorching sun. In the Bronze Inscriptions and Later Seal Character, the sun part on top changes into an eye part, as if the labourers were slaves working under the close surveillance of a slave owner. So the original meaning of 众 was "masses of slaves," but it has evolved to mean a crowd of people, or simply, a large number (of people or of things).

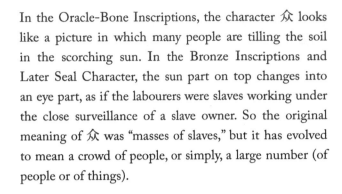

chǐ

Bronze Inscriptions

Later Seal Character

尺 is a measure of length, equal to ten 寸 or one tenth of 丈 in the Chinese System, and one third of a metre in the Metric System. In ancient times, these measures of length were based on the length of parts of a human body. In the Bronze Inscriptions, the character 尺 looks like a man with a sign on the shank, marking the length of 尺. In the Later Seal Character, the character has the same structure except some minor change in the shape. From its primary meaning has also derived the use of 尺 to refer to an instrument for measuring length—尺子 (ruler).

zuò

Ancient Script

坐

Later Seal Script

坐 means "to sit," especially "to sit on the ground." The character 坐 in the Ancient Script, as is recorded in the *Origin of Chinese Characters*, consists of two man parts and a ground part, signalling two men sitting face to face on the ground. The meaning "to travel by (a vehicle)" is one of its extended meanings.

diào

Oracle-Bone Inscriptions

Bronze Inscriptions

Later Seal Character

In the Oracle-Bone Inscriptions and Bronze Inscriptions, the character 吊 looks like a man around whom winds a long rope with a short arrow at its head. Its original meaning is unclear. In the Bronze Inscriprions, 吊 was often used to refer to one's father's younger brother. In some ancient records, it was used in the sense "to express one's condolences, sympathies." Nowadays, however, it usually means "to hang (something)."

zhòng/chóng

Bronze Inscriptions

Later Seal Character

重 is an ideograph. In the early Bronze Inscriptions, the character 重 consists of 人 and 东, like a man carrying a sack on his back strenuously, signalling that the sack is heavy. In the late Bronze Inscriptions, the two components 人 and 东 are combined, with no sign of a man carrying things on his back any more. The character 重 in the Later Seal Character, derivative from the Bronze Inscriptions, consists of 壬 (tǐng) and 东. In short, its primary meaning is "heavy," as against 轻 (light). Its extended meanings include "honest and kind," "serious" and "solemn." 重 can also be pronounced as chóng, meaning "to overlap" and "to repeat."

xiàn

Oracle-Bone Inscriptions

Bronze Inscriptions

Later Seal Character

臽 was the original form of 陷. In the Later Seal Character, the character 臽 looks like a man in a hole, signified by 臼. Its primary meaning is "to fall (into a hole)," but it can also be used as a noun, meaning "a hole," "a pitfall."

队

duì

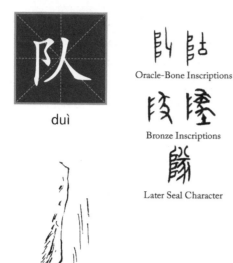

臥 訨
Oracle-Bone Inscriptions

陕 陸
Bronze Inscriptions

𨸏
Later Seal Character

队 was the original form of 坠 (zhuì). In the Oracle-Bone Inscriptions, the character 队 consists of a mound part and an upsidedown man part, signalling a man falling off a cliff. In the Bronze Inscriptions, the upside-down man part is changed into a pig part (豕). As a result, in the Later Seal Character, it becomes a phonetic compound with 阜 as the radical and 豕 as the phonetic. Its original meaning was "to fall down." This meaning, however, is now expressed by a later development 坠 (墜), as 队 is usually used in the sense of "a file of people," "a contingent."

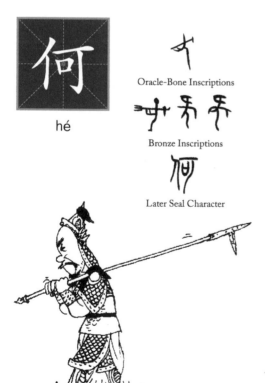

何

hé

丈
Oracle-Bone Inscriptions

丈 吊 吊
Bronze Inscriptions

何
Later Seal Character

The character 何 was originally an ideograph. In the Oracle-Bone Inscriptions and Bronze Inscriptions, the character 何 looks like a man marching with a dagger-axe on his shoulder. In the Later Seal Character it becomes a phonetic compound with 人 as the radical and 可 as the phonetic pronounced as. The original meaning of 何 was "to carry." But this meaning is now expressed by 荷 (hè), as 何 has come to be used as an interrogative pronoun or adverb, meaning "what," "who," "where," or "how."

yǒng

Oracle-Bone Inscriptions

Bronze Inscriptions

Later Seal Character

永 was the original form of 泳. In ancient writing systems, the character 永 looks like a man moving in the water, i.e. swimming. Later, this character came to be used in the sense of "a long river," and acquired the meaning of "long." Its original meaning is now expressed by a new character 泳.

qiāng

Oracle-Bone Inscriptions

Bronze Inscriptions

Later Seal Character

羌 is the name of a national minority in China, who lived in the northwest in ancient times. They were a nomadic tribe, living on the sheep. They wore clothes and hats made of sheepskin, and there were often woolen decorations on the hats. In the Oracle-Bone Inscriptions, the character 羌 looks like a man with woolen decorations on the head. Sometimes, there is a rope round the neck. This is a reflection of a fact that the Qiang and Han were enemies then, and the Qiang people would be taken prisoner and tied up when they were defeated.

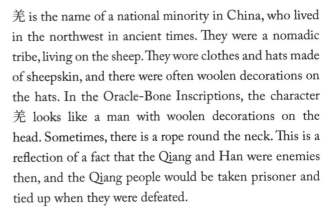

jìng

Oracle-Bone Inscriptions

Bronze Inscriptions

Later Seal Character

In the Oracle-Bone Inscriptions and early Bronze Inscriptions, the character 竞 looks like two men running shoulder to shoulder. Its primary meaning is "to strive to go ahead of sb. else," e.g. 竞逐 (to catch up and take the lead), and 竞走 (a heel-and-toe walking race). Its extended meanings include "to compete (竞争)" and "to contest (竞赛)."

pú

Oracle-Bone Inscriptions

Bronze Inscriptions

Later Seal Character

In the Oracle-Bone Inscriptions, the character 仆 looks like a man holding a winnowing pan. The part atop the man's head is 辛, an instrument of torture, signalling that the man is a prisoner of war or criminal, who has been put to torture. The tail at the buttocks of the man is a sign of insult. The dots above the winnowing pan represent the dust to be rid of. So the primary meaning of 仆 is "a slave who winnows or does other chores," e.g. 奴仆 (servant), and 仆人 (domestic servant).

shī

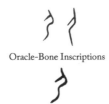

Oracle-Bone Inscriptions

Bronze Inscriptions

Later Seal Character

In the Oracle-Bone Inscriptions and Bronze Inscriptions, the character 尸 looks like the profile of a man lying upturned. Its primary meaning is "a corpse," "a dead body," that is why in the Regular Script there is the character 死 (dead) under 尸. In ancient times, the man who in the name of the dead accepted the sacrifice and worship at sacrificial rites was called 尸, and 尸 usually be acted by liegemen or the junior of the dead. Later the custom was changed. A memorial tablet or portrait of the dead was used instead. So this meaning is no longer current.

tún

Oracle-Bone Inscriptions

Later Seal Character

臀 means "buttocks." In the Oracle-Bone Inscriptions, the character 臀 looks like a man with a sign marking the position of the buttocks, similar to the composition of many other characters, such as 身 (body) and 肱 (the upper arm). According to the way of character's creation, 臀 in the Oracle-Bone Inscriptions is an indicative character. 臀 has gradually come to be a phonetic, compounded with 骨 (or 肉) as the radical and 殿 as the phonetic.

wěi

Oracle-Bone Inscriptions

Later Seal Character

In ancient times, people would dress up like wild animals, wearing horns on the head and attaching a tail at the buttocks, in order to get close to them and catch them. Later on these horns and tails became ornaments, people danced with these things on at ceremonies. In the Oracle-Bone Inscriptions, the character 尾 looks like a man with an ornamental tail at the buttocks. Its primary meaning is "the tail of an animal," from which have derived its uses to refer to the end of something or something at the back.

niào

Oracle-Bone Inscriptions

Later Seal Character

In the Oracle-Bone Inscriptions, the character 尿 looks like the side view of a man, and there are three dots in front standing for the urine passed from the body. In the Later Seal Character, the character 尿 is composed, differently from that in the Oracle-Bone Inscriptions, of 尾 (tail) and 水 (water). But they mean the same, i.e. "to urinate," or as a noun, "urine."

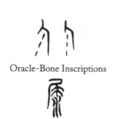

shǐ

Oracle-Bone Inscriptions

In the Oracle-Bone Inscriptions, the character 屎 looks like the side view of a man squatting. The dots under the buttocks stand for the excrement passed from the body. Hence 屎 means "excrement," "dung" or "droppings."

sǐ

Oracle-Bone Inscriptions

Bronze Inscriptions

Later Seal Character

In the Oracle-Bone Inscriptions, the left side of the character 死 looks like a man on his knees lowering his head, and the 歹 on the right stands for the skeleton of a dead man. This is a picture of the living mourning on his knees over the dead. Hence its meaning "to die," "to be dead." As anything dead will not be able to move, 死 is also used for things which are stiff, inflexible, e.g. 死板 (rigid), 死气沉沉 (lifeless), from which derives its meaning "to be determined," e.g. 死心塌地 (to be dead set).

葬

zàng

Later Seal Character

In the Later Seal Character, the character 葬 has a dead part (死) in between two grass parts (草), signalling that a dead man is buried in a wilderness of weeds. Hence the primary meaning is "to bury the dead." But it can also be used in a more general sense to refer to the ways to dispose of the dead, e.g. 火葬 (cremation), and 海葬 (sea-burial).

大

dà

Oracle-Bone Inscriptions

Bronze Inscriptions

Later Seal Character

In ancient writing systems, the character 大 looks like the frontal view of a man with the hands stretched out and the legs apart. Originally it referred to an adult or a man of lofty position. But now it refers to anything greater in size, volume, number, strength, hardness, etc., as opposed to 小 (small).

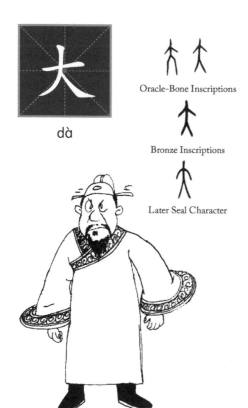

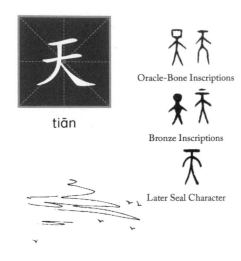

tiān

Oracle-Bone Inscriptions

Bronze Inscriptions

Later Seal Character

Similar to 元, 天 originally meant the head of a man. In the early Oracle-Bone Inscriptions and early Bronze Inscriptions, the character 天 looks like the frontal view of a man with the head especially prominent. Also like what happened to 元, this head was later simplified into a horizontal stroke, on which sometimes there was a dot to signal the position of the head. 天 originally meant the head of a man, or the top of the head, but it has gradually come to mean the sky above the human head, and even more generally the whole natural world. Anything that comes naturally may be called 天, e.g. 天文 (astronomy), 天气 (weather), 天险 (natural barrier), and 天然 (natural). Nowadays, 天 also means "day," e.g. 一整天 (the whole day), 今天 (today), and 明天 (tomorrow).

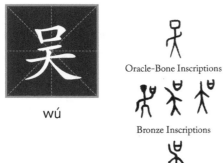

wú

Oracle-Bone Inscriptions

Bronze Inscriptions

Later Seal Character

吴 is a name of a place, also used as a name of a state or kingdom in ancient times. In the early West Zhou Dynasty, 泰伯, a son of the then king, came to live in 吴 (now known as 梅里 in Wuxi, Jiangsu Province). His descendants became powerful and established the first state named by 吴, which was destroyed by 越 (a state in present-day Zhejiang and Fujian) in 475 b.c.. The State of Wu occupied an area centred around Jiangsu, a place well-known for its handicrafts, such as earthware and ironware. That perhaps is the reason why the character 吴 in ancient writing systems looks like a man holding a piece of pottery on his shoulder. It's original meaning was the craftsman of making parthware.

夭

yāo

Oracle-Bone Inscriptions

Bronze Inscriptions

Later Seal Character

In the Oracle-Bone Inscriptions and Bronze Inscriptions, the character 夭 looks like a man running with his arms swinging forward and backward, hence its origianl meaning "to run." In the Later Seal Character, 夭 undergoes some change in its shape, looking like a man with his head tilted, and its meaning is changed as well. It has come to mean "to bend," "to break," from which has derived its meaning "to die young."

交

jiāo

Oracle-Bone Inscriptions

Bronze Inscriptions

Later Seal Character

In ancient writing systems, the character 交 looks like a man with his legs crossed, hence the primary meaning is "to cross," "to interlock." Its extended meanings include "to link" and "to associate with," e.g. 交界 (to have a common border), 交涉 (to negotiate), 交情 (friendship), 交心 (to open one's heart to), 交易 (transaction), and 交流 (to exchange).

wén

Oracle-Bone Inscriptions

Bronze Inscriptions

Later Seal Character

文 is a pictograph. In the Oracle-Bone Inscriptions and Bronze Inscriptions, the character 文 looks like the frontal view of a man with a tattoo on his chest. Hence the character 文 originally meant "a man with tattoos," from which have derived the meanings of "a decorative pattern" or lines. Its uses in words like 文字 (characters; script; writing), 文化 (culture), 文章 (article), and 文明 (civilization) are all later developments.

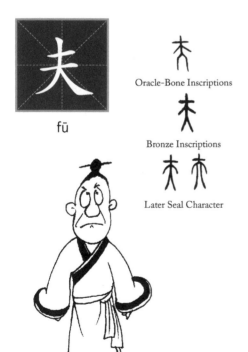

fū

Oracle-Bone Inscriptions

Bronze Inscriptions

Later Seal Character

In ancient times, it was a custom for a man of twenty to have his hair held together and to put on a hat, to show that he had reached manhood. The character 夫 consists of 大 and 一, the former meaning "man," and the latter representing the hair clasp which does the holding. In the Oracle-Bone Inscriptions and Bronze Inscriptions, the character 夫 looks like a man with his hair held together by a hair clasp. Its primary meaning, therefore, is "adult man." As a man is allowed to get married only after he has reached adulthood, 夫 also means "husband," in opposition to 妇 (woman) or 妻 (wife). An adult man would also have to serve as a forced labourer in ancient times, so 夫 is also used in the sense of "forced labourer," and more generally, any type of labourer, e.g. 渔夫 (fisherman) and 农夫 (farmer).

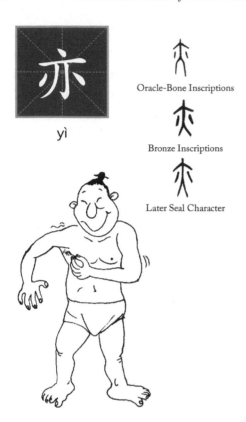

亦
yì

亣
Oracle-Bone Inscriptions

亣
Bronze Inscriptions

亣
Later Seal Character

亦 was the original form of 腋 (yè, armpit). In ancient writing systems, the character 亦 looks like the frontal view of a man with two dots under the arms showing the position of the armpits. As 亦 later came to be used as a function word, equivalent to 也 (too), another character 腋, with 月 as the radical and 夜 as the phonetic, was invented to replace 亦 for its original meaning.

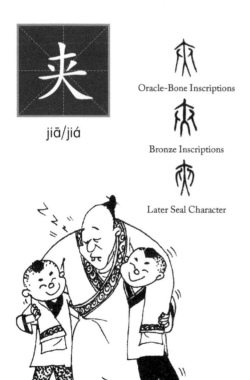

夹
jiā/jiá

夾
Oracle-Bone Inscriptions

夾
Bronze Inscriptions

夾
Later Seal Character

In ancient writing systems, the character 夹 looks like two small men supporting a big man in the middle, hence the primary meaning is "to help from the sides" or "to assist." In addition, it is used in the sense of "space between two things," e.g. 夹缝 (a space between two adjacent things) and 夹道 (passageway). And it can also be used to refer to things made up of two layers, e.g. 夹衣 (a traditional Chinese coat with a thick lining) and 夹被 (a quilt without the padding material in between).

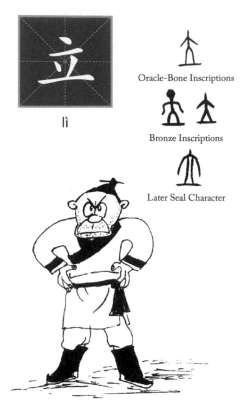

lì

Oracle-Bone Inscriptions

Bronze Inscriptions

Later Seal Character

In the Oracle-Bone Inscriptions and Bronze Inscriptions, the character 立 looks like the frontal view of a man on his feet, with a line underneath signalling the ground, hence the primary meaning is "to stand." "to set up" and "to establish" are its extended meanings, e.g. 立功 (to do a deed of merit), 立法 (to make a law), and 立威 (to build up one's prestige). In ancient times, the ascending of a new emperor to the throne was also called 立.

wèi

Oracle-Bone Inscriptions

Bronze Inscriptions

Later Seal Character

The character 位, consisting of 人 (man) and 立 (to stand), refers primarily to the place where a man stands, and the office of a king or the rank of a minister in particular. Thus the *Origin of Chinese Characters* says, "The position at court in which a man stands is known as 位." It is also used to refer to the capacity and status of a person, or more generally, to the location of anything.

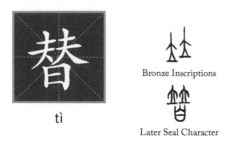

tì

Bronze Inscriptions

Later Seal Character

In the Bronze Inscriptions, the character 替 consists of two 立 and looks like two men in an arrangement of one in front of the other, signalling that one is to take the place of the other. Hence the character 替 primarily means "to replace," "to substitute for," from which have derived the senses "to discard" and "to be on the decline."

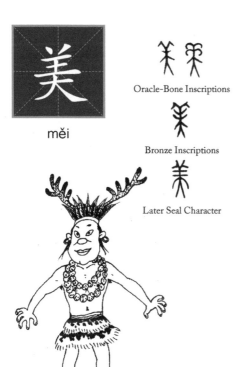

měi

Oracle-Bone Inscriptions

Bronze Inscriptions

Later Seal Character

In ancient times, people would wear horns or feathers on their heads in order to get close to wild animals and catch them. Later on horns and feathers of this type became decorations to be put on the head as a sign of beauty. This is the origin of the character 美 in the Oracle-Bone Inscriptions and Bronze Inscriptions, from which derived the later form of 美, consisting of 羊 (sheep) and 大 (man). That is to say a man with sheep horns on the head is regarded as beautiful. So, originally 美 meant the beautiful decorations of a person. Its use to refer to the looks, talents or virtue of a person is a later development. And its sense has also been extended to cover the sweet taste of food.

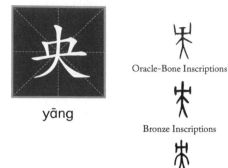

yāng

Oracle-Bone Inscriptions

Bronze Inscriptions

Later Seal Character

In the Oracle-Bone Inscriptions and Bronze Inscriptions, the character 央 looks like a man carrying something with a bamboo pole. As the things are hung from the two ends of the carrying pole, and the man is in the middle, the character 央 has the primary meaning of "middle," e.g. 中央 (central). But 央 can also mean "end," e.g. 长乐未央 (happy without end). Another extended meaning of 央 is "to ask earnestly," e.g. 央求 (to beg; to plead).

hēi

Bronze Inscriptions

Ancient Seals

Later Seal Character

In the Bronze Inscriptions, the character 黑 looks like a man sweating with heat from a fire and blackened with smoke from it. It is primarily used to refer to something blackened by smoke, and more generally, to anything that is black in colour, as against 白 (white). The colour of black is dim, so 黑 is also used in the sense of darkness, from which derive the further extended meanings of "secret" and "covered."

夷
yí

夷
Bronze Inscriptions

夷
Later Seal Character

夷 in ancient times was a general term for the national minorities in remote areas and foreigners. At that time the Han people regarded their own land as the centre, and despised and tyrannized other nationalities, who were often used as slaves or sacrifices. In ancient writing systems, these people were often referred to as 尸 (corpse), showing open contempt for them. On the other hand, the character 夷 in the Bronze Inscriptions looks like the frontal view of a man tied up with ropes, signalling that he has been captured and is used as a slave or sacrifice.

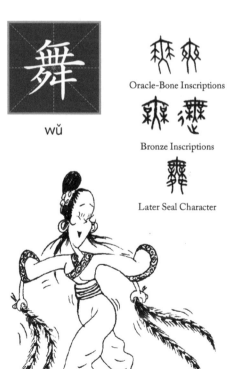

舞
wǔ

森 夾
Oracle-Bone Inscriptions

棘 懋
Bronze Inscriptions

舞
Later Seal Character

In the Oracle-Bone Inscriptions, the character 舞 looks like a man dancing with branches or ribbons in hand, hence the primary meaning is "to dance." As this character was often used in the sense of 无 ("without," the original complicated form being 無), in the Bronze Inscriptions, acomponent 辵 signalling the use of legs, was added to emphasize its primary meaning. In the Later Seal Character, on the other hand, a part representing two legs was added. So that 舞 and 无 (無) would no longer be confused. In addition, the character 舞 can also mean "to wave (舞动)" and "to wield (swords and spears) (舞弄)."

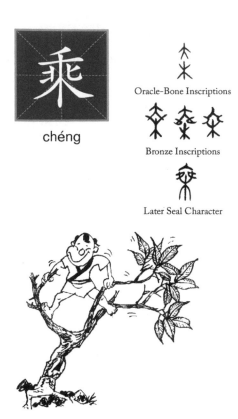

乘

chéng

Oracle-Bone Inscriptions

Bronze Inscriptions

Later Seal Character

It is said that in the remote ages, there was a sage called You Chao (Nester), who taught people to build nests on trees for homes, so as to protect themselves from the attacks of wild animals and floods. This primitive way of life, to dwell on tress, is known as nesting. In the Oracle-Bone Inscriptions and Bronze Inscriptions, the character 乘, in the shape of a man on top of a tree, is a vivid description of nesting. Hence the original meaning of 乘 was "to climb trees," from which have derived its extended meanings "to climb," "to ascend" and "to ride," e.g. 乘车 (to take a bus), 乘船 (to travel by boat) and 乘马 (to ride a horse).

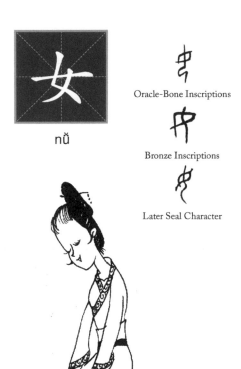

女

nǚ

Oracle-Bone Inscriptions

Bronze Inscriptions

Later Seal Character

女 means "female," opposite to 男 (male). In the old days, the female had a very low social status, and this is reflected in the form of the character 女. In the Oracle-Bone Inscriptions, this character looks like a woman on her knees, with her arms lowered and crossed, a show of complete subservience. In the later writing systems, the kneeling woman stands up, but her waist and legs are bent, still a posture displaying her meek and mild nature.

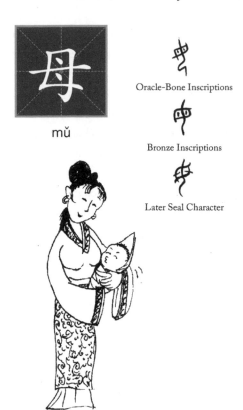

Oracle-Bone Inscriptions

Bronze Inscriptions

Later Seal Character

mǔ

In ancient writing systems, the character 母 looks like a woman on her knees, with her arms crossed in the front, and there are two dots on the chest representing the breasts. 母 primarily refers to a woman who has children, i.e. mother. From this sense, it has derived its use as a general term for senior females in the family, e.g. 伯母 (aunt), 祖母 (grandmother); and even more generally for all female animals, e.g. 母鸡 (hen) and 母牛 (cow). As mothers are able to produce the young, 母 may also be used in the sense of "origin."

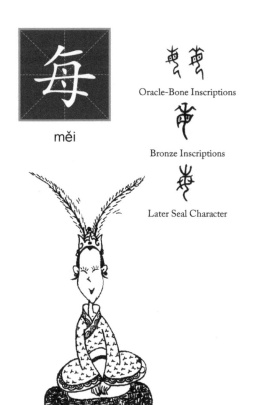

Oracle-Bone Inscriptions

Bronze Inscriptions

Later Seal Character

měi

In the Oracle-Bone Inscriptions, the character 每 looks like a woman on her knees, with her arms crossed in the front, and there are ornamental plumes on her head. In the Bronze Inscriptions, the shape of the character is changed, with two dots representing the breasts added. In other words, the lower part changes from the component 女 into 母, though the meaning is not changed, as it still signifies the female. In ancient times, it was a sign of beauty for a woman to have plumes on her head, similar to a man wearing animal horns on the head (as in the character 美), so 每 originally was used to refer to the beauty of a woman. The characters 每 and 美 were composed in the same way and had similar meanings, except that the former was used for women while the latter for men. Later on, the use of 美 spread and 每, in the sense of beauty, fell into disuse. It has come to be used as a function word instead, signalling "frequently," "every" or "each." And few people nowadays know its original meaning.

yāo/yào

Bronze Inscriptions

Later Seal Character

要 was the original form of 腰. In the Bronze Inscriptions, the lower part of the character, 女, stands for a human being, and the upper part looks like two hands on the sides, hence it refers to the waist of a person. In the Later Seal Character, the character 要, more picturelike than in the Bronze Inscriptions, looks like a person with arms akimbo. Though the original meaning of 要 was "waist," it is more usually used in the senses "to demand" and "to ask," e.g. 要求 (to demand), 要挟 (to coerse). As the waist occupies the central position in a human body, 要 pronounced as yào, also takes on the sense of "key position," from which have derived its senses of "important," "the main points" or "essentials."

qiè

Oracle-Bone Inscriptions

Bronze Inscriptions

Later Seal Character

In ancient times, prisoners of war and criminals were often used as slaves to do forced labour. The character 妾 in ancient writing systems consists of 女 (woman) and 辛 (an instrument of torture), signalling that this is a woman slave, who has been put to torture. So the original meaning of 妾 was a woman slave. The use of 妾 in the sense of concubine is an extended meaning. In the past, the character was also used by women as an expression of self-depreciation.

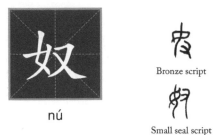

nú

Bronze script

Small seal script

In ancient times, slaves were usually prisoners of war or civilians captured from other tribes. In ancient writing systems, the character 奴 has the shape of a big hand in possession of a woman, hence its meaning is "woman slave," "servant-girl," or more generally, slave of any type.

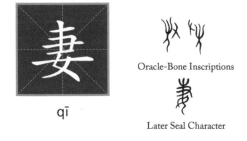

qī

Oracle-Bone Inscriptions

Later Seal Character

妻 refers to the spouse of a man, i.e. his wife. In ancient writing systems, the character 妻 looks like a man getting hold of a woman's hair. This is in fact a vivid description of the practice of marriage by capture at that time: a man would go to another tribe and abduct a woman as his wife. Since the wife was obtained by force, she would naturally have no position at home at all. It is only in civilized societies, where equality between men and women is a major concern, that wives are no longer taken by force.

hǎo/hào

Oracle-Bone Inscriptions

Bronze Inscriptions

Later Seal Character

In the traditional view, more children meant more happiness. And people were urged to observe filial piety, according to which among the three sins of an unworthy descendant, not to have any children was the biggest. So the first requirement of a good woman was to be able to bear children. The character 好 consists of 女 (woman) and 子 (child), signalling that for a woman to bear children constitutes what is good. The character 好, as an adjective, has the senses of "good" and "kind," as against 坏 (bad). It can also be used as a verb, pronounced as hào, meaning "to like," "to love," e.g. 好奇 (to be curious) and 嗜好 (to have a liking for).

qǔ

Oracle-Bone Inscriptions

Later Seal Character

娶 is both an ideograph and a phonetic compound. It consists of 取 (to get) and 女 (woman), meaning to take a woman to wife. The component 取 at the same time serves as the phonetic, in which case, 女 is seen as the radical, it thus is also a phonetic compound. 娶, for a man to get married with a woman, is opposite to 嫁, for a woman to get married with a man.

shēn

Oracle-Bone Inscriptions

Bronze Inscriptions

Later Seal Character

In the Oracle-Bone Inscriptions, the character 身 looks like a woman with a round abdomen, hence its primary meaning: to be pregnant. 身 also means the body of a human being or animal, with its extended meanings of "oneself," "personally" or "in person." Characters with 身 as a component all have to do with the body, e.g. 躬 (to bend forward; to bow), 躲 (to hide), 躺 (to lie down) and 躯 (the human body).

yùn

Oracle-Bone Inscriptions

Later Seal Character

In the Oracle-Bone Inscriptions, the character 孕 looks like the side view of a human body with 子 in the abdomen, signalling she is pregnant. In the Later Seal Character, the shape of the character is changed. The 子 inside the abdomen comes to the outside and the 人 also changes its form, ending up as an ideograph consisting of 乃 and 子 in the Regular Script. This character primarily means "to be pregnant," "to breed," but it is also used metaphorically to refer to the development of new things out of the existing ones.

育

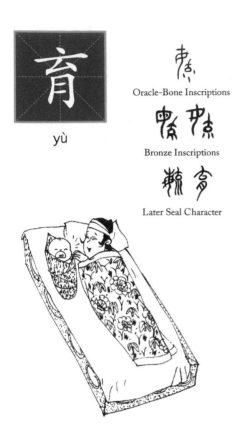

yù

Oracle-Bone Inscriptions

Bronze Inscriptions

Later Seal Character

In the Oracle-Bone Inscriptions and Bronze Inscriptions, the character 育 looks like a woman in the process of giving birth to a baby. Under the part signalling a woman, there is the component 子 with its head down signalling the newborn baby. The three dots underneath the baby signal the liquid coming along with it. 毓 was the original form of 育. The primary meaning of 育 is "to give birth to," but it is also used in the senses "to rear," "to raise" and "to bring up."

子

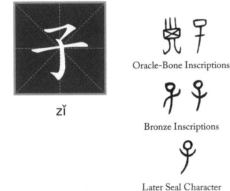

zǐ

Oracle-Bone Inscriptions

Bronze Inscriptions

Later Seal Character

In the Oracle-Bone Inscriptions and Bronze Inscriptions, the character 子 looks like a baby with a big head and a small body. In some writings, the baby in swaddling clothes is waving its arms. In others, the baby is on its feet, with very little hair and the fontanelles are not closed yet. The character 子 refers to baby, and descendants in general. But it is also used as a name of the first of the twelve Earthly Branches, a traditional Chinese system of sequence. Characters with 子 as a component most have to do with the baby or descendant, e.g. 孩 (child), 孙 (grand child), 孝 (filial piety), 孕 (to be pregnant) and 字 ([derivative] character).

Oracle-Bone Inscriptions

Later Seal Character

rǔ

In the Oracle-Bone Inscriptions, the character 乳 looks like a woman with nipples standing out and a baby in her arms, hence the primary meaning is "to breastfeed a baby." From this primary meaning derives the meaning of sucking or drinking in general, e.g. 乳血餐肤 (to suck blood and eat flesh). Its extended meanings include "milk," "breast," "to give birth to," and even "one who has just become a mother" or "newborn."

Bronze Inscriptions

Later Seal Character

zì

The character 字 consists of a house part (宀) and a baby part (子). In other words, it signals that there is a baby in a house, hence its original meaning is "giving birth to" and extended meanings is "raising" and "multiplying." In ancient times, the monadic pictographs were known as 文, while those made up of two or more monads were known as 字, in the sense that they were derivatives from monads. Nowadays, however, the two characters are no longer distinguished in this way, and 字 has become the general term for characters, or writing.

bǎo

Oracle-Bone Inscriptions

Bronze Inscriptions

Later Seal Character

A new-born baby, unable to stand on its own feet and walk, has to be put under the care of the adult. Usually the baby is carried in the arms or on the back. In the Oracle-Bone Inscriptions and early Bronze Inscriptions, the character 保 looks like a man carrying a baby on his back, with an arm stretched out to prevent it from falling. In other writing systems, the arm part is separated from the man part and becomes a dot on the right. To redress the balance, another dot is added on the left, resulting in a total destruction of the original picturelike image. In short, the original meaning of 保 was the same as 抱, i.e. to hold in the arms. The meanings "to take care of," "to raise" and "to bring up" are its earlier extended meanings, and "to protect," "to guard" and "to defend" are its later extended meanings.

ér

Oracle-Bone Inscriptions

Bronze Inscriptions

Later Seal Character

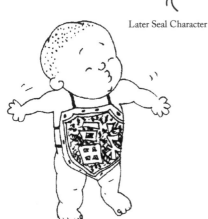

In ancient writing systems, the character 儿 looks like a baby with a big head and a small body, and the fontanelles are not closed yet. The *Origin of Chinese Characters* says, "儿 means baby. … like the fontanelles which have not been closed yet." Hence the primary meaning of 儿 is "little child." In ancient times, a boy was called 儿, and a girl 婴. But this distinction was not always kept and 儿 could sometimes refer to children of both sexes.

sūn

Oracle-Bone Inscriptions

Bronze Inscriptions

Later Seal Character

The character 孙 consists of 子 and 系. The former looks like a child and the latter is in the shape of a rope signalling connection. Hence the character 孙 signifies children in succession. 孙 primarily refers to the son of a son, i.e. grandson, but it is also used for the later generations, e.g. 曾孙 (great-grandson) and 玄孙 (great-great-grandson).

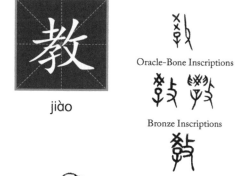

jiào

Oracle-Bone Inscriptions

Bronze Inscriptions

Later Seal Character

In ancient times, corporal punishment was a commonplace in education. The rod was regarded as a necessary instrument for teaching, as the saying goes "Spare the rod and spoil the child." The composition of the character 教 is a picturelike reflection of this practice. In ancient writing systems, its right part looks like a man holding a rod while the left is made up of 子 (child) and two crosses above representing counters for addition and subtraction. So the primary meaning of 教 is "to urge pupils to study," and it is more generally used in the senses of "giving guidance," "educating" and "teaching."

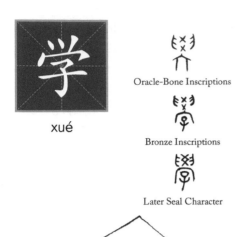

学

xué

Oracle-Bone Inscriptions

Bronze Inscriptions

Later Seal Character

学 is an ideograph. In the Oracle-Bone Inscriptions, the character 学 looks like a man setting counters in order to learn to do sums. In the Bronze Inscriptions, the component 子 is added to make it clear that it is a child who is learning to count. So its primary meaning is "to learn," and the senses of "learning," "theory" and "knowledge" are its extended meanings, e.g. 品学兼优 (of both good character and scholarship). It can also be used to refer to the place where one learns, i.e. school.

长

zhǎng/cháng

Oracle-Bone Inscriptions

Bronze Inscriptions

Later Seal Character

In the Oracle-Bone Inscriptions and Bronze Inscriptions, the character 长 looks like an old man with a walking stick in hand, and the long white beard on his chin is especially noticeable, hence the primary meaning is "old man." Its extended meanings include "senior" (older or of higher rank) and "chief." When it is used as a verb, it means "to grow," "to develop" and "to increase." 长 can also be pronounced as cháng, meaning "long."

老

lǎo

Oracle-Bone Inscriptions

Bronze Inscriptions

Later Seal Character

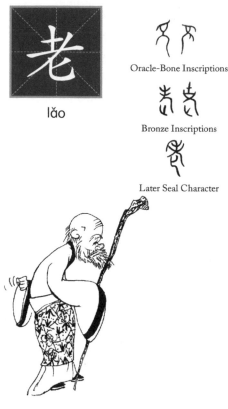

In the Oracle-Bone Inscriptions and Bronze Inscriptions, the character 老 looks like an old doddering man, back bent and a stick in hand, hence its primary meaning is "a man of old age." Its extended meanings include "old in age" contrasted with 少, 幼 (young), and "belonging to past times," contrated with 新 (new) or 嫩 (tender).

孝

xiào

Oracle-Bone Inscriptions

Bronze Inscriptions

Later Seal Character

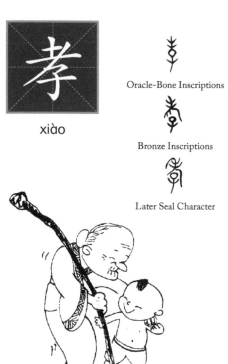

孝, filial piety, was one of the old moral concepts in Chinese feudal society, according to which children should be obedient to their parents at any time. In ancient writing systems, the character 孝 is made up of two parts: the upper part representing an old man with a long white beard and a bent back, and the lower part a child. The child is under the old man, suggesting that the former is helping the latter. To respect and help the old is one of the contents of filial piety. 孝 can also mean to observe certain codes of behaviour during the mourning period of one's seniors.

yīn

Bronze Inscriptions

Later Seal Character

In the Bronze Inscriptions, the character 殷 looks like a man giving an acupuncture treatment to a patient who has a swollen belly. Hence the original meaning is "medical treatment," from which derive the meanings "to treat" or "to adjust." In addition, 殷 also means "grand," "great number of" and "well-off."

xià

Bronze Inscriptions

Later Seal Character

In ancient writing systems, the character 夏 looks like a big man of strong limbs, who sticks out his chest with the hands on the sides. In ancient times, the Han people called themselves by the name 夏, or 华夏. The first dynasty in the Chinese recorded history is known as the Xia Dynasty. But nowadays the character 夏 is usually used as a surname. In addition, it is also used for the second season of the year, i.e. summer.

CHAPTER 2

ORGAN

页

yè

Oracle-Bone Inscriptions

Bronze Inscriptions

Later Seal Character

In the Oracle-Bone Inscriptions, the character 页 looks like a man with an enormous head, hence the original meaning was "the head of a man." Thus Xu Shen says in his *Origin of Chinese Characters*, "页 means head." Nowadays, however, the character 页 is usually used in the sense of leaf, especially as a sheet of paper in a book, or one side of a sheetpage, e.g. 册页 (an album of paintings or calligraphy) and 活页 (loose leaf). But characters with 页 as a component most have to do with its original meaning of "head," e.g. 颈 (neck), 项 (nape of the neck), 额 (forehead), 顶 (crown) and 须 (beard).

首

shǒu

Oracle-Bone Inscriptions

Bronze Inscriptions

Later Seal Character

In the Oracle-Bone Inscriptions, the character 首 is in the shape of a head, though it is more like a monkey's head than a man's. In the Bronze Inscriptions, the character 首 uses an eye and some hair to represent the head. So the primary meaning of 首 is a head, of a man or any animal. From this meaning derive the extended meanings of "leader," "beginning," "the first" and "the highest," e.g. 首届 (the first session), 首席 (chief), 首当其冲 (to be the first to be affected; to bear the brunt) and 首屈一指 (to come first on the list; to be second to none).

xiàn

Bronze Inscriptions

Later Seal Character

县 was the original form of 悬. In the Bronze Inscriptions, the character 县 is made up of a tree on the left and a head hanging from it with a rope on the right. In the Later Seal Character, the shape of the character has undergone some change. The left is an upside-down 首 (head), and the right 系 (to link). But it keeps the original meaning: "the hanging of a head" or "to chop off a head and hang it." The more general sense of the hanging of anything is its extended meaning. As 县 came to be used as a name of an administrative area—county later, a new character 悬 was created to take its place for the original meaning.

miàn

Oracle-Bone Inscriptions

Later Seal Character

In the Oracle-Bone Inscriptions, the character 面 has a big eye inside an outline of a face, hence the primary meaning is "face." However, in ancient times, 脸 (nowadays meaning the same as 面) and 面 meant differently. 脸 referred to the part between the eye and cheekbone on either side of the face, while 面 referred to the whole of the front of a head. That is why 面 can also be used for anything that is in the front, or in the outside.

yí

Oracle-Bone Inscriptions

Later Seal Character

颐 refers to the part of face known as cheek in English. In ancient writing systems, the character looks like the cheek of a face; in some of them there are even strokes representing whiskers. In the Regular Script, the part 页, signalling head, is added, to show that 颐 is part of a head. Apart from this sense, 颐 can also mean "to keep fit," e.g. 颐养 (to take care of oneself).

xū

Oracle-Bone Inscriptions

Later Seal Character

In ancient China, men were proud of their beautiful long beard. In the Bronze Inscriptions, the character 须 looks like a face with beard, hence its primary meaning is "beard." But it has come to take on the senses of "need," "must" and "should" as well.

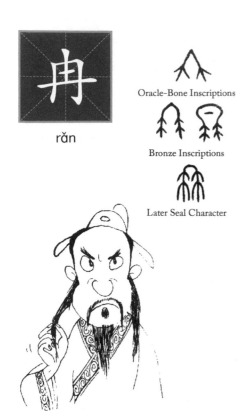

rǎn

Oracle-Bone Inscriptions

Bronze Inscriptions

Later Seal Character

冉 was the original form of 髯, referring to whiskers, sometimes to beard (known as 须) as well; though they were strictly kept apart at the beginning, 髯 referring to hair on the cheeks and 须 to that on the chin. In ancient writing systems, the character 冉 looks like hair growing on the two cheeks of a man's face. As whiskers are soft and hang down, the character 冉 has also taken on the senses of "soft" and "to hang down." And two 冉 used together means "slowly" and "gradually."

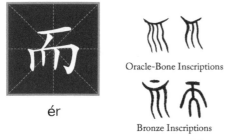

ér

Oracle-Bone Inscriptions

Bronze Inscriptions

Later Seal Character

In the Oracle-Bone Inscriptions and the Bronze Inscriptions, the character 而 looks like the beard on the chin fluttering in the wind, hence the original meaning was "beard." However this meaning is now usually expressed by 须. And the character 而 has come to be used instead as a pronoun, meaning "you"; or as a conjunction, meaning "and," "but," "if," etc.

Later Seal Character

nài

In ancient times, 耐 referred to a light form of punishment: to shave off the beard. The character 耐 consists of 而 and 寸, the former meaning "beard" and the latter "hand," hence the meaning "to take away beard by hand." However, the character has gradually come to be used in the sense "to tolerate" and "to bear," and its original meaning is no longer current.

méi

Oracle-Bone Inscriptions

Bronze Inscriptions

Later Seal Character

In the Oracle-Bone Inscriptions and Bronze Inscriptions, the character 眉 looks like either a man with his eye and eyebrow especially prominent, or is made up of simply an eye and eyebrow, hence the meaning "eyebrow." Since the time of the Later Seal Character, however, the character 眉 has undergone some change in its shape, and become less pictorial.

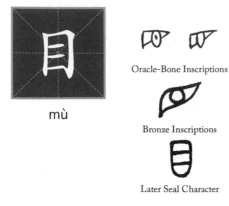

mù

Oracle-Bone Inscriptions

Bronze Inscriptions

Later Seal Character

目 is a pictograph. In the Oracle-Bone Inscriptions and Bronze Inscriptions, the character 目 is a vivid description of an eye. It was only used as a noun at the beginning, but later also used as a verb, meaning "to see things with the eye." The character 目 can also be used to refer to the holes of a fishnet, i.e. meshes, from which sense derive the senses of "clauses (of a document)," "entries (of a dictionary)" and "spicific items." Characters with 目 as a component all have to do with the eye and its function, e.g. 看 (to look at), 眉 (eyebrow), 相 (to appraise), 瞪 (to stare) and 瞥 (to shoot a glance at).

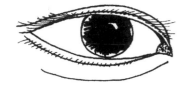

zhí

Oracle-Bone Inscriptions

Later Seal Character

In the Oracle-Bone Inscriptions, the character 直 has the shape of an eye with a straight line above it, signalling "to look straight ahead." Xu Shen says in his *Origin of Chinese Characters*, "直 means to look squarely at." Hence the original meaning of 直 was "to look straight ahead," "to look squarely at," from which have derived its extended meanings of "straight (opposite to 曲, bent)," "vertical (opposite to 橫, horizontal)," "honest," "fair-minded," "frank" and "direct."

mín

Bronze Inscriptions

Later Seal Character

In the old days, slave owners used extremely cruel methods to force slaves to work and to stop them from rebelling, e.g. to shackle them with heavy metal chains, to tie them together with ropes round their necks, to chop off one of their legs or to blind them with an awl. In the Bronze Inscriptions, the character 民 has the shape of an eye being pricked with an awl. So it was originally used to refer to slaves, but gradually its meaning was broadened to cover all the ruled, including freemen. Hence its present-day sense "common people."

máng

Ancient Seals

Later Seal Character

The character 盲 is both an ideograph and a phonetic compound. It consists of 亡 (without) and 目 (eye), signalling an eye without the pupil. On the other hand, 亡 is also its phonetic, representing its pronunciation. Xu Shen says in his *Origin of Chinese Characters*, "盲 means an eye without the pupil." An eye without the pupil will not be able to see things, hence its primary meaning is "blind."

shuì

Later Seal Character

The character 睡 is an ideograph. It consists of 目 (eye) and 垂 (to hang down), signalling to rest with one's head lowered and eyes closed. Xu Shen says in his *Origin of Chinese Characters*, "睡 means to sit dozing." Hence its original meaning was to sit dozing, but it has come to be used in the more general sense "to sleep."

相

xiàng/xiāng

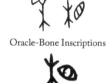

Oracle-Bone Inscriptions

Bronze Inscriptions

Later Seal Character

The character 相 is an ideograph. It consists of 木 (tree) and 目 (eye), signalling to look at the trees carefully. The primary meaning of 相 is to judge whether something is good by looking at its appearance. Later it came to mean the appearance, looks, of people or things. Besides, the character 相 can also mean to assist, and can be used as the name of a minister who assists the emperor. 相 pronounced as xiāng refers to the same actions performed by two or more than two parties and their influences on each other.

Later Seal Character

kàn

看 is a relatively new ideograph. It did not appear in the Oracle-Bone Inscriptions or Bronze Inscriptions. In the Later Seal Character, the character 看 consists of 手 (hand) and 目 (eye), signalling to look into the distance in the shade formed by a hand atop the eye. Hence its primary meaning is "to look far into the distance." But its meaning has gradually been extended to "observing and watching," and even further to "visiting the sick," or "visit in general."

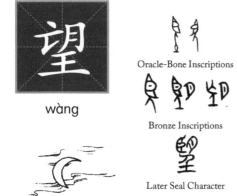

Oracle-Bone Inscriptions

Bronze Inscriptions

Later Seal Character

wàng

望 was originally an ideograph. In the Oracle-Bone Inscriptions, the character 望 looks like a man raising his head and looking into the distance on a mound. In the Bronze Inscriptions, there is also the part 月 (moon) on the upper right-hand, signalling to raise one's head and look at the moon. Hence the primary meaning of 望 is "to look up at" and "to look into the distance." As to look into the distance on a mound suggests expectation, 望 has also come to mean "to expect" and "to hope." Since the time of the Later Seal Character, the character 望 has undergone some change in its shape: the part representing eye 臣 is replaced by 亡 to indicate its pronunciation, resulting in a phonetic compound.

jiàn

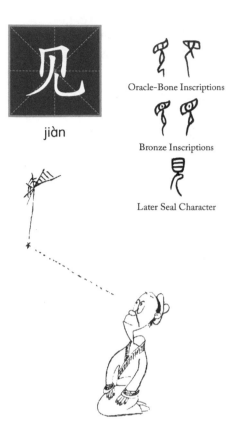

Oracle-Bone Inscriptions

Bronze Inscriptions

Later Seal Character

In ancient writing systems, the character 见 looks like a man with a big eye on the top, suggesting a man is staring at things. The primary meaning of 见 is to see, to sense something by the power of sight. Later on the sensing of something by other organs also came to be known as 见, e.g. 听见 (to hear), 见识 (knowledge) and 见解 (opinion). Besides, 见 can also be used as an auxiliary, expressing passive voice.

xiàn

Bronze Inscriptions

Later Seal Character

In the Bronze Inscriptions, the character 限 has a hill part on the left and a part depicting a man looking back on the right, suggesting that the man's sight is blocked by a hill and he is unable to look into the distance. So the primary meaning of 限 is "to block," "to obstruct," from which derive its senses "to limit" and "boundary." Besides, 限 can also be used to refer to the threshold, as it is a limit to the outsider.

Oracle-Bone Inscriptions

Bronze Inscriptions

Later Seal Character

chén

The original meaning of 臣 was man slave or captive. Thus *Shang Shu* (the Book of History) says, of slaves, "the male is called 臣 and the female 妾." From this meaning has derived its use to refer to servants. In the Oracle-Bone Inscriptions and Bronze Inscriptions, the character 臣 looks like a vertical eye. The reason is that at that time slaves were not allowed to raise their heads and look level ahead before their owners. They had to lower their heads and look upwards, hence the eye became vertical. As a vertical eye suggests submission and obedience, the character 臣 has also come to be used in these senses. In the old days all the people, including officials of various ranks, were subjects of the sovereign, so they all called themselves 臣 in front of the latter.

Later Seal Character

wò

The character 卧 consists of 人 (man) and 臣 (vertical eye), signalling a man lowering his head and looking upwards. In the Bronze Inscriptions, the character 卧, as shown in both 临 (臨) and 监 (監), has the shape of a man lowering his head and looking upwards. Hence the primary meaning of 卧 is "to lie prostrate," later it also came to mean "to lie on one's back," or "to sleep."

jiān

Oracle-Bone Inscriptions

Bronze Inscriptions

Later Seal Character

In ancient times when mirror was not yet invented, there was only one way for a man to see his own face, that is to look at one's reflection in the water. In the Oracle-Bone Inscriptions, the character 监 looks like a man staring at a basin on his knees, suggesting that the man is looking at his reflection in the water. Hence the original meaning of 监 was "to look at oneself in the water," from which derive the meaning "to observe other people and things," e.g. 监视 (to supervise; to watch) and 监督 (to superintend; to control).

lín

Bronze Inscriptions

Later Seal Character

In the Bronze Inscriptions, the character 临 looks like a man looking down at many things. In the Later Seal Character, it consists of 卧 and 品, the former representing a man looking down and the latter presents, meaning the same as that in the Bronze Inscriptions. The original meaning of 临 was "to look down at things," but it has taken on the extended meanings of "facing," "befalling," "arriving," and even those of "governing and ruling" later on.

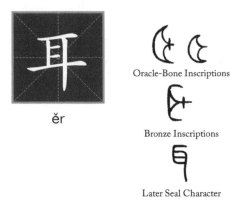

ěr

Oracle-Bone Inscriptions

Bronze Inscriptions

Later Seal Character

In the Oracle-Bone Inscriptions and Bronze Inscriptions, the character 耳 looks just like an ear, hence the meaning is "ear." The ear is the organ of hearing in human beings and animals, so characters with 耳 as a component all have to do with ear and its function of hearing, e.g. 闻 (to hear), 聂 (to whisper) and 取 (to cut off an ear).

wén

Oracle-Bone Inscriptions

Bronze Inscriptions

Later Seal Character

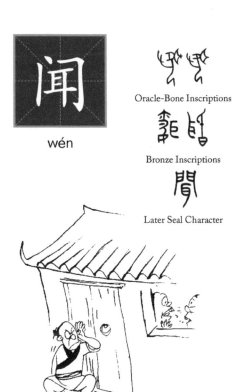

In the Oracle-Bone Inscriptions, the character 闻 looks like a man pricking up his ears. In the Later Seal Character, 闻 has 耳 (ear) as its radical and 门 (door) as its phonetic. But 门 can also be ideographic, and the character 闻 seen as such means "to put one's ear to the door of another in order to hear what is said inside," i.e. "to eavesdrop." The primary meaning of 闻 is "to listen," "to hear," but it can also be used in the extended meanings for "what has been heard," e.g. 新闻 (news), 奇闻 (something unheard of); and even for "what one knows by way of seeing and hearing," e.g. 见闻 (knowledge). In addition, 闻 can also mean "to smell," e.g. 闻香下马 (to dismount from a horse at the smell of fragrance).

shèng

Oracle-Bone Inscriptions

Bronze Inscriptions

Later Seal Character

In the Oracle-Bone Inscriptions and Bronze Inscriptions, the character 圣 looks like a man listening to someone talking. The part 口 represents the man talking, and the big ear on top of the man listening suggests that he has an acute hearing. So the character 圣 originally meant "an acute sense of hearing," but it could also mean "to be bright and intelligent" and "to have profound wisdom." In ancient times, people of noble character and great learning were known as 圣, e.g. 圣贤 (sage), 诗圣 (poet sage), 书圣 (calligrapher sage). Under the feudal system, however, 圣 was more usually used as an honorific title of the emperor, e.g. 圣上 (the emperor), 圣旨 (imperial edict) and 圣恩 (the grace of the emperor).

tīng

Oracle-Bone Inscriptions

Bronze Inscriptions

Later Seal Character

In the Oracle-Bone Inscriptions, the character 听 consists of 耳 (ear) and 口 (mouth), signalling an ear is receiving speech from a mouth. The primary meaning of 听 is "to perceive sound by the ear," but it has also taken on the meanings of "listening to" or "accepting (others' advice)," "making decisions" and "administering."

niè

Later Seal Character

聂 is an ideograph. In its original complicated form, it is made up of three ear parts (耳), signalling that many people are passing some news by word of mouth. Xu Shen says in his *Origin of Chinese Characters*, "聂 means to have a word in sb.'s ear," and that was its original meaning. Nowadays, however, it is more usually used as a surname.

shēng

Oracle-Bone Inscriptions

Later Seal Character

In the Oracle-Bone Inscriptions, the character 声 looks like a man striking a chime stone with a small mallet in hand. It has 耳 (ear) as a component, signalling that through ear one can hear the sound coming from the chime stone. It primarily means "sound," "noise," but it can also mean "music," "speech" and "message"; from which have derived the senses of "momentum" and "reputation."

取

qǔ

Oracle-Bone Inscriptions

Bronze Inscriptions

Later Seal Character

In ancient wars, the army authority would judge a soldier's contribution by the number of the enemies' heads or the captives' ears he brought back. In the Oracle-Bone Inscriptions, the character 取 looks like an ear in a hand, signalling the cutting off of an ear. From this meaning have derived its senses of "capture," "take," "accept" and "adopt."

自

zì

Oracle-Bone Inscriptions

Bronze Inscriptions

Later Seal Character

Being the original form of 鼻 (nose), the character 自 in the Oracle-Bone Inscriptions has the shape of a human nose. But it has come to be used in the sense of oneself, so a new character 鼻, made up of 自 and a phonetic 畀 (bì) has been created for the sense of nose.

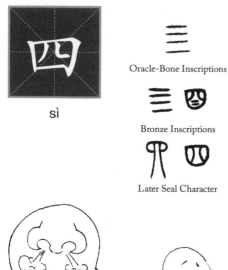

sì

三
Oracle-Bone Inscriptions

三 凹
Bronze Inscriptions

穴 四
Later Seal Character

The character 四 is a numeral, meaning "four." In the Oracle-Bone Inscriptions and Bronze Inscriptions, it is made up of four horizontal lines. Like 一 (one), 二 (two) and 三 (three), it is also indicative. But in the Later Seal Character, the character 四 is an ideograph, looking like a mouth producing sounds. Hence 四 was the original form of 呬 (xì). In this sense, the numeral 四 is a phonetic loan.

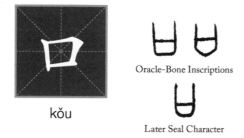

kǒu

凵凵
Oracle-Bone Inscriptions

凵
Later Seal Character

The character 口 has the shape of an open mouth of a man or an animal, hence the primary meaning is "mouth." As the mouth is an organ for a man or an animal to eat, drink and produce sounds, characters with 口 as a component are often related to eating, drinking and speaking. And it may even be used as a substitute for speech, e.g. 口舌 (exchange of words), 口角 (quarrel). Devoid of any stroke in the centre, 口 may also refer to anything with an opening, e.g. 山口 (mountain pass), 海口 (seaport), 洞口 (mouth of a cave), 关口 (strategic pass), 瓶口 (mouth of a bottle), 碗口 (top of a bowl), 疮口 (open part of a sore) and 决口 (breach; break).

qiàn

Oracle-Bone Inscriptions

Later Seal Character

In the Oracle-Bone Inscriptions, the character 欠 looks like a man on his knees, yawning with the mouth wide open. Hence the original meaning was "to open one's mouth and exhale," i.e. "to yawn." Characters with 欠 as a component, e.g. 吹 (to blow), 歌 (to sing), 歇 (to have a rest), usually have to do with the opening of the mouth and exhaling. The character 欠 in words like 欠债 (to be in debt) and 亏欠 (to have a deficit), different from the original in meaning, is a phonetic loan.

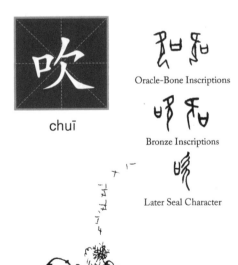

chuī

Oracle-Bone Inscriptions

Bronze Inscriptions

Later Seal Character

The character 吹 is made up of 口 (mouth) and 欠 (a man opening his mouth and exhaling). By conjoining these two parts it is brought out that the exhalation is done through the mouth. Hence its primary meaning is "to round one's lips and exhale with great strength." It may also be used to describe the natural movement of air, e.g. 风吹雨打 (the wind blowing and the rain beating). And to boast or talk big is 吹牛/吹牛皮 (literally "to blow the ox") in Chinese.

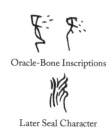

Oracle-Bone Inscriptions

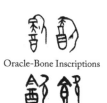

Later Seal Character

xián

The character 涎 means "salive." In the Oracle-Bone Inscriptions, this character is an ideograph, in the shape of a man opening his mouth, with water dropping from it. In the Later Seal Character, it is still an ideograph, but made up of 水 (water) and 欠 (a man with an open mouth). In the Regular Script, however, it becomes a phonetic compound, with 水 (water) as the radical and 延 as the phonetic.

Oracle-Bone Inscriptions

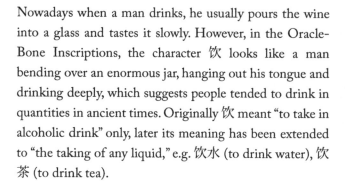

Bronze Inscriptions

Later Seal Character

yǐn

Nowadays when a man drinks, he usually pours the wine into a glass and tastes it slowly. However, in the Oracle-Bone Inscriptions, the character 饮 looks like a man bending over an enormous jar, hanging out his tongue and drinking deeply, which suggests people tended to drink in quantities in ancient times. Originally 饮 meant "to take in alcoholic drink" only, later its meaning has been extended to "the taking of any liquid," e.g. 饮水 (to drink water), 饮茶 (to drink tea).

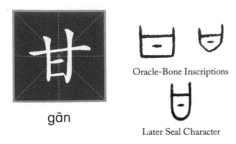

gān

Oracle-Bone Inscriptions

Later Seal Character

In ancient writing systems, the character 甘 is composed of 口 (mouth) and 一 (an indicating sign for the food in the mouth here). It primarily refers to the delicious, especially sweet, taste of some food, from which has derived its sense of (doing sth.) willingly and readily, such as 甘心.

tián

Later Seal Character

The primary meaning of 甜 is the same as 甘. The character 甜 is composed of 甘 (sweet taste) and 舌 (tongue, an organ for tasting), hence its use for something which tastes sweet. From this meaning has derived its reference to anything that is pleasant, even a sound sleep, as in (睡得真甜).

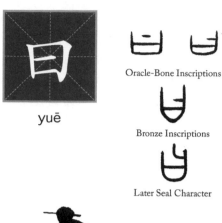

Oracle-Bone Inscriptions

Bronze Inscriptions

Later Seal Character

yuē

The character 曰 is an indicative. In ancient writing systems, the character 曰 looks like a mouth, to which is added a horizontal stroke indicating the sound coming from the mouth. Hence the primary meaning is "speaking," from which have derived its extended meanings "to be known as," "to act as," or simply "to be."

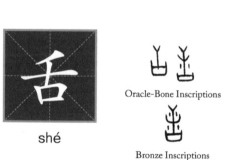

Oracle-Bone Inscriptions

Bronze Inscriptions

Later Seal Character

shé

Its primary meaning is "tongue." In the Oracle-Bone Inscriptions, the character 舌 looks like something coming out of the mouth with drops of saliva dripping, i.e. tongue. The *Origin of Chinese Characters* says, "The tongue is an organ which enables a man to speak and taste." The tongue of a human being has two important functions: to produce speech and to taste. That is why characters relating to speech and taste mostly have a component of 舌, e.g. 舐 ([fml] to lick), 舔 (to lick), and 甜 (sweet).

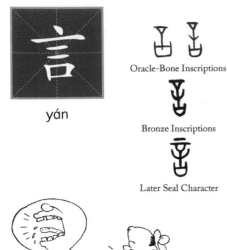

yán

Oracle-Bone Inscriptions

Bronze Inscriptions

Later Seal Character

In the Oracle-Bone Inscriptions and Bronze Inscriptions, the character 言 looks like a tongue at the top of which is added a short stroke, signalling that a man is waving his tongue, i.e. speaking. Therefore the primary meaning of 言 is "to speak," e.g. 直言不讳 (to call a spade a spade), from which has derived its use for what is talked or written about, e.g. 言简意赅 ([of speech or article] concise and comprehensive).

音

yīn

Bronze Inscriptions

Later Seal Character

音 and 言 both referred to the sound made in the mouth and meant the same at the beginning. They were interchangeable in the Bronze Inscriptions. Gradually, however, differences appeared in the usage of these two characters. 言 began to denote exclusively the activity of speaking or what is said while 音 kept its original sense, i.e. sound made in the mouth. To show the difference in writing there was an extra stroke inserted in the mouth part for 音. Nowadays 音 primarily refers to sounds, including musical sounds, and its extended meanings include "information," "message," etc.

yá

Bronze Inscriptions

Later Seal Character

牙 means "tooth." In the Later Seal Character, the character 牙 has the shape of an upper tooth interlocked with a lower tooth. In former times, 牙 was usually used to refer to the tooth of an elephant, e.g. 牙尺 (ivory ruler), 牙板 (ivory tablet) and 牙管 (ivory penholder). And 牙 was used as an abbreviation of the general's banner (牙旗).

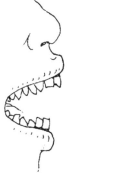

chǐ

Oracle-Bone Inscriptions

Bronze Inscriptions

Later Seal Character

齿, the same as 牙, also means "tooth." In the Oracle-Bone Inscrioptions, the character 齿, a pictograph, looks like the two rows of teeth in a mouth. In the Bronze Inscriptions and Later Seal Character, there is a phonetic 止 added on the top, resulting in a phonetic compound.

xiāo

Bronze Inscriptions

Later Seal Character

The character 嚚 consists of a head part (页) and four mouth parts (口), i.e. a man with four mouths at the corners. It signals that many people are speaking at the same time, hence the meaning is "noisy." For example, it is used in the idiom 甚嚚尘上 (noisy and dusty) to describe a situation, usually pejoratively, in which many people are talking about something at the same time.

xùn

Oracle-Bone Inscriptions

Bronze Inscriptions

Later Seal Character

In the Oracle-Bone Inscriptions and Bronze Inscriptions, the character 讯, an ideograph, looks like a man with his two hands bound at the back, plus a mouth part on the left. The man bound signifies a prisoner of war or a criminal, and the mouth stands for interrogation. Hence 讯 originally meant "to interrogate a prisoner of war or a criminal." It may also denote the prisoner of war in particular, as is used in 折首执讯 (to chop off the heads of enemies or capture them). In the Later Seal Character, it becomes a phonetic compound and the original meaning is lost. It has come to be used in the sense of "enquiry," from which derive the meaning of "message" or "information." For example, Chu Guangxi of the Tang Dynasty has the lines: 有客山中至, 言传故人讯 (a guest coming to the mount, brings news of an old friend).

shǒu

Bronze Inscriptions

Later Seal Character

The character 手 is a cover term for the upper limb of a human being, but it generally refers to the moveable part below the wrist, i.e. hand. In ancient writing systems, 手 has the shape of a man's upper limb: the upper branches denoting the five fingers and the lower part the arm. Characters with 手 (扌) as a component all indicate activities related to hand, e.g. 拿 (to take), 打 (to hit), 拍 (to pat), and 扶 (to support with the hand).

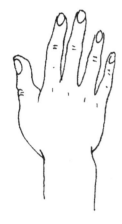

zhǎo/zhuǎ

Oracle-Bone Inscriptions

Bronze Inscriptions

Later Seal Character

As the original form of 抓, the character 爪 meant to grasp something with the palm downward at the beginning. In the Oracle-Bone Inscriptions, it looks like a hand reaching downward with the fingers branching out. In the Bronze Inscriptions, there are finger nails added at the fingertips, so 爪 has come to mean "primarily fingers," or "fingernails and toenails." Later, its meaning has been further extended to "cover the claws of animals."

gōng

Oracle-Bone Inscriptions

Later Seal Character

肱 refers to the upper arm, or sometimes the whole arm. In the Oracle-Bone Inscriptions, the character 肱 looks like an arm, with a raised sign indicating the position of elbow. This is the origin of the character 肱 in the Later Seal Character, as is recorded in the *Origin of Chinese Characters*. Its variant in the Later Seal Character is the result of an addition of 月 to the original form, which in turn becomes the basis of 肱 in the Regular Script.

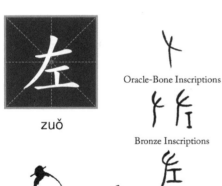

Oracle-Bone Inscriptions

Bronze Inscriptions

Later Seal Character

zuǒ

The character 左, like 右, was a pictograph at the beginning. In the Oracle-Bone Inscriptions, it looks like a hand stretching towards the left. The final form was established after the part 工 was added to it later. Hence it has the primary meaning of left hand, from which has derived its locative use to refer to anything which is on the left-hand side, opposite to 右 (right).

右

yòu

又
Oracle-Bone Inscriptions

Bronze Inscriptions

Later Seal Character

The character 右 was a pictograph at the beginning. In the Oracle-Bone Inscriptions, it looks like a hand stretching toward the left. This character could be regularized as 又, which was the original form of 右. As 又 was more usually used in the function of an adverb, a component 口 was added to it at the time of the Bronze Inscriptions to make it a separate character. So the character 右 means "right hand," or as a locative, "right-hand side," opposite to 左 (left).

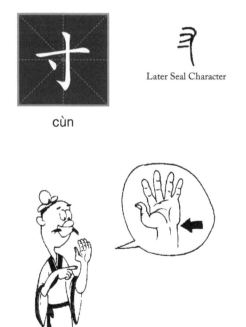

寸

cùn

Later Seal Character

The character 寸 is an indicative. In the Later Seal Character, it consists of 又 and 一; the former means "the right hand" and the latter is a sign marking the position on the lower arm about a little longer than an inch away from the wrist. This is the place where a traditional Chinese doctor feels the pulse of a patient. This shows that 寸 was originally the name of a point on the network of channels through which, according to the traditional Chinese medicine, vital energy circulates. But 寸 is also a measure of length, equal to ten 分 or one tenth of 尺 in the Chinese System, and one third or a decimetre in the Metric System. Consequently it may also be used to describe things which are short or small, as is shown in expressions like 寸土 (an inch of land), 寸步 (a tiny step) and 寸阴 (an extremely short time).

Oracle-Bone Inscriptions

Bronze Inscriptions

Later Seal Character

友

yǒu

In ancient writing systems, 友 looks like two stretching-out right hands, signalling two people are shaking hands. In the Oracle-Bone Inscriptions, there are sometimes even two horizontal stroks linking the two hands to emphasize the point. The purpose of shaking hands with someone is to show one's friendship with him, just like what happens when old friends meet nowadays. So the primary meaning of 友 is what is now known as 朋友 (friend). In ancient times, however, 朋 and 友 had different meanings: 同门为朋 (those who learn under the same teacher are 朋); 同志为友 (those who follow the same ideal are 友).

攀

pān

Later Seal Character

In the Later Seal Character, the character 攀 was originally an ideograph, using a pair of hands stretching out in opposite directions to indicate that a man is grasping at things in order to climb up. At a later stage, it changed into a phonetic compound with 手 as the radical and 樊 as the phonetic. The primary meaning of 攀, therefore, is "to climb," from which have derived its extended meanings "to take hold of," "to attach oneself to" and "to seek connections with." In addition, it may mean "to pull down and break off (twigs)" and "to pick (flowers)."

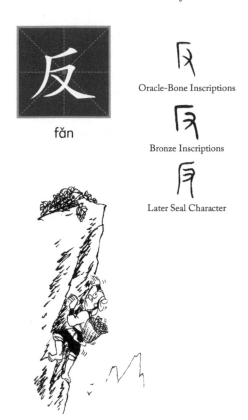

fǎn

Oracle-Bone Inscriptions

Bronze Inscriptions

Later Seal Character

反 was the original form of 扳 (pān, meaning the same as 攀). In ancient writing systems, 反 looks like a man climbing a steep cliff with hands, hence the original meaning is "to climb," from which have derived its meanings of "turn over" and "the opposite." As it is more and more used in its extended meanings, and its original meaning is falling into disuse, a new character 扳, with a component 手 (扌) added to 反, has been created to express the meaning "to climb."

zhēng

Oracle-Bone Inscriptions

Later Seal Character

In ancient writing systems, the character 争 looks like two hands, one up and the other down, fighting to get an object. The primary meaning of 争 is "to fight for," from which have derived its extended meanings "to fight," "to compete," "to argue," "to strive," etc.

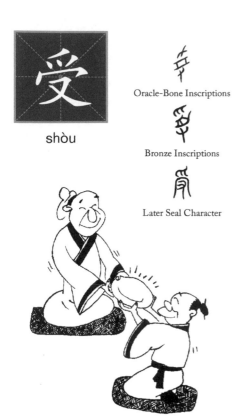

shòu

Oracle-Bone Inscriptions

Bronze Inscriptions

Later Seal Character

In the Oracle-Bone Inscriptions and Bronze Inscriptions, the character 受 consists of two hand parts and a boat part in between, signalling that one side is offering something which the other side is receiving. Hence it originally meant both giving and receiving. Later on a component 手 (扌) was added to 受, forming a new character 授 to mean "offering," "giving." And the character 受 has come to be used exclusively in the sense of "receiving."

yuán

Oracle-Bone Inscriptions

Bronze Inscriptions

Later Seal Character

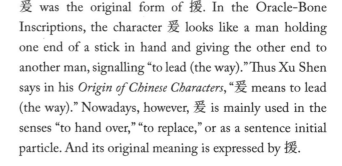

爰 was the original form of 援. In the Oracle-Bone Inscriptions, the character 爰 looks like a man holding one end of a stick in hand and giving the other end to another man, signalling "to lead (the way)." Thus Xu Shen says in his *Origin of Chinese Characters*, "爰 means to lead (the way)." Nowadays, however, 爰 is mainly used in the senses "to hand over," "to replace," or as a sentence initial particle. And its original meaning is expressed by 援.

dòu

Oracle-Bone Inscriptions

Later Seal Character

In the Oracle-Bone Inscriptions, the character 斗 looks like two men in a fight, grasping each other's hair and grappling together. Its primary meaning is "to exchange blows," "to wrestle," but it is also used in the general sense of fight. As the original complicated form of 斗 in the Regular Script is very similar to that of 门 (鬥) (door), a measure word 斗 has come to be used as its simplified form to make the distinction between them more noticeable.

nào

Later Seal Character

The character 闹 is an ideograph. In the Later Seal Character, it consists of 市 (market) and 鬥 (fight), signalling people are fighting in the market. As the original complicated form of 鬥 in the Regular Script is very similar to that of 门 (鬥) (door), the simplified form of 闹 is mistakenly changed into a composition of 市 and 门. The primary meaning of 闹 is "noisy," "unquiet," from which have derived the senses of "quarrel," "make trouble," etc.

若

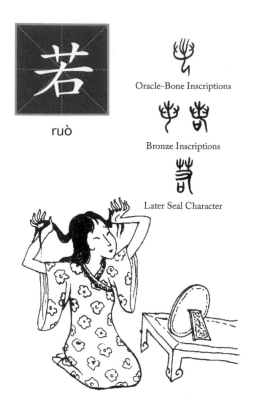

ruò

Oracle-Bone Inscriptions

Bronze Inscriptions

Later Seal Character

In the Oracle-Bone Inscriptions, the character 若 looks like a man combing his hair with his two hands. Through combing the hair may become smooth, hence 若 originally meant "smooth" and "obedient," "conformable" were its extended meanings. In the Oracle-Bone Inscriptions, it is used in the sense "(to accomplish something.) smoothly and successfully." Nowadays, however, it means "like," "the same as," and its original meaning has fallen into disuse.

俘

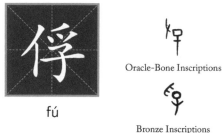

fú

Oracle-Bone Inscriptions

Bronze Inscriptions

Later Seal Character

In the Oracle-Bone Inscriptions and Bronze Inscriptions, the character 俘, consisting of 爪 (to grasp) and 子 (man), looks like a hand capturing a man. Sometimes, it has 彳 (to walk) as its component, signalling to drive someone along the road. The primary meaning of 俘 is "to capture people in the war," but it is also used to refer to those captured, i.e. captives.

付

fù

Bronze Inscriptions

Later Seal Character

In the Bronze Inscriptions, the character 付, consisting of 人 (man) and 又 (the right hand), looks like a man handing over something to another. Sometimes it has 寸 instead of 又, but means the same. Hence the primary meaning of 付 is "to hand over, to give."

及

jí

Oracle-Bone Inscriptions

Bronze Inscriptions

Later Seal Character

What the character 及 expresses is: a man catches up from behind and seizes the man who was previously running in the front. The original meaning of 及, therefore, was "to catch up with," from which have derived the meanings "reach" or "come up to." But it can also be used as a conjunction, similar to 和 or 与 (and).

fú

Bronze Inscriptions

Later Seal Character

In the Bronze Inscriptions, the character 扶, consisting of 夫 (man) and 又 (the right hand), looks like a man supporting another with his hand. In the Later Seal Character, it changes to a phonetic compound, with 手 as its radical and 夫 as its phonetic. The primary meaning of 扶 is "to support," from which have derived its extended meanings "to help sustain," "to foster," "to prop up" and "to depend."

chéng

Oracle-Bone Inscriptions

Bronze Inscriptions

Later Seal Character

In the Oracle-Bone Inscriptions and Bronze Inscriptions, the character 承 looks like two hands holding a man on his knees. The primary meaning of 承 is "to hold," from which have derived its extended meanings "to accept," "to undertake," "to continue" and "to succeed (to something)."

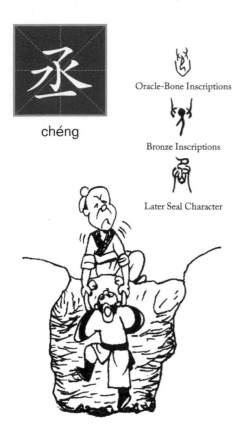

丞

chéng

Oracle-Bone Inscriptions

Bronze Inscriptions

Later Seal Character

In the Oracle-Bone Inscriptions, the character 丞 looks like a man in a pitfall, and there are two hands on top in an attempt to save him. In the Bronze Inscriptions, the part representing the pitfall is omitted, but the meaning "to save someone with the hands" is not changed. Hence the original meaning of 丞 was to save. In other words, it was the original form of 拯. And "to assist and help" is one of its extended meanings. In the past 丞 was also used as a noun to refer to the assistant officers in the central or local governments, e.g. 大理寺丞 (assistant director of Dalisi Bureau), 府丞 (vice mayor) and 县丞 (county magistrate's assistant).

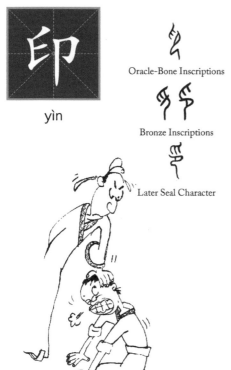

印

yìn

Oracle-Bone Inscriptions

Bronze Inscriptions

Later Seal Character

In the Oracle-Bone Inscriptions and Bronze Inscriptions, the character 印 looks like a hand pressing the head of a man. Hence its original meaning is "to depress." In other words, 印 was the original form of 抑. But it was later on used with reference to a seal or stamp, which had to be depressed in order to leave any mark. Before the Qin Dynasty, seals were generally known as 玺 (xǐ). However, after the unification of China by the First Emperor of Qin, it was stipulated that only the seal of the emperor could be called 玺, and all the others would have to be called 印. And the character 印 is also used for other marks which result from the act of depressing, e.g. 手印 (finger print) and 脚印 (foot print).

妥

tuǒ

Oracle-Bone Inscriptions

Bronze Inscriptions

Later Seal Character

In ancient writing systems, the character 妥 looks like a woman on her knees obediently, whose head is pressed by a hand. The primary meaning of 妥 is "obedient," "submissive," from which have derived its extended meanings of "steady" and "reliable."

奚

xī

Oracle-Bone Inscriptions

Bronze Inscriptions

Later Seal Character

In ancient writing systems, the character 奚 looks like a man around whose neck is a rope and the other end of the rope is in the hand of another man. It was a commonplace in the slave society to bind a man with a rope and to lead him to work so that he could not run away. And those who were bound were slaves, who had no freedom whatsoever. So the original meaning of 奚 was "slave." But it could also be used with reference to any freeman who had committed a crime and become a servant to an officer. The character 奚, now used as a surname, perhaps also originated from the slave system.

zú

Oracle-Bone Inscriptions

Bronze Inscriptions

Later Seal Character

足 is a pictograph. In the Oracle-Bone Inscriptions, the character 足 has the shape of a complete human foot: from toe to heel, even including the ankle. In the Bronze Inscriptions, the character is simplified: only the toe is retained, the other parts being reduced to a circle. The primary meaning of 足 is "foot," but it is also used in the senses of "substantial," "sufficient" and "enough." Characters with 足 as a component all have to do with foot and activities connected with it, e.g. 跟 (to follow), 蹈 (to dance), 路 (road), 跳 (to jump) and 践 (to trample).

zhǐ

Oracle-Bone Inscriptions

Bronze Inscriptions

Later Seal Character

In the Oracle-Bone Inscriptions, the character 止 has the shape of a human toe. Hence it primarily refers to the toe, but it is also used in a general sense to refer to the foot. As 止 means the foot which stays in place, it also takes on the meanings "to stop," "to be at a standstill" and "to rest." Characters with 止 as a component all have to do with activities connected with the foot, e.g. 步 (step), 此 (here), 陟 (to ascend a height) and 涉 (to wade).

步

bù

Oracle-Bone Inscriptions

Bronze Inscriptions

Later Seal Character

In the Oracle-Bone Inscriptions and Bronze Inscriptions, the character 步 looks like two toes, one in front of the other, signalling the two feet are moving forward alternatively. Hence its primary meaning is "to walk." 步 may also be used as a noun referring to the distance covered in walking. But how long this distance is varies with the system used. According to an informal system, 步 is equal to two steps while one step is known as 跬 (kuǐ). Thus Xun Zi (Hsün Tzu) says, "不积跬步, 无以致千里 (Without the accumulation of single steps, one cannot travel the distance of a thousand miles)." In the formal system of the Zhou Dynasty, 步 is equal to eight 尺 whereas in that of the Qin Dynasty, it is six 尺 long and three hundred 步 constitute 里 (equal to 500 hundred metres in the Metric System).

走

zǒu

Bronze Inscriptions

Stone-Drum Inscriptions

Later Seal Character

In the Bronze Inscriptions, the upper part of the character 走 looks like a man running forward with his arms swinging, and the lower part 止 stands for the foot. Hence the original meaning of 走 was "to run," or "to run away." In Classical Chinese, 走 meant "to run" while "to walk" (the present-day meaning of 走) was expressed by the character 行. It was not until the Song Dynasty that the meaning of 走 was gradually shifted from "run" to "walk." Characters with 走 as a component most have to do with running, e.g. 趋 (to hurry), 赴 (to go), 赶 (to rush), 超 (to overtake) and 趣 ([arch.] to hurry).

qǐ

Oracle-Bone Inscriptions

Later Seal Character

In the Oracle-Bone Inscriptions, the character 企 looks like a man with his foot especially prominent, signalling that the man is standing on tiptoe. Sometimes, the foot is separated from the body, resulting in a two part character consisting of 人 (man) and 止 (foot). This is the origin of the form in the Later Seal Character. The original meaning of 企 was "to stand on tiptoe." But it is now more usually used in the sense "to expect."

bēn

Bronze Inscriptions

Stone-Drum Inscriptions

Later Seal Character

In the Bronze Inscriptions, the character 奔 is made up of a part like a man running with his arms swinging (夭) and three toe parts (止), signalling that many people are running together. In the Stone-Drum Inscriptions, it is made up of three 夭 and three 止, and the meaning of many people on the run is brought out more clearly. Hence the original meaning of 奔 is "many people on the run," from which have derived its extended meanings "to run fast," "to hurry" and "to flee from home." However, the three toes were mistakenly changed into three clusters of grass in the Later Seal Character, resulting in a change of image from many people on the run to one man running on grass.

xiān

Oracle-Bone Inscriptions

Bronze Inscriptions

Later Seal Character

In ancient writing systems, the character 先 has a toe part on top of a man part, signalling that a man has taken a step ahead of another. Hence the primary meaning of 先 is "before in position," as against 后 (back). But it can also mean "before in time," i.e. "earlier."

zhī

Oracle-Bone Inscriptions

Bronze Inscriptions

Later Seal Character

In the Oracle-Bone Inscriptions, the chatacter 之 has a foot part on top of a horizontal line. The former signifies the action to take a step forward and the latter denotes the starting point. Hence the original meaning of 之 was "to go to (a place)." However it is more usually used as a particle in the functions of pronoun, conjunction, preposition, adverb, etc., rather than in its original sense.

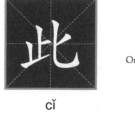

此

cǐ

Oracle-Bone Inscriptions

Bronze Inscriptions

Later Seal Character

In ancient writing systems, the character 此 consists of 止 and 人. 止 means "toe" or "foot," but it may also mean "to stop." In the Oracle-Bone Inscriptions, this character was used to refer to a man standing still, and, perhaps more so, the place where a man stood. But that was its original meaning. Nowadays it is used as a demonstrative, meaning "this," opposite to 彼 or 那 (that), or an adverb, meaning "in this way."

正

zhèng

Oracle-Bone Inscriptions

Bronze Inscriptions

Later Seal Character

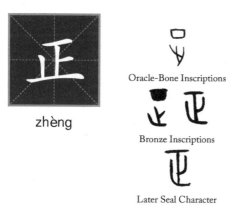

正 is the original form of 征. In the Oracle-Bone Inscriptions, the upper part of the character 正, the square, stands for a town with walls on its four sides, and the lower part 止 means to take steps towards the town and attack it. In the Bronze Inscriptions, its upper part is either repalced by a solid square or simplified into a horizontal line, gradually losing its pictorial flavour. The original meaning of 正 was "to go on an expedition," especially a punitive one. But it is now usually used in the sense of "upright," "straight," as against 偏 (slanting), 斜 (tilted). It can also be used to refer to the right side, opposite to 反 (the reverse side).

逆

nì

Oracle-Bone Inscriptions

Bronze Inscriptions

Later Seal Character

In the Oracle-Bone Inscriptions, the upper part of the character 逆 looks like a man coming towards here, while the lower part 止 suggests going towards there. Hence the original meaning of 逆 was "to go to meet." For example, there is a line "吕翎逆君于秦 (Lü Sheng went to meet the King in Qin)" in *Guo Yu.* When one goes to meet another, the two of them go in opposite directions. So 逆 takes on the meanings of "opposite" and "contrary."

达

dá

Oracle-Bone Inscriptions

Bronze Inscriptions

Later Seal Character

In the Oracle-Bone Inscriptions, the character 达 consists of a man part (大) and a road part (彳), signalling a man is walking on a road. To emphasize the point, sometimes a component 止 is added. So the original meaning of 达 was "to walk on a road," with the implication "to reach," "to arrive," e.g. 四通八达 (to extend in all directions) and 抵达 (to arrive). But it is also used in the sense "to understand thoroughly," e.g. 达观 (to take things philosophically), 达识 (insightful); and in the sense "to convey," e.g. 转达 (to pass on), 传达 (to relay) and 词不达意 (The words fail to convey the idea).

yí

Oracle-Bone Inscriptions

Bronze Inscriptions

Later Seal Character

In the Oracle-Bone Inscriptions, the character 疑 looks like a man standing with the support of a walking stick and looking at the sides, signalling that he is not decided where to go. Sometimes it has a component 彳 to emphasize the point that the man has lost his way. The primary meaning of 疑 is "confusion" and "undecided," from which has derived its sense of "doubt."

zhì

Oracle-Bone Inscriptions

Bronze Inscriptions

Later Seal Character

In ancient writing systems, the character 陟 looks like two feet ascending a height one after another. It primarily means is "to ascend a height," but is also used in the sense "to rise socially."

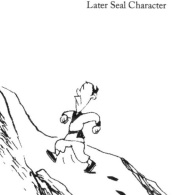

jiàng/xiáng

Oracle-Bone Inscriptions

Bronze Inscriptions

Later Seal Character

In the Oracle-Bone Inscriptions and Bronze Inscriptions, the character 降 looks like two feet descending from a height one after another. The primary meaning of 降, opposite to 陟, is "to descend," from which have derived its extended meanings "to fall," "to lower" and "to belittle." In addition, 降, pronounced as xiáng, may mean "to subdue," "to surrender," etc.

shè

Oracle-Bone Inscriptions

Bronze Inscriptions

Later Seal Character

In the Oracle-Bone Inscriptions and Bronze Inscriptions, the character 涉 has a part like a meandering flow of water on each side of which is a foot part, signalling that a man is wading through it. In the Later Seal Character, the character 涉 has 步 (to walk) in between two 水 (water), also signalling "to wade through water." But its meaning has been extended to cover the senses "to travel," "to reach," "to face," "to enter" and "to connect."

wèi

Bronze Inscriptions

Later Seal Character

胃 refers to the stomach, the organ in which food is digested. The character 胃 is both a pictograph and ideograph. In ancient writing systems, its upper part looks like a bag containing food to be digested represented by the four dots in it; its lower part 月 (a variant of 肉, flesh), suggesting that the stomach is a fleshy organ.

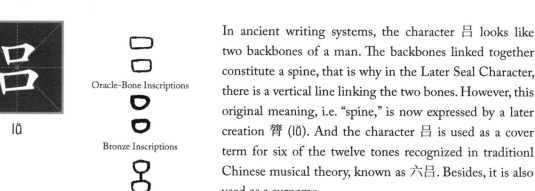

lǚ

Oracle-Bone Inscriptions

Bronze Inscriptions

Later Seal Character

In ancient writing systems, the character 呂 looks like two backbones of a man. The backbones linked together constitute a spine, that is why in the Later Seal Character, there is a vertical line linking the two bones. However, this original meaning, i.e. "spine," is now expressed by a later creation 膂 (lǚ). And the character 呂 is used as a cover term for six of the twelve tones recognized in traditionl Chinese musical theory, known as 六呂. Besides, it is also used as a surname.

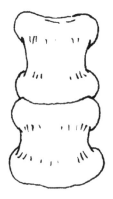

jǐ

Later Seal Character

脊 refers to the spine, the row of bones in the centre of the back of a man. In the Later Seal Character, the upper part of the character 脊 has the shape of a spine in between back muscles, and the lower part is 肉 (月) (flesh), suggesting that the spine is part of a human body. The primary meaning of 脊 is "spine," but it is also used metaphorically for anything that has a rising middle part, e.g. 山脊 (mountain ridge), 屋脊 (the ridge of a roof).

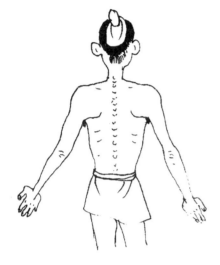

xìn

Oracle-Bone Inscriptions

Bronze Inscriptions

Later Seal Character

囟 refers to the fontanelle, the membranous space in an infant's skull at angles of parietal bones. In the Later Seal Character, the character 囟 looks like a human skull seen from above, the cross in it represents the fontanelles.

sī

Ancient Seals

Later Seal Character

In ancient times, people mistakenly thought that the heart was the organ for thinking, and characters which had something to do with thinking, ideas and feelings all had 心 as a component. It is only in modern times that people realize it is the brain that does the thinking. In the Later Seal Character, the character 思 consists of 囟 and 心, the former referring to the brain here and the latter the heart. In other words, thinking is seen as a process performed by the brain and heart together. In the Regular Script, 思 consists of 田 and 心, resulting from an erroneous derivation. The primary meaning of 思 is "to think," from which have derived the senses: "to think of," "to cherish the memory of" and "train of thought."

xīn

Oracle-Bone Inscriptions

Bronze Inscriptions

Later Seal Character

心 refers to the heart. In ancient writing systems, the character 心 has the shape of a heart. The heart is the most important organ of a human body. And people in ancient times mistook it for an organ for thinking, so the character 心 is also a cover term for thinking, ideas and feelings. The heart is situated in the centre of a human chest, hence 心 also means "centre" and "central." Characters with 心 (忄, 小) as a component most have to do with human thinking, ideas and feelings, e.g. 志 (aspiration), 忠 (loyalty), 性 (temperament), 怕 (afraid), 恭 (respectful), 忝 (regretfully), etc.

yōu

Bronze Inscriptions

Later Seal Character

In the Bronze Inscriptions, the character 忧 looks like a man covering his face with a hand, signalling there are worried expressions on the face. Sometimes, it has 心 (heart) as a component, signalling that the man is in a gloomy mood. Hence 忧 means "worried," "depressed," but it can also refer to things which make one worried.

mèng

Oracle-Bone Inscriptions

Later Seal Character

梦 means "dream," the things one experiences during sleep. In ancient times, when medical science was at a low stage of development, people did not know much about the causes of illness, and they often linked illness with nightmare. They thought terrible dreams were omens of coming illness of disaster. In the Oracle-Bone Inscriptions, the character 梦 looks like a man on a bed, with open eyes and loose hair, and moving his hands and legs in confusion, signalling that the man is in a dream.

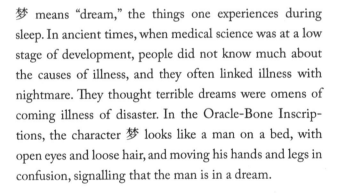

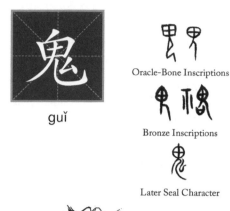

guǐ

Oracle-Bone Inscriptions

Bronze Inscriptions

Later Seal Character

People in the past believed that men would become ghosts after death. In the Oracle-Bone Inscriptions, the lower part of the character 鬼 has the shape of a man, but its upper part, the head, is monstrous and disproportionately big, signalling that it is a big-headed ghost changed from a dead man. The primary meaning of 鬼 is "the soul of a man after death." As the soul lives in the nether world and has no fixed form, the character 鬼 can also mean "mysterious," "cunning" and "resourceful." Characters with 鬼 as a component most have to do with ghost and soul, e.g. 魂 (soul), 魄 (spirit), 魔 (devil), and 魅 (demon).

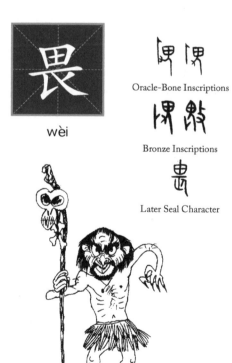

wèi

Oracle-Bone Inscriptions

Bronze Inscriptions

Later Seal Character

In the Oracle-Bone Inscriptions and Bronze Inscriptions, the character 畏 looks like a monstrous, big headed ghost with a stick in hand, suggesting an awe-inspiring appearance. Hence 畏 originally meant, the same as 威, "awe-inspiring." But in the present-day usage, it has taken on the meanings of "frightening," "fearsome," "worried" and even "respect."

异

yì

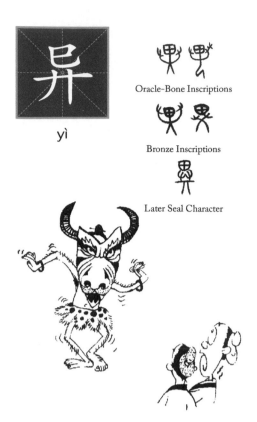

Oracle-Bone Inscriptions

Bronze Inscriptions

Later Seal Character

In ancient times, witchcraft was a commonplace. When a wizard performed magic, he would wear a fierce looking mask and dance, in order to drive away evil demons. In the Oracle-Bone Inscriptions, the character 异 looks like a man dancing with a big, fierce-looking mask. As the mask looks ferocious, different from the normal face, the character 异 takes on the meanings of "strange," "unusual," "different" and "special," too.

CHAPTER 3

INSTRUMENTS

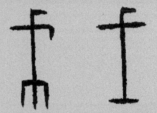

戈

gē

Oracle-Bone Inscriptions

Bronze Inscriptions

Later Seal Character

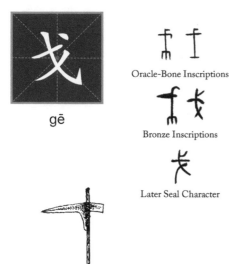

戈 is a type of ancient weapon, widely used in the Shang Dynasty. With a long handle and a horizontal blade at the head, it may be used to strike or hook. In the Oracle-Bone Inscriptions and early Bronze Inscriptions, the character 戈 has the shape of this weapon. It is one of the main weapons in ancient China. For example, Xun Zi (Hsuntzu) says, "There is no weapon other than 戈, 矛, 弓 and 矢 in ancient times." Characters with 戈 as a component most have to do with weapon, war and fight, e.g. 戟 (a spearlike weapon), 武 (military), 戎 (army), 戒 (to guard against), 戍 (to defend) and 伐 (to attack).

戒

jiè

Oracle-Bone Inscriptions

Bronze Inscriptions

Later Seal Character

In ancient writing systems, the character 戒 looks like a man holding a weapon in his hands. Its primary meaning is "to guard against," from which has derived its extended meaning "to warn." But it can also be used in the senses "to prohibit" and "to give up," e.g. 戒烟 (to give up smoking), 戒酒 (to give up drinking).

咸

xián

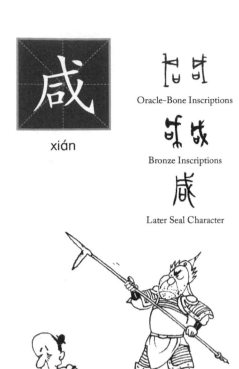

Oracle-Bone Inscriptions

Bronze Inscriptions

Later Seal Character

The character 咸 consists of 戌 and 口. Judging from the Oracle-Bone Inscriptions and Bronze Inscriptions, 戌 is a big axe with a long handle, and 口 denotes the head of a man here. Hence 咸 meant originally to use an axe to chop off a head, i.g. to kill. Xu Shen says in his *Origin of Chinese Characters*, "咸 means all, the whole lot." This gloss of 咸 in the sense of "all," "the whole lot," is in fact a derivative from its original meaning "to kill everyone."

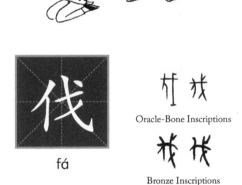

伐

fá

Oracle-Bone Inscriptions

Bronze Inscriptions

Later Seal Character

伐 is an ideograph, consisting of 人 and 戈. In the Oracle-Bone Inscriptions and Bronze Inscriptions, the character 伐 looks like a man chopping the head of an enemy with 戈. The primary meaning of 伐 is "to chop," from which have derived its extended meanings "to strike" and "to attack." In addition, 伐 can also mean "victory," "achievement" and "to boast of (one's achievements)."

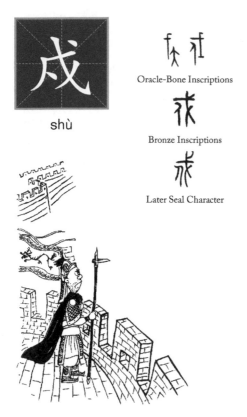

戌

shù

Oracle-Bone Inscriptions

Bronze Inscriptions

Later Seal Character

In ancient writing systems, the character 戍, consisting of 人 and 戈, looks like a man carrying 戈, signalling he is defending his land. Hence the primary meaning of 戍 is "to defend," "to guard the frontiers."

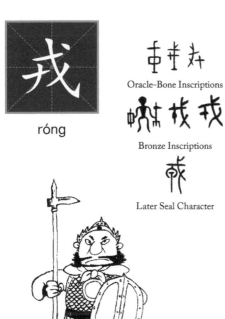

戎

róng

Oracle-Bone Inscriptions

Bronze Inscriptions

Later Seal Character

In the early Bronze Inscriptions, the character 戎 is a pictograph, looking like a man holding 戈 (an affensive weapon) in one hand and 盾 (a shield) in the other. Later the man part is omitted. In the Oracle-Bone Inscriptions, the character 戎 is only a combination of 戈 and 盾. In the late Bronze Inscriptions, the shield part is reduced to a cross (十), similar to the original form of 甲. That is why the character 戎 in the Later Seal Character consists of 甲 and 戈 by mistake. 戎 is a general term for arms, but it can also be used to refer to war and army. Besides, 戎 was also a cover term for the national minorities in the northwest in the past.

wǔ

Oracle-Bone Inscriptions

Bronze Inscriptions

Later Seal Character

武 is the opposite of 文 (civil). In ancient writing systems, the character 武 consists of 戈 and 止. 戈 is a cover term for weapon, and 止 (foot) here means "to go forward." So the primary meaning of 武 is "military operation." It is a general term for activities connected with army and fighting. It can also be used in the sense of "valiant" and "vigorous."

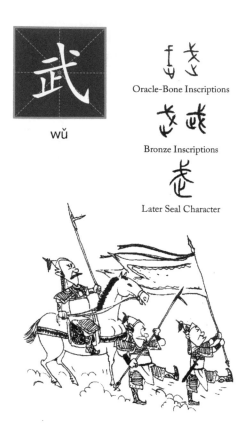

战

zhàn

Bronze Inscriptions

Later Seal Character

The character 战 consists of 单 (單) and 戈. The former, 单, an instrument for catching animals, may also be used as a weapon, and the latter, 戈, is a common weapon. The combination of 单 and 戈 means "to use weapons against each other," so the primary meaning of 战 is "two armies engaged in a battle," i.e. "fight," or "war." It may also refer to any activity in which different sides are competing for a prize.

wǒ

Oracle-Bone Inscriptions

Bronze Inscriptions

Later Seal Character

What is 我? From the shape of the character 我 in the Oracle-Bone Inscriptions, we know that it is a type of weapon. It has a long handle and a blade like the teeth of a saw, used for the execution of criminals or the dismemberment of animals in ancient times. This weapon is rarely seen in later ages, so the original meaning of 我 is rarely used. It is more ususlly used as a pronoun to refer to the first person, the speaker himself.

yuè

Oracle-Bone Inscriptions

Bronze Inscriptions

Later Seal Character

The original form of 钺, is an ancient weapon, made of bronze or iron, looking like a big broad axe. There were various types of axe in ancient times, of different shapes and uses. The character in the Oracle-Bone Inscriptions and Bronze Inscriptions looks like a weapon with a long handle and round blade, a member of the axe family.

sui

Oracle-Bone Inscriptions

Bronze Inscriptions

Later Seal Character

In the Oracle-Bone Inscriptions and early Bronze Inscriptions, the character 岁 looks like an axe-type weapon with a long handle. The two dots in the blade position indicate that the blade bends at the two ends and the dotted positions are devoid of anything. Though originally referring to a type of axe, 岁 is more usually used in the sense of "age," "year" and more generally "time." Later, there are two foot parts (止) added, suggesting that time passes like a man walking from one place to another.

wáng

Oracle-Bone Inscriptions

Bronze Inscriptions

Later Seal Character

王 was the title of the monarch in ancient times. In the Oracle-Bone Inscriptions and Bronze Inscriptions, the character 王 looks like an axetype weapon—钺, an instrument for the execution of criminals. As military commanders used it to direct the army and urge the soldiers to charge forward, 钺 became a symbol of power, and the one who had 钺 in his hand was known as 王. In the primitive society, the military commander, i.e. 王 was the highest ruler of a land. By the time of the dynasties of Xia, Shang and Zhou, only the monarch of a country could be referred to as 王. In the Warring States period, however, the rulers of the states all called themselves 王. Then the First Emperor of Qin unified China, and he changed the title from 王 to 皇帝 (emperor). After that 王 became the highest title granted to princes or ministers of great achievements, no longer the title of the monarch.

shì

Oracle-Bone Inscriptions

Later Seal Character

In the early Bronze Inscriptions, the character 士, like 王, is in the shape of an axe. While 王 refers to a big broad axe, a symbol of power, however, 士 refers to ordinary axetype weapons. The primary meaning of 士 is "the warrior or law executor, who holds a weapon in hand," e.g. 士卒 (soldiers), 士师 (jailer). But it is also used in the general sense of adult man, e.g. 士女 (men and women). In addition, 士 may also refer to a social stratum, beyond ordinary people, e.g. 士族 (gentry) and 士子 (scholar).

bīng

Oracle-Bone Inscriptions

Bronze Inscriptions

Later Seal Character

In Oracle-Bone Inscriptions, the character 兵 looks like a man holding a sharp weapon—axe, so its primary meaning is "the weapon using in war," from which have derived its extended meaning "soldiers," "army," "military affairs," and "war."

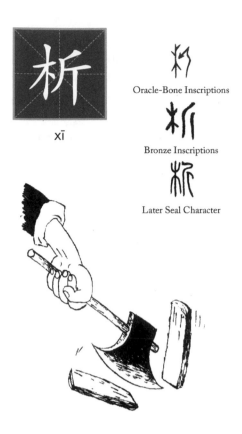

析
xī

析
Oracle-Bone Inscriptions

析
Bronze Inscriptions

析
Later Seal Character

In the Oracle-Bone Inscriptions, the character 析 has a tree part (木) on the left and an axe with a crooked handle (斤) on the right, signalling the splitting a tree with an axe. From the original meaning of "splitting" have derived the extended meaning of "separation and segmentation," e.g. 分崩离析 (to fall to pieces). And it may also be used in the sense "to analyse." Thus Tao Yuanming writes in his poem *"House-moving,"* "奇文共欣赏, 疑义相与析 (A remarkable work should be shared and its subleties discussed)."

折
zhé

折
Oracle-Bone Inscriptions

折 折
Bronze Inscriptions

折 折
Later Seal Character

In the Oracle-Bone Inscriptions, the character 折 looks like a small tree being cut down with an axe. From this original meaning derives its meaning "to break." To break something one may use an axe, or simply use one's hand. And to break something with one's hand, one will first have to bend it. So the character 折 has also taken on the meaning "to bend," e.g. 曲折 (winding), 转折 (to turn), 折叠 (to fold). It can also be used metaphorically in the sense of "convinced." From the meaning "to break" it have also derived the meanings "to die young (夭折)," "loss (损失)," "setback (挫折)," "deficit (亏损)," etc.

新

xīn

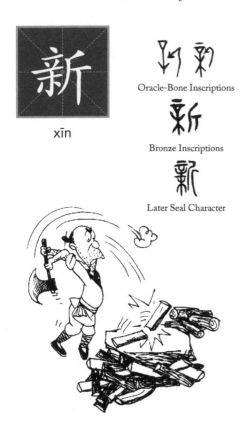

Oracle-Bone Inscriptions

Bronze Inscriptions

Later Seal Character

新 was the original form of 薪. In the Oracle-Bone Inscriptions and Bronze Inscriptions, the character 薪 has an axe part (斤) on the right, and a part representing a piece of wood on the left, signalling the splitting of wood with an axe. The original meaning of 新 was "wood split up," i.e. "firewood." But 新 is often used in the sense of "new," opposite to 旧 (old), so a new character 薪 has been created to express its original meaning.

匠

jiàng

Later Seal Character

The character 匠 consists of 匚 and 斤; the former stands for the open toolbox of a carpenter and the latter one of his tools—axe. So the primary meaning of 匠 is "carpenter." Gradually, however, anyone with a special skill or of great achievement in one field may be referred to as 匠, e.g. 铁匠 (blacksmith), 能工巧匠 (skillful craftsman) and 巨匠 (great master).

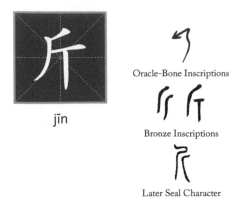

jīn

Oracle-Bone Inscriptions

Bronze Inscriptions

Later Seal Character

In the Oracle-Bone Inscriptions, the character 斤 looks like an axe with a crooked handle, and the arrow on it signals that it is very sharp. The original meaning of 斤 was "axe," used as a weapon in ancient times. Characters with 斤 as a component most have to do with the axe and its uses, e.g. 斧 (axe), 新 (firewood), 断 (to break), 析 (to split), 折 (to bend) and 斫 (to cut). Nowadays, however, 斤 is more usually used as a measure of weight.

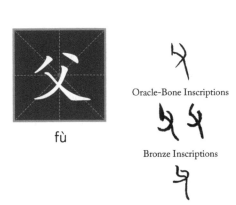

fù

Oracle-Bone Inscriptions

Bronze Inscriptions

Later Seal Character

父 was the original form of 斧. In the Bronze Inscriptions, the character 父 looks like a hand holding a stone axe. In the primitive society, the stone axe was one of the most important weapons and tools. And it was the responsibilty of the adult man to fight with the enemy and to work in the fields with the stone axe, hence 父 became a term of address for the adult man. Gradually, it has taken on the present-day meaning of "father."

辛

xīn

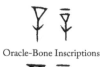

Oracle-Bone Inscriptions

Bronze Inscriptions

Later Seal Character

Judging from the early Bronze Inscriptions, the character 辛 looks like something with a round end and a pointed head, referring to an instrument of torture for tattooing the face of a criminal. But this character is now mainly used as a name of the eighth Heavenly Stem, part of a traditional Chinese system of sequense. In addition, 辛 also has the meaning of "hot in taste," and can refer to vegetables which taste hot. Its meaning can be further extended to cover "sad," "bitter" and "hard." Characters with 辛 as a component most have to do with torture and hot taste, e.g. 辜 (guilt), 辟 (to cut) and 辣 (hot taste).

辟

pī/bì/pì

Oracle-Bone Inscriptions

Bronze Inscriptions

Later Seal Character

辟 was the orignial form of 劈. In the Oracle-Bone Inscriptions and Bronze Inscriptions, the character 辟 has a man on his knees on the left and a knife for the execution of death penalty on the right. Sometimes, at the lower part in between the man and the knife there is a little square or circle, which stands for the head cut off. Therefore the character 辟 is a vivid description of the execution of a criminal, and it originally meant "to cut," "to chop." But it may also refer to other forms of punishment, e.g. 劓 (yì) 辟 (to cut off the nose), 墨辟 (to tattoo the face with insulting words), from which have derived its meanings of "law," "legal system" and its use to refer to the highest law executor, the monarch. That is why the present-day term 复辟 means the restoration of a dethroned monarch. In addition, 辟 can also mean "to call up," e.g. 辟召 (to draft).

máo

Bronze Inscriptions

Later Seal Character

矛 is a type of ancient weapon, which has a long handle at the end of which is a spearhead made of bronze or iron. In the Bronze Inscriptions, the character 矛 looks like a picture of this weapon. Characters with 矛 as a component all have to do with this weapon and its uses, e.g. 矜 (qín, the handle of a spear), 矟 (shuò, lance).

shū

Bronze Inscriptions

Later Seal Character

殳 is a type of ancient weapon with a hooked edge at the head. It is usually made of bamboo, but sometimes made of bronze or other metal as well. In the Bronze Inscriptions, the character 殳 looks like a man holding this weapon in hand. Characters with 殳 as a component usually have to do with hitting, killing and striking, e.g. 殴 (to hit), 毁 (to destroy), 杀 (殺, to kill, the original complicated form being) and 段 (segment).

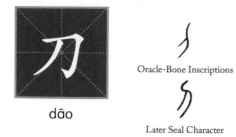

刀
dāo

Oracle-Bone Inscriptions

Later Seal Character

刀, originally the name of a type of sword, is a general term for any tool which functions as a knife, i.e. to cut or chop. In ancient writing systems, the character 刀 looks like a chopper with a short handle and an arching edge. Characters with 刀 (刂) as a component most have to do with the knife and its uses, e.g. 刃 (edge), 刑 (to kill), 剁 (to chop up), 利 (sharp), 剖 (to cut open), 剥 (to peel), etc.

刃
rèn

Oracle-Bone Inscriptions

Later Seal Character

The character 刃 is an indicative. It is composed of a knife part and a sign indicating the position of edge. Hence the primary meaning of 刃 is "the point or edge of a knife." But it can also refer the knife as a whole, e.g. 利刃 (a sharp knife), 白刃 (naked sword). And it can be used as a verb, meaning "to kill with a knife."

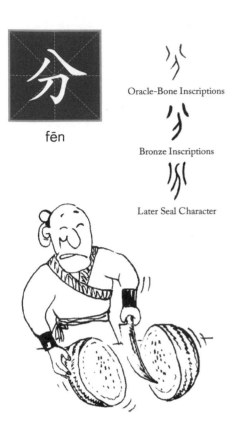

fēn

Oracle-Bone Inscriptions

Bronze Inscriptions

Later Seal Character

The character 分 consists of 八 (to separate) and 刀 (knife), signalling to divide something into two parts with a knife. The primary meaning of 分, opposite to 合 (to combine), is "to segment something into several parts" or "to separate things which are otherwise connected." From this meaning have derived its extended meanings "to distinguish" and "to distribute."

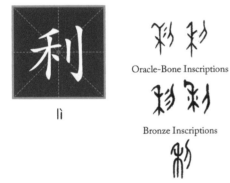

lì

Oracle-Bone Inscriptions

Bronze Inscriptions

Later Seal Character

In ancient writing systems, the character 利 consists of 禾 (standing grain) and 刀 (knife), signalling to cut the grain with a knife. To cut down the grain, the knife must be sharp enough. So the character 利 means "sharp" and "acute" primarily. But it can also be used in the senses of "benefit (利益)," "advantage (功用)," "smooth (顺利)" and "lucky (吉利)."

别

bié

Oracle-Bone Inscriptions

Later Seal Character

In the Oracle-Bone Inscriptions, the right part of the character 别 looks like a heap of bones and the left a knife, signalling to separate bone from flesh with a knife. Hence the original meaning of 别 was "to pick bone," from which have derived the extended meanings: "to separate," "to distinguish," "branches," "differences" and "types."

刖

yuè

Oracle-Bone Inscriptions

Later Seal Character

刖 refers to an ancient form of punishment: to cut away a leg. In the Oracle-Bone Inscriptions, the character 刖 looks like a man's leg being severed with a saw, a vivid description of the cruel punishment. In the Later Seal Character, the character 刖 consists of 肉 (flesh) and 刀 (knife); though still an ideograph, there is no longer any trace of picture-like image. From the main use of 刖 as a name of punishment has derived the more general sense of the cutting off of anything.

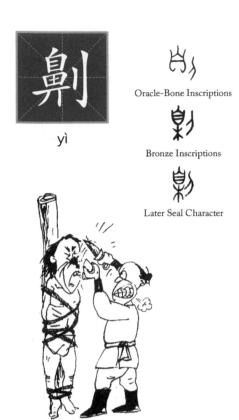

yì

岜彡
Oracle-Bone Inscriptions

Bronze Inscriptions

Later Seal Character

In the Oracle-Bone Inscriptions, the character 劓 consists of 刀 (knife) and 自 (the original form of 鼻, nose), signalling to cut off a nose with a knife. It was one of the five common punishments in ancient times to cut off the nose of a man. According to the law at that time, anyone who disobeyed orders, changed regulations without permission, stole things or wounded others would have his nose cut off as a punishment.

契

qì

扪
Oracle-Bone Inscriptions

契
Later Seal Character

In ancient writing systems, the character 契 has a knife part on the right and a vertical stroke with three horizontal strokes on the left, depicting vividly one of the ways of recording events beside tying knots in a rope, i.e. marking with a knife. In the Regular Script, 契 has an additional component 木 (wood), signalling the marks are made on wood. Later on, the component 木 was mistakenly written as 大, hence the present form of 契. From its original meaning of marking with a knife, 契 has evolved to refer to things which have marks on, especially those recording agreements between different sides, i.e. contracts. It can also be used as a verb, meaning "to agree."

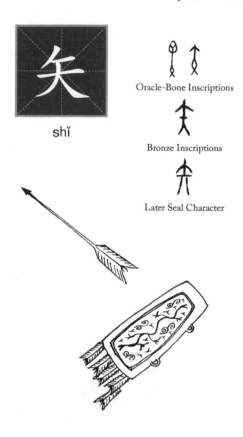

矢

shǐ

Oracle-Bone Inscriptions

Bronze Inscriptions

Later Seal Character

矢 refers, the same as 箭, to a very important weapon: arrow. In ancient times, however, there was a little difference between 矢 and 箭: the former is made of wood and the latter bamboo. In the Oracle-Bone Inscriptions and Bronze Inscriptions, the character 矢 looks like an arrow, with its head, shaft and tail all present. And "arrow" is its main meaning, e.g. 有的放矢 (to shoot the arrow at the target; to have a definite object in view). As 矢 and 誓 (to vow) sounded the same in ancient times, 矢 is sometimes used in the sense of 誓.

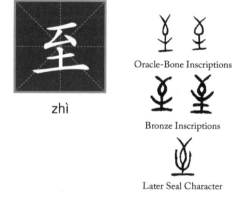

至

zhì

Oracle-Bone Inscriptions

Bronze Inscriptions

Later Seal Character

In the Oracle-Bone Inscriptions and Bronze Inscriptions, the character 至 looks like an upside-down arrow on a horizontal line standing for the ground, signalling an arrow has reached the ground. Therefore, the primary meaning of 至 is "to reach," from which have derived its meanings of "the extreme point" and "the most."

射

shè

Oracle-Bone Inscriptions

Bronze Inscriptions

Later Seal Character

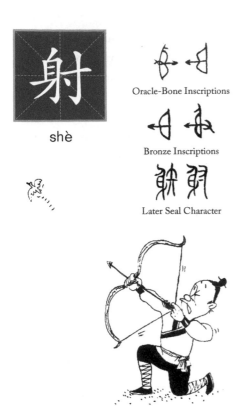

Wu Zetian (Wu Tse-t'ien), Empress of the Tang Dynasty, fond of coining new characters and altering existing ones, once said to her ministers, "The characters 射 and 矮 should exchange their meanings. 射 should mean 矮 (short), since its components are 身 (body) and 寸 (a measure of length, a little longer than an inch), and a man of about an inch is short. On the other hand, 矮 should mean 射 (to shoot), since its components are 矢 (arrow) and 委 (to let go), and to let go an arrow means to shoot." In most of the ancient writing systems, however, the character 射 looks like a man drawing a bow. It is only in the Later Seal Character that the part signalling bow and arrow, by mistake, becomes bodylike and the part signalling hand becomes 寸. The original picturelike image has disappeared all together. And it is no longer possible to judge its meaning from its shape. That is why Wu Zetian made herself a laughing stock by her suggestion.

疾

jí

Oracle-Bone Inscriptions

Bronze Inscriptions

Later Seal Character

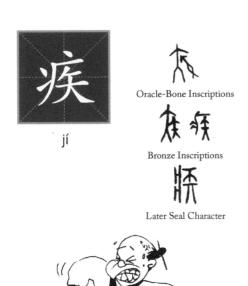

疾 was originally an ideograph. In both the Oracle-Bone Inscriptions and Bronze Inscriptions, the character 疾 looks like a man hit by an arrow under the armpit, signalling to be wounded by an arrow. It can also refer to wound in general. In the Later Seal Character, however, the character 疾 becomes a phonetic compound, with 疒 (illness) as the radical and 矢 as the phonetic, and its meaning is also changed from "wound" to "ailment." Though at the beginning 疾 meant some what differently from 病, which referred to serious illness. As the original meaning of 疾 was "to shoot someone with an arrow and arrows fly fast," 疾 can also mean "fast" and "quick."

侯

hóu

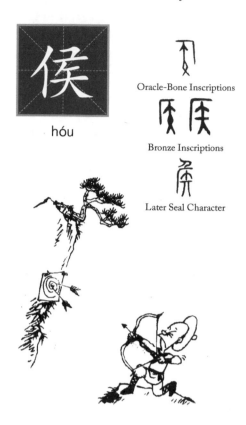

Oracle-Bone Inscriptions

Bronze Inscriptions

Later Seal Character

In the Oracle-Bone Inscriptions and Bronze Inscriptions, the character 侯 looks like an arrow flying to the target, hence the original meaning was "target for archery." In ancient times, bow and arrow was a very important weapon, and those who were good at shooting were usually selected as leaders. As 侯 meant target, those who were good at hitting the target were also known as 侯. In the Chinese system of nobility, 侯 ranks the second, equivalent to marquis. But it can also be used as a general term for high officers and noble lords.

函

hán

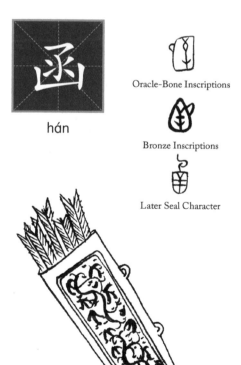

Oracle-Bone Inscriptions

Bronze Inscriptions

Later Seal Character

In the Oracle-Bone Inscriptions and Bronze Inscriptions, the character 函 looks like a bag containing an arrow, i.e. a quiver. The quiver has an eyelet on its side so that it may be attached to the belt of a man. From this original meaning of "quiver" have derived its more general meanings: "to contain," and "container," especially "envelope." Nowadays it is more usually used in the sense of "letter"—the contained in an envelope.

fú

Oracle-Bone Inscriptions

Bronze Inscriptions

Later Seal Character

In the Oracle-Bone Inscriptions and Bronze Inscriptions, the character, an ideograph, looks like a rack for holding arrows. And that is its primary meaning. In the Later Seal Character, it becomes a phonetic compound, with 竹 (bamboo) as its radical as it is usually made of bamboo, and 服 as its phonetic.

gōng

Oracle-Bone Inscriptions

Bronze Inscriptions

Later Seal Character

弓 refers to the weapon used for shooting an arrow, i.e. bow. In the Oracle-Bone Inscriptions, the character 弓 is in the shape of a complete bow with its string and back. In the Bronze Inscriptions and early Bronze Inscriptions, the character 弓 looks like a bow with its back only, a stringless bow. As the bow back is curved in later Bronze Inscriptions and Later Seal Character, the character 弓 has also taken on the meaning of "curve." Characters with 弓 as a component all have to do with the bow and its uses, e.g. 弦 (string), 弹 (pellet), 张 (to stretch), 弛 (to relax), 弩 (volleybow), etc.

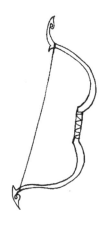

引

yǐn

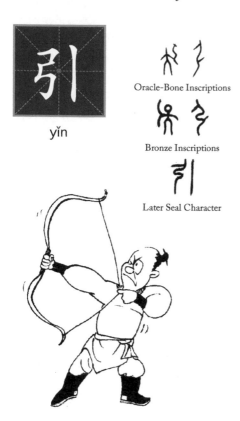

Oracle-Bone Inscriptions

Bronze Inscriptions

Later Seal Character

In the Oracle-Bone Inscriptions and early Bronze Inscriptions, the character 引 looks like a man drawing a bow. In the late Bronze Inscriptions, the man part is left out, but a short stroke is added to the bow part to signal the drawing of it. The primary meaning of 引 is "to draw a bow," but it is also used in the more general sense of pulling. Other extended meanings of 引 include "to lengthen," "to elongate," "to lead" and "to persuade."

弦

Later Seal Character

xián

弦 refers to the stringlike material, made of ox sinew or silk, stretched between the two ends of a bow back for shooting an arrow. In the Later Seal Character, the character 弦 consists of 弓 (bow) and 玄 (silk cord), signalling a string made of silk. Apart from this use, the character 弦 may also refer to the strings stretched across a musical instrument to give sound, or any other stringlike things.

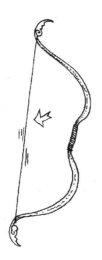

弹

dàn/tán

Oracle-Bone Inscriptions

Later Seal Character

In the Oracle-Bone Inscriptions, the character 弹 looks like a pellet on a bow-string, ready to be shot. In the Later Seal Character, it becomes a phonetic compound with 弓 as the radical and 单 as the phonetic. The character 弹 primarily refers to the pellet, or the catapult, the instrument for shooting a pellet. But it may also be used as a verb, pronounced as tán, meaning "to shoot a pellet," from which have derived its senses of "plucking (a stringed musical instrument)" and "playing (a keyboard musical instrument)."

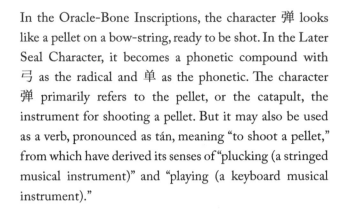

盾

dùn

Oracle-Bone Inscriptions

Bronze Inscriptions

Later Seal Character

盾 refers to the shield, an instrument for protecting oneself from arrows, blows, etc. In the Oracle-Bone Inscriptions and early Bronze Inscriptions, the character 盾 sometimes has "+" as the radical and 豚 as the phonetic, and "+" is a sign for shield.

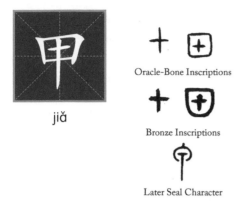

jiǎ

Oracle-Bone Inscriptions

Bronze Inscriptions

Later Seal Character

甲 means "armour," the protective covering made of leather and metal, worn in former times by soldiers in fighting to prevent themselves from getting wounded. In the Oracle-Bone Inscriptions and Bronze Inscriptions, the character 甲 looks like plates of armour linked together; and sometimes it is simply represented by a cross. 甲 primarily refers to armour, from which has derived its use for the hard shells of animals, e.g. 龟甲 (tortoise-shell), 甲壳 (crust), 指甲 (nail). The character 甲 is also the name of one of the ten Heavenly Stems, a traditional Chinese system of sequence. As it ranks first there, 甲 has taken on the meaning of first as well.

介

jiè

Oracle-Bone Inscriptions

Bronze Inscriptions

Later Seal Character

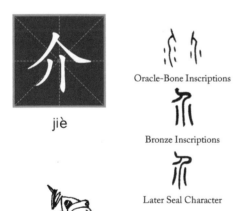

In ancient writing systems, the character 介 looks like the side view of a man in between two dots standing for armour. The original meaning of 介 was "the armour worn by men." As the armour covers the man, in other words, the man is in between the front and back parts of armour, 介 has also taken on the meaning of "in between," e.g. 介居 (to be situated between). In addition, 介 can also mean "upright and outspoken" and "proud and aloof."

niè

Oracle-Bone Inscriptions

Bronze Inscriptions

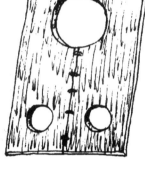

Later Seal Character

幸 originally referred to a manacle, which is an instrument of torture being used for lock prisoners up in ancient times. In Oracle-Bone Inscriptions, the character 幸 looks like a picture that a manacle has two 辖 at both ends. Hence its original meaning was "manacle." In Regular Script, 幸 as a radical be written as 幸. Charaters with 幸 (幸) as a component most have to do with detention, e.g. 执 (執), 报 (報), 圉.

执

zhí

Oracle-Bone Inscriptions

Bronze Inscriptions

Later Seal Character

In the Oracle-Bone Inscriptions, the character 执 looks like a man with his two hands in handcuffs. The original meaning of 执 was "to arrest," from which have derived its extended meanings of "hold," "grasp," "master," "administer," "execute," "stick to," etc.

xíng

Bronze Inscriptions

Later Seal Character

刑 means punishment, especially corporal punishment. In Bronze Inscriptions, the character 刑 consists of "井" and 刀 as radicals, the "井" part looks like a cage, and the 刀 part refers to corporal punishment. So 刑 signals a man in a cage or bearing corporal punishment, in the Later Seal Character, 刑 becomes, by mistake, a phonetic compound with 刀 (knife) as the radical and 井 (well) as the phonetic. In the *Origin of Chinese Characters*, "刑, means penalty, consists of 井 and 刀 as radicals." In *Yi* says "井, means law, and 刀 is the phonetic part."

yǔ

Oracle-Bone Inscriptions

Bronze Inscriptions

Later Seal Character

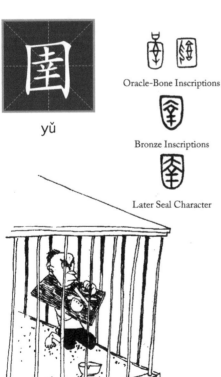

The character 圄 consists of 口 and 幸. The former stands for prison and the latter fetters and handcuffs. Hence the primary meaning is "prison." In the Oracle-Bone Inscriptions, the character 圄 looks like a man with handcuffs in a prison cell. That is why prison in former times is also known as 囹圄 or 囹圉. In addition, 圉 can also mean "to breed horses."

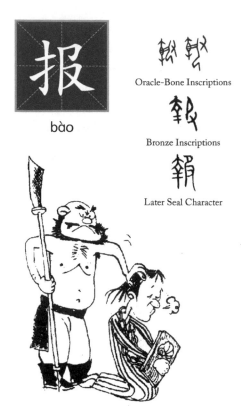

报

bào

Oracle-Bone Inscriptions

Bronze Inscriptions

鞝

Later Seal Character

In the Oracle-Bone Inscriptions, the character 报 looks like a handcuffed offender on his knees, who is about to be sentenced, and there is a man pressing his head from behind so as to make him obedient. The original meaning of 报 was "to sentence an offender according to his crime." To sentence an offender, one must report it to the higher authorities and publicly declare it. Hence the character 报 has taken on the meanings of "report" and "inform" as well.

鞭

biān

Bronze Inscriptions

鞭

Later Seal Character

鞭 refers to the whip, an instrument for driving cattle along or hitting people. In the Bronze Inscriptions, the character 鞭, an ideograph, looks like a man with a whip in hand, or a man beating another with a whip. So 鞭 may also be used as a verb, meaning "to beat with a whip."

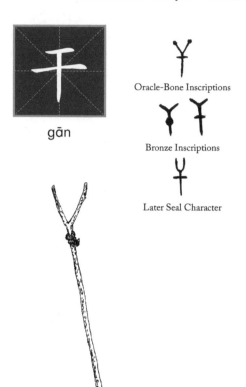

gān

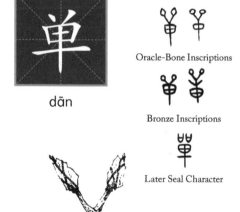

干

Oracle-Bone Inscriptions

Bronze Inscriptions

Later Seal Character

In ancient writing systems, the character 干 looks like a two-tined fork with a long handle. This forklike weapon may be used both to attack the enemy and to protect oneself. But its meaning has evolved over the years and it has come to refer to defensive weapons only, a substitute for 盾 (shield), in other words. Nevertheless, 干 is a weapon; and used as a verb it means "to violate," e.g. 干犯 (to offend), 干涉 (to interfere) and 干预 (to intervene) etc.

单

dān

Oracle-Bone Inscriptions

Bronze Inscriptions

Later Seal Character

单 was an instrument for hunting or fighting in ancient times. In the Oracle-Bone Inscriptions and Bronze Inscriptions, the character 单 looks like a two tined fork with a long handle. One may stab animals or people with its forks or hit them by throwing the stone fastened to its head. This type of weapon was very common in the primitive society, but rarely seen in later ages. So its original meaning has died out, and 单 is nowadays more usually used in the senses of "alone," "single," "thin," etc.

wǎng

Oracle-Bone Inscriptions

Bronze Inscriptions

Later Seal Character

网 means "net," an instrument for catching fish or birds. In the Oracle-Bone Inscriptions, the character 网 looks exactly like a net, strings woven together between two sticks with regular spaces. In the Bronze Inscriptions, its structure is simplified, while in the Regular Script it undergoes an opposite process, added with a thread part (纟) as its radical, and a phonetic part 罔. Characters with 网 and it's variant 罒 as a component most have to do with the net and its uses, e.g. 罗 (a net for catching birds), 罟 (gǔ, fishing net) and 罾 (zēng, a fishing net with wood or bamboo sticks as framework).

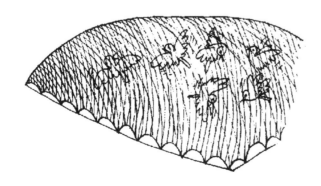

luó

Bronze Inscriptions

Later Seal Character

In the Oracle-Bone Inscriptions, the character 罗 looks like a net on a bird, signalling to catch a bird with a net. And that is its primary meaning, e.g. 门可罗雀 (<lit.> One can catch sparrows on the doorstep; Visitors are few and far between.), 网罗人才 (to enlist able men). 罗 may also be used as a noun, e.g. 天罗地网 (nets above and snares below).

毕

bì

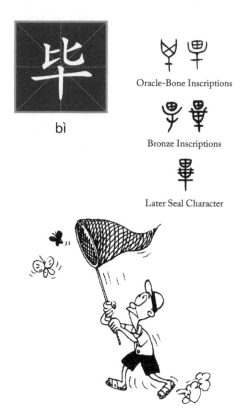

毕 was a small net with a handle for catching birds in former times. In the Oracle-Bone Inscriptions, the character 毕 looks like a picture of this type of net; sometimes it has the part 又, signalling it is to be held by a hand. In the Bronze Inscriptions, it has a component 田 (field), indicating it is an instrument for hunting in the fields. Thus, Xu Shen says in his *Origin of Chinese Characters*, "毕 is a net for field hunting." However, this character is nowadays more usually used in the sense of "end," "completion" and "all," whereas its original meaning is lost.

Oracle-Bone Inscriptions

Bronze Inscriptions

Later Seal Character

禽

qín

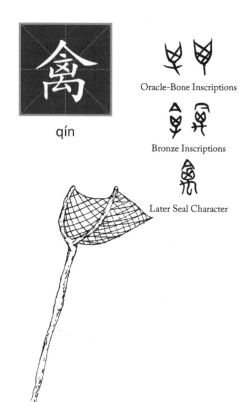

Oracle-Bone Inscriptions

Bronze Inscriptions

Later Seal Character

In the Oracle-Bone Inscriptions, the character 禽 looks like a net with a handle, an instrument for catching birds. The original meaning of 禽 was "net for catching birds," but it can also be used as a verb, meaning the same as 擒, "to catch." 禽 is also a general term for birds, sometimes it may even cover the meaning of beasts as well.

刚

gāng

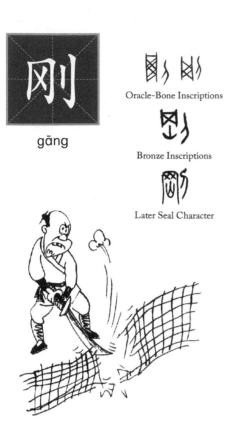

Oracle-Bone Inscriptions

Bronze Inscriptions

Later Seal Character

In the Oracle-Bone Inscriptions, the character 刚 looks like a net beside a knife, signalling hard and sharp. In the Bronze Inscriptions, a mountain part (山) is added to reinforce its sense of firmness.

午

wǔ

Oracle-Bone Inscriptions

Bronze Inscriptions

Later Seal Character

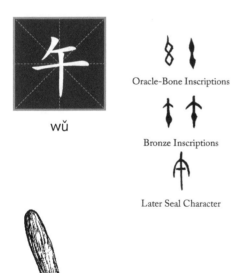

午 was the original form of 杵, referring to the pestle. In the Oracle-Bone Inscriptions and Bronze Inscriptions, the character 午 looks like a pestle, whose two ends are rounded and bigger than the middle. As a pestle is used for husking rice, characters with 午 as a component most have a sense of "offending" and "violating," e.g. 忤 (disobedient), 迕 (to go against). But 午 is now mainly used as a name of the seventh Earthly Branch, a traditional Chinese system of sequence, and its original meaning is expressed by 杵.

春

chōng

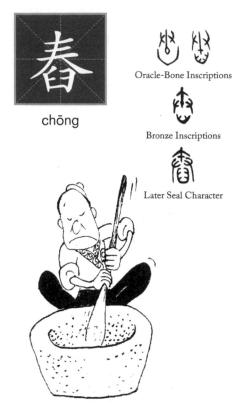

Oracle-Bone Inscriptions

Bronze Inscriptions

Later Seal Character

春 means "to husk rice." This was done by hand before the invention of husking machines. In ancient writing systems, the character 春 looks like a picture of this activity: two hands holding a pestle on top of a mortar, signalling to remove the husks of grain by striking with a pestle in a mortar.

臼

jiù

Ancient Pottery Inscriptions
(Pre-Qin Period)

Later Seal Character

臼 means "mortar," a vessel made from stone, for containing grain to be husked. In ancient writing systems, the character 臼 has the shape of a mortar. It refers to mortar and mortarlike things at that. Characters with 臼 as a component most have to do with mortarlike things, e.g. 舀 (ladle), 春 (to husk) and 臽 (pitfall).

yǎo

Later Seal Character

The character 舀, an ideograph, consists of 爪 (hand) and 臼 (mortar). In the Later Seal Character, the character 舀 looks like the grasping of rice from a mortar with a hand. Its original meaning was "to lift things from a mortar." But its meaning has been shifted and it now means "to get something, especially liquid, with a ladle or spoon."

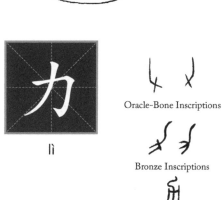

力

lì

Oracle-Bone Inscriptions

Bronze Inscriptions

Later Seal Character

In the Oracle-Bone Inscriptions, the character 力 looks like a farm implement for ploughing: the upper part is the handle, the lower part is the ploughshare, and the vertical stroke suggests the place to step on. In other words, the original meaning of 力 was "耒 (plough)." As it takes a great deal of strength to turn over land with a plough, the character 力 has taken on the meaning of "strength," from which derive the meanings of "ability," "power," etc.

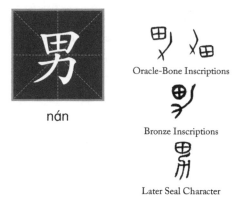

nán

Oracle-Bone Inscriptions

Bronze Inscriptions

Later Seal Character

The character 男 consists of 田 (field) and 力 (plough). It was a tradition for men to till the fields and women to weave cloth in former times. So the character 力, to plough the fields, has come to refer to the people who do the ploughing i.e. adult men. Later its meaning has been broadened to cover the whole male sex, opposite to 女 (female). But it may also refer to son in particular.

lěi

Bronze Inscriptions

Later Seal Character

耒 was a spadelike tool with a forked head for breaking land in ancient times. In the early Bronze Inscriptions, the character 耒 looks like a hand (又) holding a forked plough (力). In the Later Seal Character, the hand part is simplified into three left-falling strokes and the plough part becomes wood (木) by mistake. This mistaken structure is the origin of the character 耒 in the Regular Script. Characters with 耒 as a component all have to do with farming tools or crops, e.g. 耜 (sì, a spadelike tool), 耕 (to plough), 耤 (cultivation), 耦 (ǒu, two men ploughing side by side).

jí

Oracle-Bone Inscriptions

Bronze Inscriptions

Later Seal Character

In the Oracle-Bone Inscriptions, the character, an ideograph, looks like a farmer turning over land strenuously with a plough, hence its meaning is "to cultivate the ground." In the Bronze Inscritpions, the part 昔 is added to indicate its pronunciation. In the Later Seal Character, its structure is simplified, resulting in a phonetic compound with 耒 as the radical and 昔 as the phonetic. But in ancient books, the character was usually written as 藉, e.g. 藉田 (also 籍田, field cultivated by the emperor in name).

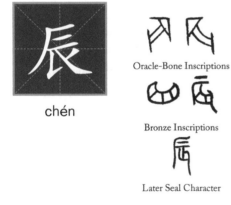

辰

chén

Oracle-Bone Inscriptions

Bronze Inscriptions

Later Seal Character

辰 was the original form of 蜃 (giant clam). Thus the character 辰 in the Bronze Inscriptions is in the shape of a clam. Giant clams have big and hard shells, which can be used as tools for weeding. For example, Huainan Zi records, "In the past people sharpened ploughs to turn over land and whetted clams to remove weeds." However, the character 辰 is now mainly used as a name of the fifth Earthly Branch, a traditional Chinese system of sequence. It is also a general term for the celestial bodies like the sun, moon and stars, and may refer to time or days.

nóng

Oracle-Bone Inscriptions

Bronze Inscriptions

Later Seal Character

In the Oracle-Bone Inscriptions, the character 农 looks like the removal of weeds between crops with a clam, signalling cultivation. In the Bronze Inscriptions, it has 田 (field) as a component, and the meaning "to cultivate land" is expressed more clearly. Apart from this primary meaning, 农 may also refer to the people who do the cultivation, i.e. farmers.

qí

Oracle-Bone Inscriptions

Bronze Inscriptions

Later Seal Character

In the Oracle-Bone Inscriptions, the character 其 looks like a pan, an instrument for winnowing. In other words, 其 was the original form of 箕 (winnowing pan). As it is made of bamboo, a bamboo part is added to 其 to form 箕. And the character 其 is how mainly used as a third person pronoun, especially in the possessive case; a conjunction, expressing presupposition or contrast; or an adverb, expressing assumption or wish.

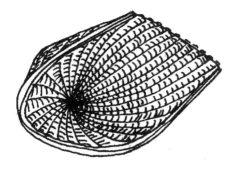

kuài

Later Seal Character

The character 块 was originally an ideograph. In the Later Seal Character, it looks like a basket containing lumps of soil. And "lumps of soil" is its primary meaning. But it has changed into a phonetic compound later. For example, the variant in the Later Seal Character has 土 (soil) as its radical and 鬼 as its phonetic; and its simplified form has 土 as the radical and 夬 (guài) as the phonetic. 块 is also used generally for anything which is in the shape of a lump, e.g. 铁块 (lumps of iron), 煤块 (lump coal), 石块 (stone). In addition, it can mean "proud and aloof" and "open and upright."

kāng

Oracle-Bone Inscriptions

Bronze Inscriptions

康 was the original form of 糠. In the Oracle-Bone Inscriptions, the character 康 looks like a winnowing pan with four dots standing for husks below it, signalling to blow off the husks with a winnowing pan. These husks, or bran, are known as 糠, hence 康 originally referred to husks. The character 康, however, is now mainly used in the senses of "peace and happiness," "plentiful" and "broad." Its original meaning is expressed by 糠.

fèn

Oracle-Bone Inscriptions

Later Seal Character

In the Oracle-Bone Inscriptions, the character 糞 looks like a man sweeping away the dirt with a broom and a dustpan. Hence its orignal meaning was "to clean" and "to sweep away the dirt." As what is swept away is dirty, the character 糞 is also used to refer to excrement and urine; or as a verb, meaning "to apply manure."

qì

Oracle-Bone Inscriptions

Bronze Inscriptions

Later Seal Character

In the Oracle-Bone Inscriptions, the character 弃 looks like two hands holding a dustpan in which is a dead newborn, and the dots around it stand for birth water, signalling to throw away a dead baby. Hence the primary meaning of 弃 is "to throw away," from which have derived the meanings "to discard," and "to go against."

zhǒu

Oracle-Bone Inscriptions

Bronze Inscriptions

Later Seal Character

帚 means "broom." In the Oracle-Bone Inscriptions and Bronze Inscriptions, the character 帚, a pictograph, looks like an upsidedown broom: the upper part is the head and the lower part is the stick; sometimes there is an additional horizontal stroke signalling the binding string. In the Later Seal Character, it has undergone some change in its shape, losing its picturelike image. As it was the responsibility of the housewife to clean the room in former times, 帚 (broom) was used together with 女 (female) to form the character 婦 (woman, now simplified as 妇).

fù

Oracle-Bone Inscriptions

Bronze Inscriptions

Later Seal Character

It was an old tradition for the man to work in the fields and the woman to work at home. While the man tills the land or goes hunting outside, the woman weaves cloth, sweeps the floor and does the cooking at home. That is why in the Oracle-Bone Inscriptions and Bronze Inscriptions, the character 妇 looks like a woman holding a broom. It is the housewife's responsibility to do the domestic chores, so 妇 primarily means "married woman" or "wife."

qīn

Oracle-Bone Inscriptions

Bronze Inscriptions

Later Seal Character

In the Oracle-Bone Inscriptions, the character 侵 looks like a man driving cattle with a broom, signalling the annexation of other's property. Its primary meaning is "to occupy" and "to seize," from which have derived the extended meanings of "invade," "attack," "bully" and "persecute."

xīng/xìng

Oracle-Bone Inscriptions

Bronze Inscriptions

Later Seal Character

In the Oracle-Bone Inscriptions and Bronze Inscriptions, the character 兴 looks like many hands lifting a tamping plate together. This is a vivid description of many people building together an earth wall by tamping. Sometimes there is a mouth part (口) in the character to signal that they are chanting while tamping. Hence the original meaning of 兴 was "to lift," from which have derived the extended meanings of "rise," "set up," "flourish" and "thrive."

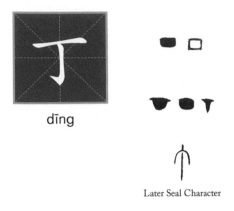

丁 is a most simple Chinese character, consisting of a horizontal stroke and a vertical hook. It is so easy to write and recognize that almost everybody should be able to know it, hence the idiom 目不识丁 (ignorant of even the character 丁; utterly ignorant) is often used to mock those who lack knowledge. However, you may not know what 丁 meant originally if I do not tell you. In the Oracle-Bone Inscriptions and Bronze Inscriptions, the character 丁 has the shape of a nail: seen from the top, it is round (or square); and seen from the side, it is like a wedge. Therefore 丁 was the original form of 钉 and meant "nail" at the beginning.

dīng

Later Seal Character

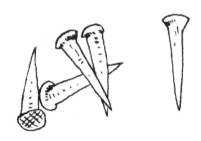

Oracle-Bone Inscriptions

Later Seal Character

zhuān

In the Oracle-Bone Inscriptions, the character 专 looks like a hand turning round a spindle, signalling to twist the thread in spinning with a spindle. The original meaning of 专 was "spindle." In Chinese characters, which with 专 as a component have the meaning of "to rotate," "to turn round," or "to move and pass," such as 抟, 团 (團), 转 and 传. And 专 could be used as a noun, meaning "the brick which is used for fix the spinning wheel standing on the ground." Nowadays, however, it is more usually used in the senses of "alone," "pure" and "single."

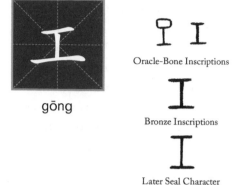

gōng

Oracle-Bone Inscriptions

Bronze Inscriptions

Later Seal Character

In ancient times, the character 工 looks like a square rule, so its primary meaning is "square rule," from which have derived the extended meaning "carpenter," or "craftsman." Sometimes it can refer to "labour." The craftsman must work with great care and skill, and the character 工 has further taken on the meanings of "careful" and "skillful."

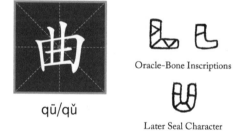

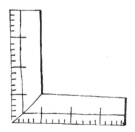

qū/qǔ

Oracle-Bone Inscriptions

Later Seal Character

In the Oracle-Bone Inscriptions and Bronze Inscriptions, the character 曲 looks like a carpenter's square. Its primary meaning is "bent," opposite to 直 (straight), from which have derived its senses of "winding," "hidden" and "indirect." Pronounced as qǔ, 曲 can also refer to the tune of a song.

jù

Bronze Inscriptions

Later Seal Character

巨 was the original form of 矩, referring to the carpenter's square. Thus Xun Zi (Hsün-Tzu) says, "The circles are as perfect as drawn with a pair of compasses, and the squares with a carpenter's square." In the Bronze Inscriptions the character 巨 looks like a man holding a carpenter's square in hand. However the character 巨 is now mainly used in the sense of "huge" and "gigantic," and its original meaning is expressed by 矩.

zhàng

Later Seal Character

In the Later Seal Character, the character 丈 consists of 十 (ruler) and 又 (hand), signalling to measure length with a ruler in hand. The primary meaning of 丈 is "to measure," but it is also used as a measure of length, equal to ten 尺 or one tenth of 引 in the Chinese System, and three metres and one third in the Metric System. In addition, 丈 can also be used as an honorific term for the adult man, especially the aged.

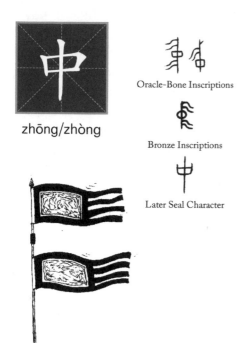

中

zhōng/zhòng

中 Oracle-Bone Inscriptions

中 Bronze Inscriptions

中 Later Seal Character

In ancient China, a banner may consist of several streamers known as 㫃. The number of streamers in a banner is determined by the rank of the owner, and the banner of a king may have as many as twelve streamers. In the Oracle-Bone Inscriptions and Bronze Inscriptions, the character 中 looks like a banner with several streamers, and there is a piece of wood bound to the middle of the mast to make it stronger. This wood is known as 中, but as it is situated in the middle part of the mast, the character 中 takes on the meaning of "middle," "central," from which derive its meanings of "inside" and "amidst." To adopt a moderate approach in politics, not adhering to any extreme views is also known as 中, e.g. 中行 (the middle course), 中庸 ((the doctrine of) the mean).

旅

lǚ

Oracle-Bone Inscriptions

Bronze Inscriptions

Later Seal Character

In former times, when soldiers were about to go to battle, they would assemble under a banner and listen to the orders first. In the Oracle-Bone Inscriptions and Bronze Inscriptions, the character 旅 looks like a group of people assembling under a banner. So the primary meaning of 旅 is "a group of soldiers," expecially a brigade of 500 soldiers. But it may refer to troops in general as well. In addition, 旅 may also mean "a crowd of people" or "travel."

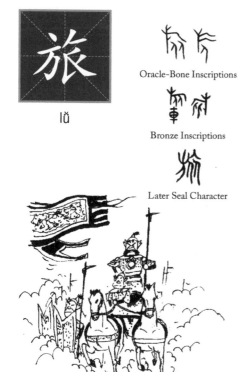

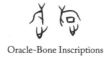

xuán

Oracle-Bone Inscriptions

Bronze Inscriptions

Later Seal Character

In the Oracle-Bone Inscriptions and Bronze Inscriptions, the character 旋 looks like a foot under a banner, signalling people are marching forward with a banner in the lead; and the character 旋 maybe consists of 正 (征) as a radical, signalling people go on an expedition. In the Later Seal Character, 正 part changed to 疋 (or 足). The primary meaning of 旋 is "the returning of army in triumph," but it can also mean "returning in general." An extended meaning of it is "to revolve."

yóu

Oracle-Bone Inscriptions

Bronze Inscriptions

Later Seal Character

In ancient times, whenever there was an outdoor activity or military operation, banners and drums would be used to add to its grandness. In the Oracle-Bone Inscriptions and early Bronze Inscriptions, the character 游 looks like a man marching forward with a banner in hand, and the streamers are fluttering in the wind. The original meaning of 游 was "to march with a banner," but it could also refer to streamers in particular, though strictly speaking the true character for this sense is 斿. In the Bronze Inscriptions, sometimes there is a foot part (止) in the character, the modern derivative being, 遊 signalling movement on foot. In the Later Seal Character, the character may have 水 (water) as its radical, signalling movement in water. Nowadays, however, there is no longer any distinction between 斿, 遊 and 游, which are all written as 游.

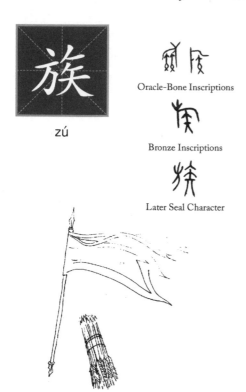

zú

Oracle-Bone Inscriptions

Bronze Inscriptions

Later Seal Character

In ancient times, a tribe or a clan was not only a group of people of the same blood, but also a military organization. In the Oracle-Bone Inscriptions and Bronze Inscriptions, the character 族 looks like arrows under a banner; arrows stand for arms and the banner represents a place where people assemble. The primary meaning of 族 is "tribe," "clan" or "family." When it is used as a verb, it means "to gather" and "to assemble."

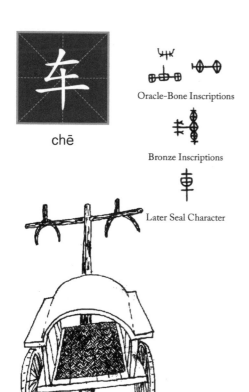

chē

Oracle-Bone Inscriptions

Bronze Inscriptions

Later Seal Character

车 refers to the means of transportation which has wheels and runs along roads. In the Oracle-Bone Inscriptions and Bronze Inscriptions, the character 车 looks like a cart with all its components such as carriage, wheels, axle, shaft and yoke. In the Later Seal Character, it is reduced to something with carriage, wheels and axle only. Characters with 车 as a component most have to do with 车 and its uses, e.g. 轨 (track), 轮 (wheel), 转 (to turn), 载 (to carry) and 军 (army).

Bronze Inscriptions

Later Seal Character

liǎng

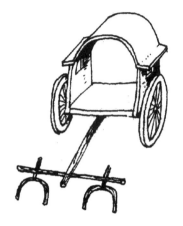

两 was the original form of 辆. In former times, a cart was usually drawn by two horses, so there was usually a yoke for two horses in a cart. And the character 两 looks like such a yoke in the Bronze Inscriptions. Hence 两 originally could be used as a substitute for cart. But it is more usually used as a numeral, meaning "two." In the past, it could also be used as a classifier for vehicles, a function assumed nowadays by 辆. In addition 两 is a measure of weight, equal to ten 钱 or one tenth of 斤 in the Chinese System, and 50 grams in the Metric System.

Bronze Inscriptions

Later Seal Character

niǎn

In the Bronze Inscriptions, the character 辇 looks like a cart drawn by two men, hence its original meaning "cart drawn by men." Since the Qin and Han dynasties, however, the character 辇 has come to be used specially for the carriage of the emperor or empress, e.g. 帝辇 (emperor's carriage), 凤辇 (empress' carriage).

yú

Oracle-Bone Inscriptions

Later Seal Character

In ancient writing systems, the character 輿 looks like four hands carrying a sedan. Its original meaning was "to carry a sedan," and it could be used in the general sense of carrying. But it could also refer to the sedan or carriage. In addition 輿 was a name of the sixth rank in an old ten-rank system of people, referring to people of low social status, in other words, common people.

hōng

Later Seal Character

The character 轟 in its original complicated form is made up of three cart parts, signalling that many carts are running together, making a great noise. Used as an onomatopoeic word, it refers to the noise made by the carts running at the same time, or any similar noise. When used as a verb, it can mean "to thunder," "to bomb," "to shell," "to drive," etc.

zhōu

Oracle-Bone Inscriptions

Bronze Inscriptions

Later Seal Character

In the Oracle-Bone Inscriptions and Bronze Inscriptions, the character 舟 looks like a simple boat, hence its primary meaning is "boat." It can also refer to the saucer, known as 茶舟 in former times and also 茶船 nowadays. Characters with 舟 as a component most have to do with the boat and its uses, e.g. 航 (to sail), 舫 (boat), 舰 (warship), 艇 (light boat) and 艘 (a classifier for boats).

yú

Bronze Inscriptions

Later Seal Character

In the Bronze Inscriptions, the character 俞 has a boat part on the left and a chisellike part on the right, with a dot beside standing for bits of wood cut off. The original meaning of 俞 was "to make a boat by cutting a deep hollow in a log," and it could also refer to the dugout canoe. However, it is more usually used as an exclamation in classical Chinese, and as a surname in modern Chinese, while its original meaning is lost.

qián

Bronze Inscriptions

Later Seal Character

前 is an ideograph. In ancient writing systems, the character 前 consists of 止 (foot) and 舟 (boat); the former means "to move forward" and the latter "to go by boat." The primary meaning of 前 is "to move forward," but it can also mean "before in position or time," opposite to 后 (after).

háng

Oracle-Bone Inscriptions

Later Seal Character

In the Oracle-Bone Inscriptions, the character 航 looks like a man punting a boat with a long pole. Its primary meaning is "to punt a boat," "to sail." But it may also mean "boat," especially "twinboat" (方舟). In the Later Seal Character, the character 航 becomes a phonetic compound. That is why Xu Shen says in his *Origin of Chinese Characters*, "航, or 方舟, has 方 as its radical and 亢 as its phonetic." In addition 航 can also mean "to travel in the air."

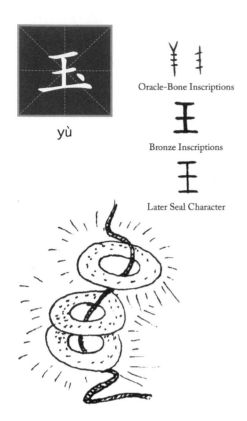

玉

yù

Ý Ì
Oracle-Bone Inscriptions

王
Bronze Inscriptions

王
Later Seal Character

In the Oracle-Bone Inscriptions, the character 玉 looks like a number of jade articles strung together with a thread, hence its primary meaning is "jade article," or simply "jade." As a precious stone, jade is often made into ornaments or sculptures. Thus people often use 玉 as a modifier for beautiful or precious objects, e.g. 玉颜 (good looks), 玉体 (fair body), 玉女 (beautiful girl). Characters with 玉 as a component most have to do with jade, e.g. 环 (ring; hoop), 珍 (treasure), 琳 (beautiful jade), 琼 (fine jade) and 球 (ball).

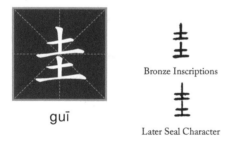

圭

guī

圭
Bronze Inscriptions

圭
Later Seal Character

圭 is a tablet of jade held in hand by ancient rulers on ceremonial occasions. With its pointed head and broad base, it looks like the character 土. That is why the character 圭 has two 土, one upon the other. The character 圭 sometimes has 玉 as a component, emphasizing that it is made of jade.

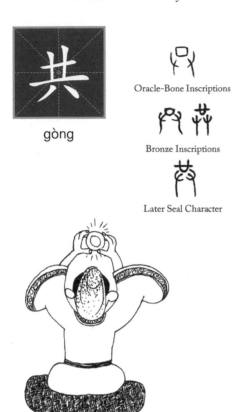

共

gòng

Oracle-Bone Inscriptions

Bronze Inscriptions

Later Seal Character

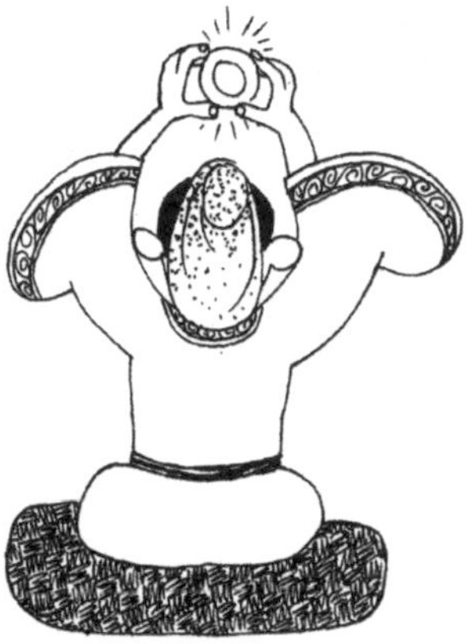

共 was the original form of 拱 or 供. In the Oracle-Bone Inscriptions and the early Bronze Inscriptions, the character 共 looks like a man holding a piece of jade in two hands. Jade is of great value, and is often used of the offerings to ancestors at memorial ceremonies. Hence 共 originally meant "to hold a jade object as an offering," from which derived its extended meanings "to encircle" and "to surround and protect" now written as 拱, and "to supply" now written as 供. When holding something, both hands are used at the same time, so 共 has also taken on the meaning of "being together," e.g. 同舟共济 (to cross a river in the same boat; people in the same situation help each other).

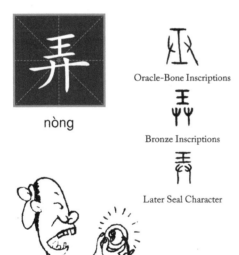

弄

nòng

Oracle-Bone Inscriptions

Bronze Inscriptions

Later Seal Character

In ancient writing systems, the character 弄 looks like two hands playing with a piece of jade, hence its original meaning is "to play with jade," or "to play in general." In the past those who had jade objects to play with must be very rich, such as kings, ministers, generals, and their family members, so to play with jade was a highbrow cultural activity. Nowadays, however, the character 弄 often has pejorative sense, e.g. 弄权 (to manipulate power for personal ends), 愚弄 (to make a fool of), 戏弄 (to play tricks on), 弄巧成拙 (to try to be clever only to end up with a blunder).

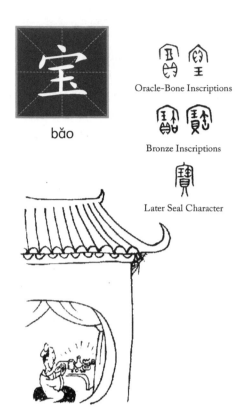

bǎo

Oracle-Bone Inscriptions

Bronze Inscriptions

Later Seal Character

In the Oracle-Bone Inscriptions, the character 宝 looks like a shell and a piece of jade in a house. Used as a medium for exchanging goods in ancient times, the seashell was a symbol of wealth, and jade objects were rare and precious. So the form of 宝 suggests that the owner of the house has great treasure and wealth. In the Bronze Inscriptions, there is a part 缶 added to indicate its pronunciation, resulting in a phonetic compound. The character 宝 in the Regular Script also has this structure. But in the modern simplified form, the parts 贝 and 缶 are left out, changing it back to an ideograph, consisting of 宀 (house) and 玉 (jade).

班

Bronze Inscriptions

Later Seal Character

bān

In ancient writing systems, the character 班 looks like two pieces of jade with a knife in the middle, signalling to divide a jade stone with a knife. The original meaning of 班 was "to divide a jade stone," from which have derived the senses of "distribution," "dispersal" and "arrangement." 班 may also be used as a noun, meaning "rank," "grade," or referring to a unit of the army-squad.

bèi

Oracle-Bone Inscriptions

Bronze Inscriptions

Later Seal Character

贝 means "shellfish," though it mainly referred to those types living in the sea in ancient China. In the Oracle-Bone Inscriptions and Bronze Inscriptions, the character 贝 looks like a seashell. Far away from the sea, it was not easy for people of central China in ancient times to obtain a seashell. And seashells were seen as valuable ornaments to be made into necklaces and worn by rich people. The seashell was also one of the oldest currencies and a symbol of wealth. Characters with 贝 as a component most have to do with money or treasure, e.g. 财 (property), 货 (goods), 贯 (a string of a thousand coins), 贸 (trade), 贵 (expensive), 赁 (to rent) and 贷 (loan).

péng

Oracle-Bone Inscriptions

Bronze Inscriptions

Later Seal Character

In former times, five shells formed a string, and two strings of shells were known as 朋. In the Oracle-Bone Inscriptions and Bronze Inscriptions, the character 朋 looks like two strings of shells, which was what it originally meant. Later it was used as a monetary unit, as is shown in the *Classic of Poetry*, "When encountering a friend, a hundred péng I was offered." Nowadays, however, 朋 is more usually used in the senses of "friend," "party," "comrade," or as a verb, meaning "to associate."

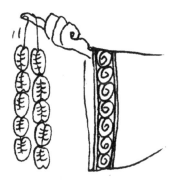

dé

Oracle-Bone Inscriptions

Bronze Inscriptions

Later Seal Character

The seashell, used as a currency in ancient times, was precious, and difficult to obtain. In the Oracle-Bone Inscriptions, the character 得 looks like a hand grasping a seashell, signalling success in obtaining something, hence its primary meaning is "obtaining." In the Bronze Inscriptions, it sometimes has a part 彳 added, indicating it refers to an action.

yīng

Bronze Inscriptions

Later Seal Character

The seashell was precious, and difficult to come by in ancient times. It was used as an ornament, strung together and worn on the neck by women, as well as a currency. The character 嬰 consists of two shell parts (贝) and a woman part (女), signalling the necklace of shells worn by women. Thus the *Origin of Chinese Characters* says, "嬰 means necklace." Nowadays, however, it refers to the newborn baby, and the female baby in particular.

zhù

Oracle-Bone Inscriptions

Bronze Inscriptions

Later Seal Character

In the Oracle-Bone Inscriptions, the character 貯, an ideograph, looks like a shell in a chest, hence its primary meaning "to store." In the Bronze Inscriptions, it has undergone some change in the form, the shell part (贝) is put under the chest part (宁, zhù). In the Later Seal Character, the chest part (宁) is moved to the right of the shell part (贝), resulting in a phonetic compound, with 贝 as the radical and 宁 as the phonetic.

măi

Oracle-Bone Inscriptions

Bronze Inscriptions

Later Seal Character

In ancient writing systems, the character 买 consists of a net part (网) and a shell part (贝), signalling to obtain something with a net in exchange for a shell. The shell was used as a currency, a medium for exchanging goods in former times. So 买 means "to buy," "to obtain something in exchange for money," opposite to 卖 (to sell).

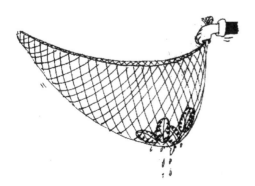

负

fù

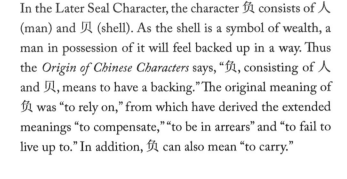

Later Seal Character

In the Later Seal Character, the character 负 consists of 人 (man) and 贝 (shell). As the shell is a symbol of wealth, a man in possession of it will feel backed up in a way. Thus the *Origin of Chinese Characters* says, "负, consisting of 人 and 贝, means to have a backing." The original meaning of 负 was "to rely on," from which have derived the extended meanings "to compensate," "to be in arrears" and "to fail to live up to." In addition, 负 can also mean "to carry."

实

shí

Bronze Inscriptions

Later Seal Character

Xu Shen says in his the *Origin of Chinese Characters*, "实 means rich." In the Bronze Inscriptions, the character 实 consists of 宀 (house), 田 (field) and 贝 (shell), signalling the family has fields and money. In the Later Seal Character, the character consists of 宀 (house) and 贯 (a string of a thousand coins), also signalling rich. Thus the original meaning of 实 was "rich," "substantial," or "wealth," "property." Its extended meanings include "full," opposite to 空 (empty); and "real," opposite to 假 (false).

Later Seal Character

jī

In ancient times, there were no chairs or tables. People would sit on the ground, and there was something beside to support one's back or arm. This object is thin and long, and has short legs, something like a tea table. The character 几 in the Later Seal Character looks like such a small table. Nowadays, however, the character 几 is mainly used as the simplified form of 幾, pronounced as jǐ and meaning "a few."

chǔ

Bronze Inscriptions

Later Seal Character

In the Bronze Inscriptions, the character 处 looks like a man sitting on a stool, sometimes with 虎 as its phonetic. The original meaning of 处 was "to sit," from which have derived its extended meanings of "situate," "reside" and "get along with." But it is mainly used in the senses of "manage" and "deal with" nowadays.

chuáng

Oracle-Bone Inscriptions

Later Seal Character

In former times 床 referred to an article of furniture for both sitting and sleeping. In the Oracle-Bone Inscriptions, the character 床 looks like a bed on end, with both its board and posts. In the Later Seal Character, a wood part (木) is added to it, signalling that it is made of wood. The vulgarism in the Regular Script is written as 床, which is the origin of the modern simplified form.

xí

Ancient Script

Later Seal Character

席 refers to a matlike cushion, made of reed, bamboo or straw, on which people can sit or lie. The character 席 in the Ancient Script as is recorded in the *Origin of Chinese Characters* looks like a straw mat under the roof of a house. The primary meaning of 席 is "matlike cushion," from which have derived the meanings of "seat," "order of seats" and "feast."

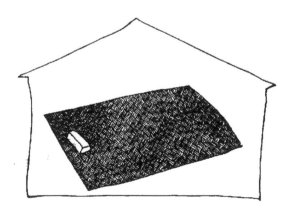

因
yīn

Oracle-Bone Inscriptions

Bronze Inscriptions

Later Seal Character

因 was the original form of 茵. In ancient writing systems, the character 因 looks like a man lying on a matlike cushion. Its original meaning was "straw mat." As a mat is something supporting a man, the character 因 has taken on the senses "to rely on," "on the basis of," "to depend," "to follow," and even the senses of "cause" and "reason."

鼓
gǔ

Oracle-Bone Inscriptions

Bronze Inscriptions

Later Seal Character

鼓 means "drum," a percussion instrument consisting of a skin stretched tight over the two sides of a hollow circular frame. In former times, the army general used the drum to signal the beginning of attack against the enemy and the bell to withdraw the troops. In ancient writing systems, the character 鼓 looks like a man beating a drum with a drumstick. From its primary meaning of "beating a drum" have derived the extended meanings "to beat," "to strike" and "to play (a musical instrument)," e.g. 鼓掌 (to clap one's hands), 鼓瑟 (to pluck the stringed instrument sè). It can also mean "to agitate (鼓动)," "to encourage (鼓励)" and "to inspire (鼓舞)." As the drum has a rounded body, the character 鼓 is also used in the sense of "bulging out," e.g. 鼓腹 (to bulge the stomach).

péng

Oracle-Bone Inscriptions

Bronze Inscriptions

Later Seal Character

In the Oracle-Bone Inscriptions and Bronze Inscriptions, the character 彭 has a drum part on the left and some dots on the right, signalling the sound produced by beating the drum. So 彭 is an onomatopoeic word for the sound of a drum. From this meaning has derived its use for the sound produced by rushing water, e.g. 汹涌彭湃 (surging and turbulent water), in which 彭 may also be written as 澎.

xǐ

Oracle-Bone Inscriptions

Bronze Inscriptions

Later Seal Character

In the Oracle-Bone Inscriptions, the character 喜 looks like a drum on a square frame, with some dots on the two sides standing for the sound produced, signalling the beating of a drum on an occasion of celebration. From this primary meaning of "celebration" have derived its extended meanings: "happy," "joyous" and "to like."

hé

Oracle-Bone Inscriptions

Bronze Inscriptions

Later Seal Character

In ancient writing systems, the character 和 has a wind instrument made of bamboo pipes on the left, and the phonetic 禾 on the right. The primary meaning of 和 is, therefore, "harmonious tune," from which have derived the meanings of "mild" and "gentle."

yuè/lè

Oracle-Bone Inscriptions

Bronze Inscriptions

Later Seal Character

It is understandable that the ancient stringed instruments were very simple. According to legend, "Shun invented a five-stringed plucked instrument for the tunes of the South." And King Wen and King Wu of the Zhou Dyansty each added a string to it, resulting in a seven-stringed plucked instrument of today. In the Oracle-Bone Inscriptions and Bronze Inscriptions, the character 乐 looks like a musical instrument consisting of strings stretched over a piece of wood. This character not only referred to the seven-stringed instrument but all types of musical instrument. And nowadays it means "music." As music is pleasing to the ear and gives people satisfaction, the character 乐 used as a verb, pronounced as lè, can mean "to be happy, cheerful or joyful."

qín

Later Seal Character

琴 is an ancient stringed instrument. In the Later Seal Character, the character 琴 looks like a diagram of this musical instrument seen from one end: the circular part at the bottom stands for its body and the two 王 parts at the top for the string holders. But it can also be used as a general term for some musical instruments, e.g. 钢琴 (piano), 提琴 (violin), 胡琴 (Chinese fiddle) and 口琴 (mouth organ).

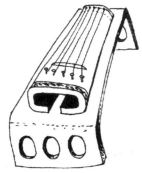

gēng

Oracle-Bone Inscriptions

Bronze Inscriptions

Later Seal Character

Judging from the early Oracle-Bone Inscriptions and early Bronze Inscriptions, the character 庚 refers to a musical instrument like a rattle-drum. There is a threaded bead on each side, which will hit the body and rattle when the instrument is rocked. However, this character is now mainly used as a name of the seventh Heavenly Stem, a traditional Chinese system of sequence, and its original meaning is lost.

qìng

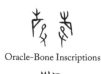

Oracle-Bone Inscriptions

Later Seal Character

磬, in the shape of a carpenter's square, is an ancient percussion instrument, made of jade, stone or metal. In the Oracle-Bone Inscriptions, the character 磬 looks like a man striking the hanging chime stone with a mallet. In the Later Seal Character, it has a stone part (石) added, signalling that it is usually made of stone. As this instrument has a bent like the carpenter's square, the character 磬 can also mean "to bend over."

yè

Bronze Inscriptions

Later Seal Character

业 refers to a frame which has teeth on the top for holding musical instruments such as bells, drums and chime stones, and whose posts are in the shape of a man supporting a beam with his two hands. In the Bronze Inscriptions, the character 业 looks like a sketch of this instrument frame. In the Later Seal Character, however, its manlike posts are changed into a wood part (木) by mistake, losing its original image. Its meaning is also changed, and is nowadays more usually used in the senses of "business," "profession," "industry" and "course of study."

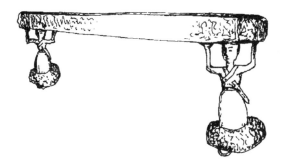

尹

yǐn

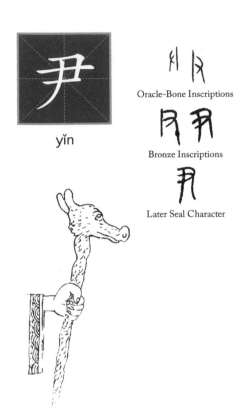

八 𠂤

Oracle-Bone Inscriptions

尹 尹

Bronze Inscriptions

尹

Later Seal Character

尹 is an ideograph. In ancient writing systems, the character 尹 looks like a man holding a sceptre in hand. The sceptre is a symbol of power. A man who has a sceptre in hand is a man in charge, so 尹 has the meaning of "governing." The character 尹 is often used as an official title, e.g. 京兆尹 (head of the capital city), 县尹 (county magistrate). And the use of 尹 as a surname comes from the official title.

君

jūn

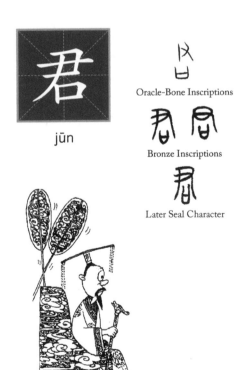

八
日

Oracle-Bone Inscriptions

君 君

Bronze Inscriptions

君

Later Seal Character

The character 君 consists of 尹 and 口, the former signalling to direct people to do something with a baton in hand and the latter to issue orders. Hence 君 refers to people who are in a position to odrer others, especially the highest ruler of a country. But it may also be used as an honorific term, e.g. 严君 (my father), 家君 (my father), 夫君 (my husband). When it is used as a verb, it means "to rule" and "to dominate."

笔

bǐ

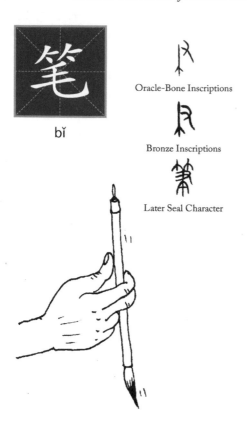

Oracle-Bone Inscriptions

Bronze Inscriptions

Later Seal Character

笔 refers to the instrument for writing, i.e. pen. In China the first type of pen is known as 毛笔 (writing brush). Judging from the archaeological excavations, the writing brush was first used in the period of Warring States. But we may well assume from other sources that the use of writing brush might date as far back as the end of the primitive society. In the Oracle-Bone Inscriptions and Bronze Inscriptions, the character 笔 looks like a hand with a writing brush in its grasp; the three-tined part at the head standing for its hair part. Early writing brushes had wooden shafts. Starting with Meng Tian in the Qin Dynasty, however, bamboo shafts took the place of wooden ones. That is why in the Later Seal Character a bamboo part (竹) is added to the character. In the modern simplified form a new structure consisting of 竹 (bamboo) and 毛 (hair) is used.

画

huà

Oracle-Bone Inscriptions

Bronze Inscriptions

Later Seal Character

In the Oracle-Bone Inscriptions and Bronze Inscriptions, the character 画 looks like a man drawing crosses with a writing brush, hence the primary meaning "drawing." As the character 画 also means "to delimit," which is now usually expressed by 划, in the late Bronze Inscriptions and Later Seal Character there is a field part (田) added, signalling the delimitation of boundaries between fields.

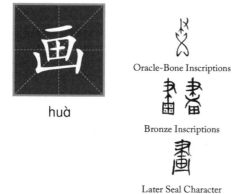

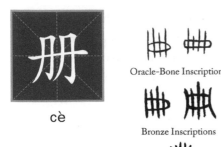

cè

Oracle-Bone Inscriptions

Bronze Inscriptions

Later Seal Character

Before the invention of paper, one of the main materials used for writing in China was bamboo slips. And the slips bound together make a book. In ancient writing systems, the character 册 has the shape of many bamboo slips bound together, hence its meaning "book" and "volume."

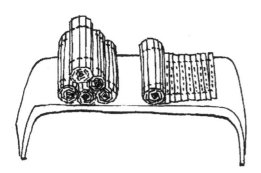

diǎn

Oracle-Bone Inscriptions

Bronze Inscriptions

Later Seal Character

In the Oracle-Bone Inscriptions, the character 典 looks like two hands holding a book. In the Bronze Inscriptions and Later Seal Character, the structure of the character is changed: the book is on a table, instead of two hands. But the meaning is not changed. That is 典 refers to books recording codes of laws and regulations. And it is also used to refer to the provisions and regulations in these books, or general codes of behaviour. Used as a verb, it means "to be in charge of," "to be engaged in" or "to mortgage something."

Later Seal Character

shān

When people wrote on bamboo slips with a writing brush, they used a knife to scrape the wrong characters. And that is what is meant by the character 删, consisting of 册 (book) and 刀 (knife). From its primary meaning of "deleting" have derived the meanings "to abridge" and "to abbreviate."

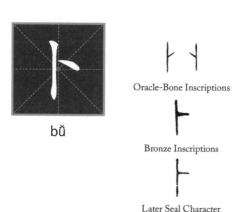

bǔ

Oracle-Bone Inscriptions

Bronze Inscriptions

Later Seal Character

In former times people were superstitious and would try to have the result foretold before doing anything. In China, one of the ways to foretell the future is to bake a tortoiseshell gently until it cracks. And the direction, length and other features of the cracks would be seen as omens of the future event: whether it would result in success or failure. In ancient writing systems, the character 卜 looks like the cracks on a baked tortoise-shell. In this sense it is a pictograph. But the pronunciation of 卜 is like the sound produced when a tortoise-shell cracks, and in this sense, it may be seen as an onomatopoeia. From its meaning of future-telling have derived its senses of "predict," "estimate" and "select."

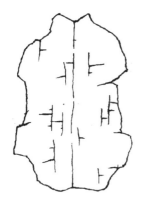

zhān/zhàn

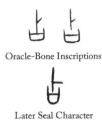
Oracle-Bone Inscriptions

Later Seal Character

The character 占 consists of 卜 and 口, signalling that in the act of future-telling, one needs to express the omen through speech organs. Hence 占 primarily means "to express omen in words." But it may refer to the activity of future-telling in general. All forms of future-telling, whether using tortoise-shell, yarrow stem, copper cash or elephant-tooth tablet, may be referred to as 占, e.g. 占卦 (divination), 占课 (to divine by tossing coins). In addition 占 may be pronounced as zhàn, meaning "to occupy," "to possess," the original complicated form being 佔.

qiě

Oracle-Bone Inscriptions

Bronze Inscriptions

Later Seal Character

且 was the original form of 祖. In ancient writing systems, the character 且 looks like a memorial tablet, which was used to represent the soul of an ancestor in a memorial ceremony, hence its original meaning "ancestor." As it is related to gods and spirits, a spirit part (示) is added to show its meaning more clearly, resulting in a new character 祖. The original 且, instead, is used now as a conjunction, e.g. 并且 (and... as well), 况且 (moreover), 尚且 (even) and 而且 (but also); or used in the senses of "for the time being (暂且)," "tentatively (姑且)." Its pronunciation is also changed from zǔ to qiě.

shì

Oracle-Bone Inscriptions

Later Seal Character

People in former times were superstitious and would call on gods and spirits for guidance and protection in anything they were going to do, so there were often sacrifice-offering ceremonies. In the Oracle-Bone Inscriptions, the character 示 looks like a stone table made of a stone plate on top of a stone stand. This is a type of altar used in sacrifice-offering ceremonies for presenting offerings, hence the original meaning of 示 "stone table," or "spirit stone (灵石)." Characters with 示 as a component most have to do with offering sacrifices to gods and ancestors, e.g. 福 (blessing), 祭 (to offer a sacrifice) and 祝 (to pray). People usually offer sacrifices to gods and ancestors in order to tell them their difficulties so that gods and ancestors would help them overcome the difficulties. As a result, the character 示 has taken on the sense of "show," "present," e.g. 示威 (to display one's strength), 示弱 (to give the impression of being weak) and 指示 (to direct).

zhù

Oracle-Bone Inscriptions

Bronze Inscriptions

Later Seal Character

In ancient writing systems, the character 祝 looks like a man on his knees saying his prayers before the altar. Hence the primary meaning of 祝 is "to pray" and "to plead with gods for blessing," from which have derived the extended meanings "to express good wishes," "to congratulate" and "to celebrate." In addition the person who is in charge of a sacrifice-offering is also known as 祝. And this may be the origin of the surname 祝, i.e. they adopted their family name from their occupation.

fú

Oracle-Bone Inscriptions

Bronze Inscriptions

Later Seal Character

In the Oracle-Bone Inscriptions, the character 福 looks like two hands placing a jar of wine onto an altar, signalling to offer wine to gods in the hope of obtaining blessing, hence the meaning is "blessing." In ancient times, there were five types of blessing as is recorded in *Shang Shu* (the Book of History), "The five types of blessing are: longevity, wealth, peace, virtue and to die a natural death." But it can also be used for happiness or good fortune in general, opposite to 祸 (misfortune). Thus *Lao Zi* (Lao-Tzu) says, "Good fortune lieth within bad, bad fortune lurketh with good."

jì/zhài

Oracle-Bone Inscriptions

Bronze Inscriptions

Later Seal Character

祭, an ideograph, looks like a man placing a piece of meat onto an altar, signalling to offer meat and wine to gods and ancestors. But it also refers to the memorial ceremony for the dead, e.g. 祭奠 (to hold a memorial ceremony for), 公祭 (a public memorial meeting). In addition, 祭 is a surname, but it is pronounced as zhài, instead of jì.

diàn

Oracle-Bone Inscriptions

Bronze Inscriptions

Later Seal Character

In the Oracle-Bone Inscriptions and Bronze Inscriptions, the character 奠 looks like a jar of wine on an altar, signalling to offer wine and meat to gods and ancestors. From this primary meaning have derived the extended meanings "to present."

zūn

Oracle-Bone Inscriptions

Bronze Inscriptions

Later Seal Character

尊, as the original form of 樽, referred to a jarlike wine container. In ancient writing systems, the character 尊 looks like a man holding a big jar with his two hands, signalling to offer wine to others. In the Regular Script, the twin-hand part becomes a singlehand part (寸). The original meaning of 尊 was "to offer wine with both hands, suggesting respect for the other." From this meaning have derived the senses of "respected," "noble," and its use for elders and betters.

yǒu

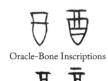

Oracle-Bone Inscriptions

Bronze Inscriptions

Later Seal Character

In the Oracle-Bone Inscriptions and Bronze Inscriptions, the character 酉 looks like a wine jar, hence its original meaning is "wine jar" or "wine pot." However, this character is now mainly used as a name of the tenth Earthly Branch, a traditional Chinese system of sequence. Characters with 酉 as a component most have to do with wine, e.g. 酣 (to drink to one's heart's content), 醉 (drunk), 釀 (wine-making), 酌 (to drink) and 配 (to mix a drink).

jiǔ

Oracle-Bone Inscriptions

Bronze Inscriptions

Later Seal Character

酒 is a general term for alcoholic drink made from grains or fruits, e.g. 米酒 (rice wine), 葡萄酒 (wine). The character 酒 consists of 水 and 酉, the former standing for water and the latter the jar for containing wine, hence its primary meaning "alcoholic drink."

酌

zhuó

Bronze Inscriptions

Later Seal Character

The character 酌 consists of 酉 and 勺, the former standing for a wine jar and the latter a ladle for lifting wine, hence the original meaning is "to fetch wine." But it is now used in the senses of "pouring out wine," "drinking wine," and even as a substitute for the character 酒 (wine). In addition, 酌 is also used in the senses "to consider" and "to estimate."

配

pèi

Oracle-Bone Inscriptions

Bronze Inscriptions

Later Seal Character

In the Bronze Inscriptions, the character 配 looks like a man squatting beside a wine jar, signalling to prepare a drink by adding water or other ingredients to spirit, hence the primary meaning is "to mix an alcoholic drink." As to mix a drink, one needs to put different things together, the character 配 has taken on the meaning of "combining," "pairing," e.g. 婚配 (to join in marriage).

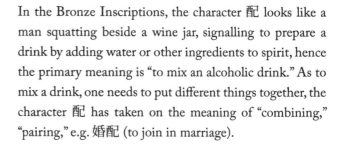

fù

Bronze Inscriptions

Later Seal Character

In the Bronze Inscriptions, the character 富 looks like a wine jar inside a house. It is a sign of wealth to have wine in the family, hence the primary meaning of 富 is "rich" and "in possession of wealth," opposite to 贫 (poor). It may also mean "wealth," "possessions," "abundant" and "plentiful."

jué

Oracle-Bone Inscriptions

Bronze Inscriptions

Later Seal Character

爵 refers to an ancient utensil for drinking, which has a v-shaped lip, a handle, and three legs in the bottom and two ornamental posts at the top. It was very popular in the Shang Dynasty and used as a gift form the king to the lords when they were given their titles. That is why the character 爵 has come to mean "title of nobility." For example, the *Book of Rites* says, "The king has made five ranks of nobility: duke, marquis, earl, viscount and baron."

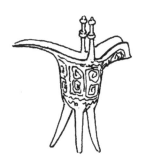

jiǎ

Oracle-Bone Inscriptions

Bronze Inscriptions

Later Seal Character

斝 refers to an ancient utensil for drinking, which has a round mouth, a flat bottom, three legs, two posts, and a handle. In the Oracle-Bone Inscriptions and Bronze Inscriptions, the character is in the shape of this utensil. In the Later Seal Character, however, it has a new form, with 斗 as a component.

hú

Oracle-Bone Inscriptions

Bronze Inscriptions

Later Seal Character

壶 refers to a vessel for liquids, made of baked clay or metal, e.g. 茶壶 (teapot), 酒壶 (wine pot). In ancient writing systems, the character 壶 is in the shape of a wine pot, with a narrow neck, a round belly, two ears, and a lid on the top and a stand at the bottom.

fǒu

Oracle-Bone Inscriptions

Bronze Inscriptions

Later Seal Character

Before burning earthenware, pottery's clay must be pounded and be made of greenware. And the workers put the greenware into a kiln to burn. In Oracle-Bone Inscriptions and Later Seal Character, the character 缶 consists of 午 and 凵 as radicals, signalling to pound pottery's clay with a pestle in a dish. Its original meaning is "greenware." Characters with 缶 as a component most have to do with earthen ware, e.g. 窑 (kiln), 缸 (earthen vat), 缺 (gap), 罅 (xià, crack) 磬 (qìng, chime stone), 罂 (yīng, an earthenware container). In later system, 缶 refers to the earthenware with a round belly, a small mouth, and a lid. The *Origin of Chinese Characters* says, "缶, means an earthen ware for containing wine. In Qin, people beat 缶 to increase the sense of rhythm of songs." 缶 refers the bronze vessels which looks like it either. In Bronze Inscriptions, 缶 consists of 金 as a radical, meaning bronze 缶 in particular.

dǐng

Oracle-Bone Inscriptions

Bronze Inscriptions

Later Seal Character

鼎 refers to an ancient cooking-vessel, usually with three legs, two loop handles and a big belly. In the Oracle-Bone Inscriptions and early Bronze Inscriptions, the character 鼎 looks like a vivid picture of this vessel. In ancient times, this vessel was an important utensil at ancestral temples for offering sacrifices, as well as a daily cooking vessel. As such it was further seen as a symbol of state power. That is why the image of 鼎 has profound cultural implications in Chinese history.

yuán

Oracle-Bone Inscriptions

Bronze Inscriptions

Later Seal Character

员 was the original form of 圆. In the Oracle-Bone Inscriptions and Bronze Inscriptions, the character 员 looks like a cooking-vessel with a circle above it, indicating that the mouth of the vessel is round. In the Later Seal Character, the character 员, resulting from a wrong development, has 贝 as a component. As the original meaning of 员 was "round vessel," it might also refer to a circle or other circular things. But the character 员 is now more usually used in the senses of "person engaged in some activity" and "specified number of people or things." Its original meaning is expressed by another character 圆.

败

bài

Oracle-Bone Inscriptions

Bronze Inscriptions

Later Seal Character

In the Oracle-Bone Inscriptions, the character 败 looks like a man striking a cooking-vessel (or seashell) with a stick. The bronze cooking-vessel (an important utensil in daily life and sacrifice-offering ceremonies) and seashell (the currency at that time) were both valuable objects. To strike them with a stick signals to destroy, and that is the primary meaning of 败. But 败 is a character of many senses, e.g. food becoming unfit to eat may be referred to as 腐败 or 败味; dead twigs and withered leaves are known as 残枝败叶; an army suffering a defeat is 战败; and to encounter a failure in work is 失败.

则

zé

Bronze Inscriptions

Later Seal Character

Before the invention of paper, people used to inscribe important documents and legal provisions on bronze objects like bells and cooking-vessels. In the Oracle-Bone Inscriptions, the character 则 consists of a cooking-vessel pant and a knife part, signalling to inscribe characters on the bronze object. In the Later Seal Character, the cooking-vessel part becomes a seashell part by mistake, making it incapable of revealing meaning through form. As the writing inscribed on bronze objects are usually legal documeats, the character 则 has taken on the sense of "rule" and "regulation." It is also used in the sense of "standard" and "norm." Used as a verb, it means "to follow the example of."

具

jù

Oracle-Bone Inscriptions

Bronze Inscriptions

Later Seal Character

As an important cooking utensil, 鼎 was used extensively in feasts and sacrifice-offering ceremonies. In the Oracle-Bone Inscriptions, the character 具 looks like two hands lifting a cooking-vessel, hence its original meaning is "to carry utensils," from which have derived the senses "to provide," "to supply," "to prepare" and "to complete." Meanwhile it may refer to table-ware, or implements in general. In the Bronze Inscriptions, however, the cooking-vessel part (鼎) by mistake becomes a seashell part (贝), which in turn becomes an eye part (目), destroying the original association between form and meaning completely.

huò

Oracle-Bone Inscriptions

Bronze Inscriptions

Later Seal Character

In the Oracle-Bone Inscriptions, the character 鑊 looks like a hand putting a bird into a utensil to be cooked. But in the Bronze Inscriptions, it changes from an ideograph into a phonetic compound. Its original meaning was "to cook," and it is also used in the sense of a big cooking utensil, i.e. cauldron.

lì

Oracle-Bone Inscriptions

Bronze Inscriptions

Later Seal Character

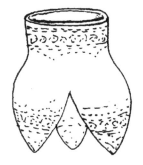

鬲 refers to an ancient cooking utensil, made of baked clay or bronze, similar to 鼎 in shape: with three legs and a big belly. It differs from 鼎 in that its legs are thick and hollow inside, like bags, hence the name "bag-legged vessel." In the Oracle-Bone Inscriptions and Bronze Inscriptions, the character 鬲 looks like a picture of this vessel. Characters with 鬲 as a component most have to do with cooking, e.g. 融 (to melt), 鬻 (yù, rice gruel), 鬵 (xín, cauldron), 鬺 (shāng, to boil; to cook).

che

Oracle-Bone Inscriptions

Bronze Inscriptions

Later Seal Character

彻 was originally a variant form of 撤. In the Oracle-Bone Inscriptions and Bronze Inscriptions, the character 彻 consists of 鬲 (a cooking utensil) and 又 (hand), signalling to take away the utensil with hand. The original meaning of 彻 was "to take away," but it is now mainly used in the sense of "thorough" and "penetrating."

yǎn

Oracle-Bone Inscriptions

Bronze Inscriptions

Later Seal Character

甗 refers to an ancient steaming utensil, which consists of two layers: the upper layer is similar to 甑 (zèng, a steaming utensil) with a perforated bottom and the lower layer is 鬲. In the Oracle-Bone Inscriptions and early Bronze Inscriptions, the character is a pictograph in the shape of this utensil. Later, however, it became a phonetic compound, resulting in a more complex form.

zēng/céng

Oracle-Bone Inscriptions

Later Seal Character

曾 was the original form of 甑 (zèng), referring to an ancient steaming utensil. In the Oracle-Bone Inscriptions, the character 曾 has a part 田 standing for its perforated bottom, and the two strokes atop represent steam, hence its original meaning was "to steam food." But it also refers to family relations three stages away, e.g. 曾祖 (great-grandfather), 曾孙 (great-grandson). 曾 may also be pronounced as céng, used as an adverb, meaning "having had the experience of," e.g. 曾经.

dòu

Oracle-Bone Inscriptions

Bronze Inscriptions

Later Seal Character

豆 referred to an ancient high-legged dinner plate, which was often used in sacrifice-offering ceremonies as well. In the Oracle-Bone Inscriptions and Bronze Inscriptions, the character 豆 looks like a vessel consisting of a deep plate on the top and a ringlike stand at the bottom, and the stroke inside the plate stands for food. The character 豆 was also an ancient measure of volume, for example, *Zuo Zhuan* (*Spring and Autumn* with Commentary by Tsu Chiuming) says, "There were originally four measures of volume: 豆, 区 (ōu), 釜 and 钟; and four shēng (升) make a dòu (豆)." Nowadays, however, 豆 mainly refers to the plant of bean family.

登

dēng

Oracle-Bone Inscriptions

Bronze Inscriptions

Later Seal Character

In the Oracle-Bone Inscriptions and Bronze Inscriptions, the character 登 consists of three parts: two feet part, a high-legged plate part and two hands part; signalling to go forward and present the offering in the plate. The original meaning of 登 was "to present offerings upwards," from which have derived its extended meanings "to go upwards," "to ascend" and "to advance."

豊

lǐ

Oracle-Bone Inscriptions

Bronze Inscriptions

Later Seal Character

Xu Shen says in his *Origin of Chinese Characters*, "豊 is a utensil used in ceremonies." In ancient writing systems, the character looks like a high-legged plate (豆) full of jade objects. These jade objects were meant to be offered to gods and spirits, so the character referred to utensils used in sacrifice-offering ceremonies. Characters with 豊 as a component most have to do with sacrifice-offering ceremonies, for example, the wine used in these ceremonies is known as 醴, and the ritual acts in these ceremonies are known as 礼 (the original complicated form being 禮).

Oracle-Bone Inscriptions

Bronze Inscriptions

Later Seal Character

fēng

In ancient writing systems, the character 丰 looks like a highlegged plate (豆) full of rice ears or wheat ears, signalling there is a bumper harvest of crops. The primary meaning of 丰 is "bumper harvest," and its extended meanings include "luxuriant," "substantial" and "rich."

Oracle-Bone Inscriptions

Bronze Inscriptions

Later Seal Character

guǐ

簋 refers to an ancient vessel, with a round belly, big mouth and ringlike stand, usually made of bronze. In the western Zhou Dynasty and the Spring and Autumn Period, 簋 usually be used with 鼎, and the usage figure relates to the user's status. For example, King had nine 鼎 and eight 簋, the feudal princes had seven 鼎 and six 簋, senior officials had five 鼎 and four 簋, and junior officials had three 鼎 and two 簋. In the Oracle-Bone Inscriptions and Bronze Inscriptions, the character 簋 looks like a man taking food with a spoon from such a vessel. In the Later Seal Character, it consists of 竹 (bamboo) and 皿 (vessel), perhaps reflecting the fact that at that time 簋 was made of bamboo.

即

Oracle-Bone Inscriptions

Bronze Inscriptions

Later Seal Character

jí

In the Oracle-Bone Inscriptions and Bronze Inscriptions, the character 即 has a high-legged plate (豆) full of food on the left and a man on his knees on the right, signalling the man is about to eat. Hence its original meaning was "to dine." In order to eat food, one must get close to it, so 即 has taken on the meanings of "approaching," "close to," e.g. 若即若离 (to appear to be neither close nor far apart), 可望而不可即 (within sight but beyond reach). It may also be used as an adverb, meaning "immediately" and "at once."

既

Oracle-Bone Inscriptions

Bronze Inscriptions

Later Seal Character

jì

The character 既 has a plate part on the left and a man part on the right. The high-legged plate is covered by a lid and the man on his knees is turning away his head, not looking at it any more. This signals that the man has finished eating and is ready to leave. So the primary meaning of 既 was "to eat up." And its extended meanings include "to finish," "to complete" and "to be over." It may also be used as an adverb, meaning "already."

xiǎng

Oracle-Bone Inscriptions

Bronze Inscriptions

Later Seal Character

In the Oracle-Bone Inscriptions and Bronze Inscriptions, the character 飨 looks like two men sitting around a food container and eating. Hence its original meaning is "two men eating together," from which has derived the meaning "to treat somebody to food and wine." In the Later Seal Character, the character 飨 is a phonetic compound, with the phonetic on top of the radical. Nowadays, the phonetic part is simplified and moved to the left of the radical.

shí

Oracle-Bone Inscriptions

Bronze Inscriptions

Later Seal Character

In the Oracle-Bone Inscriptions, the character 食 looks like a highlegged plate full of food with its angled lid lifted above it. Hence its primary meaning is "food to be eaten," from which has derived the meaning "to eat." Characters with 食 as a component all have to do with food and eating, e.g. 饭 (cooked rice), 饮 (to drink), 饼 (a round flat cake), 饱 (to have eaten one's fill), 飨 (to treat someone to dinner) and 餐 (to eat).

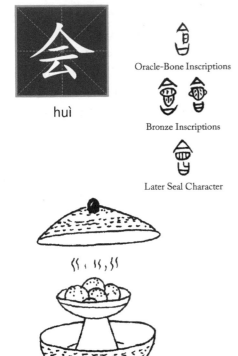

huì

Oracle-Bone Inscriptions

Bronze Inscriptions

Later Seal Character

In the Oracle-Bone Inscriptions and Bronze Inscriptions, the character 会 consists of three parts: the lid of a container, the thing contained and the belly of a container, signalling that the different parts match well. So the character 会 means "to get together," "to assemble" and "to meet." It may also refer to some activities or organizations in which people get together, e.g. 晚会 (evening party), 报告会 (public lecture), 工会 (trade union). In addition, 会 may also mean "to understand," "to be able to," e.g. 体会 (to realize), 能说会道 (to have the gift of the gab).

hé

Oracle-Bone Inscriptions

Bronze Inscriptions

Later Seal Character

In ancient writing systems, the character 合 looks like the lid and belly of a container put together. Its primary meaning is "to combine," "to close," and its extended meanings include "to get together" and "to join."

 níng/nìng

Oracle-Bone Inscriptions

Bronze Inscriptions

Later Seal Character

In the Oracle-Bone Inscriptions, the character 宁 looks like a house in which there is an vessel on a table, signalling that it is a peaceful and quiet place. In the Bronze Inscriptions, a heart part (心) is added to emphasize the point that it is "the heart"—the inside of a man that is quiet. Hence the primary meaning of 宁 is "quiet." 宁 may also be used as an adverb, pronounced as nìng, meaning "rather," "would rather."

fán

Oracle-Bone Inscriptions

Bronze Inscriptions

Later Seal Character

凡 was the original form of 盘, referring to a shallow plate with a ringlike stand. In the Oracle-Bone Inscriptions and Bronze Inscriptions, the character 凡 is in the shape of such a plate. Nowadays, however, it is more usually used in the senses of "in general," "ordinary," and its original sense is expressed by 盘.

pán

Oracle-Bone Inscriptions

Bronze Inscriptions

Later Seal Character

盘 refers to an ancient shallow plate with a ringlike stand. In the Oracle-Bone Inscriptions, the character 盘 consists of 凡 and 攴 as radicals, looks like a man taking food from such a plate with a spoon. In the Bronze Inscriptions, the plate part by mistake becomes a boat part; sometimes there is a vessel part (皿) added to indicate its use, or a metal part (金) to indicate its material. In the Later Seal Character, the character has 木 as a component, signalling that it is made of wood. In addition, 盘 may also mean "to rotate," "to twine," "to interrogate" and "to calculate."

匜

yí

Bronze Inscriptions

Later Seal Character

匜 refers to an ancient utensil for washing hands. It is in the shape of a gourd ladle, with a lip and handle. When washing, one pours out water from it, which runs through one's hands to a basin below. In the Bronze Inscriptions, the character looks like such a ladle; sometimes there is a vessel part (皿) indicating its use, or a metal part (金) indicating its material.

mǐn

Oracle-Bone Inscriptions

Bronze Inscriptions

Later Seal Character

In the Oracle-Bone Inscriptions, the character 皿 looks like a vessel with a ringlike stand. In the Bronze Inscriptions, there is sometimes a metal part (金) added to indicate that it is made of metal such as bronze. So the character 皿 is a general term for vessels such as bowls and plates. Characters with 皿 as a component most have to do with vessels and their uses, e.g. 盂 (broad-mouthed jar), 盆 (basin), 盛 (to fill [a vessel]), 盥 (to wash [one's hands and face]), 溢 (to overflow) and 盈 (to be filled with).

yì

Oracle-Bone Inscriptions

Bronze Inscriptions

Later Seal Character

益 was the original form of 溢. In ancient writing systems, the character 益 looks like a vessel overflowing with water. Hence the original meaning is "the overflow of water" or "the rise of water level." As water overflows only when there is too much of it, the character 益 has also taken on the meanings of "rich," "abundant," "to increase," "benefit" and "profit."

guàn

Oracle-Bone Inscriptions

Bronze Inscriptions

Later Seal Character

In the Bronze Inscriptions, the character 盥 looks like water running down through two hands and there is a basin below, hence the primary meaning is "washing one's hands." For example, the *Book of Rites* says, "盥 means washing one's hands with running water, which ends in a basin below." Nowadays, however, the character 盥 may also refer to the washing of one's face. And the room known as 洗手间, or 盥洗室 (washroom) is a place where one washes one's face as well as hands.

xiě/xuè

Oracle-Bone Inscriptions

Bronze Inscriptions

Later Seal Character

In the Oracle-Bone Inscriptions, the character 血 looks like drops of blood dripping into a vessel, hence its meaning is "blood."

jìn

Oracle-Bone Inscriptions

Bronze Inscriptions

Later Seal Character

In the Oracle-Bone inscriptions, the character 尽 looks like a man brushing a vessel with bamboo branches in hand, signalling the vessel is empty. Thus the *Origin of Chinese Characters* says, "尽 means a vessel is empty." From this primary meaning have derived its extended senses of "exhausted," "end," "complete" and "to the limit."

yì

Oracle-Bone Inscriptions

Bronze Inscriptions

Later Seal Character

In the Oracle-Bone Inscriptions, the character 易 looks like water being poured from one vessel to another. However this character has undergone a series of changes in its form. At the end there is left only the part with a loop handle and three dots standing for drops of water. That is why the character 易 in the Later Seal Character has assumed a completely different form from that in the Oracle-Bone Inscriptions. The original meaning of 易 was "to give," but it is also used in the senses of "change" and "exchange." The more usual sense of it, however, is "easy," opposite to 难 (difficult).

gài

Bronze Inscriptions

Later Seal Character

In the Bronze Inscriptions, the character 盖 looks like a vessel with something above it, hence its primary meaning is "the thing on top of a vessel," i.e. "cover." In the Later Seal Character, it has a grass part, referring to a type of cover made of cogongrass. It may also refer to covers in general, such as 车盖 (canopy), 伞盖 (umbrella). When it is used as a verb, it means "to cover," "to top" and "to surpass."

dǒu

Oracle-Bone Inscriptions

Bronze Inscriptions

Later Seal Character

In the Oracle-Bone Inscriptions and Bronze Inscriptions, the character 斗 looks like a dipper with a long handle. In ancient times this type of dipper was not only used to lift wine but also to measure the amount of grain. So 斗 is also a measure of capacity, equal to ten 升 or one tenth of 石 in the Chinese System, and a decalitre in the Metric System. As the group of seven stars seen only from the northern part of the world are in the shape of a dipper, they are known as 北斗星 (the Big Dipper). Characters with 斗 as a component most have to do with the measuring dipper, e.g. 斛 (a squaremouthed vessel, used as a measure of capacity equal to five 斗), 料 (to measure the amount of rice grain with 斗), 斟 (to lift wine with a ladle).

liào

Bronze Inscriptions

Later Seal Character

The character 料, an ideograph, consists of 米 (rice) and 斗 (measuring dipper), signalling to measure the amount of rice grain with a dipper. But 料 may also be used in the sense of measuring in general and has taken on the senses "to calculate," "to estimate," "to predict" and "to speculate." In addition, it may mean "to take care of" and "to put in order." As a noun, it may refer to the material to make something.

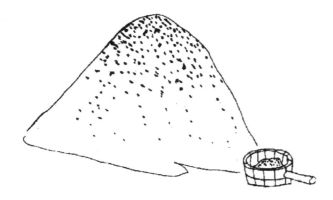

sháo

Oracle-Bone Inscriptions

Later Seal Character

勺 means "ladle," a tool for lifting things, consisting of a small bowl with a handle. In the Oracle-Bone Inscriptions, the character 勺 looks like a picture of such a tool, the dot in it standing for the food it holds. It may also be used as a verb, meaning "to lift something out of a container with a ladle."

bì

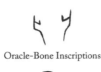

Oracle-Bone Inscriptions

Bronze Inscriptions

Later Seal Character

匕 refers to an ancient spoonlike tool, with a shallow bowl and a bent handle. In the Oracle-Bone Inscriptions and Bronze Inscriptions, the character 匕 is in the shape of such a spoon. As it looks very similar to the man part in 妣, the character 匕 in the Later Seal Character mistakenly changes to an other-way-round man part.

zhǐ

Oracle-Bone Inscriptions

Bronze Inscriptions

Later Seal Character

In the Oracle-Bone Inscriptions and Bronze Inscriptions, the character 旨 consists of 匕 (spoon) and 口 (mouth), signalling to eat with a spoon. Sometimes the character 旨 has 甘 (sweet taste) as a component, signalling that the food is delicious. The original meaning of 旨 was "sweet taste" or "delicacy," but it is now more usually used in the senses of "intention," "purpose," "aim" and "purport."

zǔ

Oracle-Bone Inscriptions

Bronze Inscriptions

Later Seal Character

俎 refers to an ancient table for presenting sacrifices such as beef and mutton at offering ceremonies. In the Bronze Inscriptions, the character 俎 looks like such a table on end: the right is the surface board and the left legs. As a utensil for sacrifice offering, this table is also seen as a ritual object. In daily life, however, it is more usually used as a chopping block.

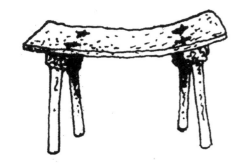

yòng

Oracle-Bone Inscriptions

Bronze Inscriptions

Later Seal Character

用 was the original form of 桶. In the Oracle-Bone Inscriptions, Bronze Inscriptions and Later Seal Character, the character 用 looks like a tub in each case. As the tub is a common object for daily use, the character 用 has taken on the meanings "to use," "to employ," "function" and "expenses."

qū/ōu

Oracle-Bone Inscriptions

Bronze Inscriptions

Later Seal Character

In the Oracle-Bone Inscriptions, the character 区 looks like a cupboard for storing things. Its original meaning was "to store" or "the place to store things," from which have derived the meanings of "region" and "district." Used as a verb, it means "to distinguish" and "to differentiate." In addition, 区 pronounced as ōu refers to an ancient measure of capacity.

zhù

Oracle-Bone Inscriptions

Bronze Inscriptions

Later Seal Character

In the Oracle-Bone Inscriptions and Bronze Inscriptions, the character 铸 looks like a man pouring a crucible of melted bronze into a mould below with the hands, hence the primary meaning is "casting." In the Later Seal Character, the character 铸 becomes a phonetic compound, with 金 (metal) as the radical and 寿 as the phonetic. Apart from its primary meaning, 铸 is also used in the general sense of making things out of a mould.

qì

Bronze Inscriptions

Later Seal Character

The character 器 is made up of a 犬 and four 口, the former referring to the dog and the latter standing for vessels, signalling a number of vessels guarded by a dog. At the beginning, it might refer to pottery only. For example *Lao Zi* (Lao-Tzu) says, "埏埴 (shānzhí) 以为 器 (One mixes clay with water to make a pot)." Later, its meaning was broadened and it could refer to any utensil or instrument. Thus the *Analects of Confucius* says, "工欲善其 事, 必先利其器 (A workman must first sharpen his tools if he is to do his work well)." But it is also used in a more general sense, referring to anything tangible and concrete, opposite to the abstract notion—道 (way; reason). So the *Book of Changes* says, "形而上者谓之道, 形而下者谓之器 (The formless, intangible is known as dào, and the formal, tangible is known as qì)."

guàn/guān

Later Seal Character

In the Later Seal Character, the character 冠 is made up of three parts: a hat part (冖) on the top, a man part (元) on the left and a hand part (寸) on the right; signalling a man is putting on a hat. Hence its primary meaning is "to put on a hat." Apart from this verbal sense, it may also refer to headgear in general. As a hat is put on the head, the character 冠 has also taken on the sense of "the first" and "the best."

Oracle-Bone Inscriptions

Bronze Inscriptions

miǎn

免 was the original form of 冕. In the Oracle-Bone Inscriptions and Bronze Inscriptions, the character 免 looks like a man with a top hat on; sometimes there are even feathers on the top as ornaments. Hence its original meaning is "top hat." Nowadays, however, the character 免 is mainly used in the senses "to remove," "to take off," "to avoid," "to dismiss" and "to exempt." Its original meaning is expressed by 冕.

Bronze Inscriptions

Later Seal Character

mào

冒 was the original form of 帽. In the Bronze Inscriptions, the character 冒 has an eye below a covering, signalling that it is a headgear. As the headgear is put on the head, the character 冒 also means "to cover." On the other hand, from the sense of "atop the head," 冒 have derived the senses "to contradict," "to offend," "to stand out," "to pretend to be," etc. In addition, it may also mean "to make bold to," "to act with out due consideration," and "to act in spite of difficulties" (e.g. 冒雨 "to brave the storm," 冒险 "to take a risk (to do sth)").

zhòu

Bronze Inscriptions

Later Seal Character

In the Bronze Inscriptions, the character 胄 looks like a head with a helmet on, and the eye is not covered by it. Hence its primary meaning is "helmet," also known as 兜鍪 (móu), a headgear worn by soldiers in fighting. But 胄 may also refer to the descendants of kings and lords, e.g. 帝胄 (a scion of royalty), 贵胄 (a scion of nobility).

huáng

Bronze Inscriptions

Later Seal Character

In the Bronze Inscriptions, the character 皇 has a king part (王) below a hat with ornaments, signalling it is a hat worn by kings, i.e. crown. For example, the *Book of Rites* records, "有虞氏皇而祭 (You Yu, also known as Shun, put on the crown and presided over the ceremony)." From this original meaning has derived its use to refer to rulers such as emperors and kings, e.g. 三皇五帝 (the earliest eight rulers in Chinese recorded history) and 皇帝 (emperor). As the crown is magnificent with ornaments, the character 皇 has also taken on the meanings of "splendid" and "magnificent," e.g. 冠冕堂皇 ([lit.] magnificent crowns). It is also used in the senses of "great" and "reverend," e.g. 皇天 (Heaven) and 皇考 (forefather).

sī

Oracle-Bone Inscriptions

Bronze Inscriptions

Later Seal Character

丝 means "silk." In the Oracle-Bone Inscriptions, the character 丝 looks like two strings made of silk. It may also refer to things which are thin and long, e.g. 柳丝 (fine willow branches), 蛛丝 (spider thread). 丝 is also a measure of weight, equal to ten 忽 or one tenth of 毫 in the Chinese System, and half a milligramme in the Metric System.

jīng

Bronze Inscriptions

Later Seal Character

In the Bronze Inscriptions, the character 经, a pictograph, originally looked like three warp threads fixed on a loom. Later, a silk part (纟) was added to it, resulting in a phonetic compound. The primary meaning of 经 is "the thread running along the length of cloth," as against 纬, the thread running across the cloth. The two characters 经 and 纬 are also used metaphorically for roads. Those going northwards or southwards are known as 经 and those going eastwards or westwards 纬. From this meaning have derived its senses of "main road," "common practice," "rule," "regulation" and "principle." Besides it may also be used as a verb, meaning "to experience," "to measure" and "to manage."

suǒ

Oracle-Bone Inscriptions

Bronze Inscriptions

Later Seal Character

In the Oracle-Bone Inscriptions, the character 索 looks like a rope made by twisting, or two hands twisting a rope. In the Bronze Inscriptions, a house part is added at the top to signal that people twist ropes inside a house. In the past 索 and 绳 meant differently, the former referred to thick ones and the latter thin ones. As ropes may be used to link things and lead one thing to another, the character 索 has also taken on the senses "to search," e.g. 按图索骥 (to look for a steed with the aid of its picture; to try to locate something by following up a clue); and "to ask for."

xì

Oracle-Bone Inscriptions

Later Seal Character

In Oracle-Bone Inscriptions and Bronze Inscriptions, the character 系 looks like a man's neck bounding with a rope. Hence its primary meaning is "to bind," from which has derived the extended meaning "to link" and "to continue." In the *Origin of Chinese Characters* says, "係, meaning to bind, consists of 人 as the radical and 系 as its phonetic." So 系 can be a phonetic either.

jué

Bronze Inscriptions

結

Later Seal Character

In the Bronze Inscriptions, the character 绝 is an ideograph, looking like a knife cutting short two silk strings. In the Later Seal Character, 绝 becomes a phonetic compound, with 系 as the radical and 色 as the phonetic. The primary meaning of 绝 is "to cut off," from which have derived the senses: "to separate," "to exhaust," "unique" and "extremely."

巾

Oracle-Bone Inscriptions

巾

Bronze Inscriptions

巾

Later Seal Character

jīn

巾 is a pictograph. In ancient writing systems, it looks like a piece of cloth hanging there. It primarily refers to a piece of cloth for washing one's face, i.e. a towel, but it may also refer to a scarf or kerchief. Characters with 巾 as a component all have to do with cloth, e.g. 布 (cloth), 市 (fú, towelshaped clothing), 幅 (classifier for cloth), 常 (<a variant of 裳> lower garment), 帷 (curtain), 幕 (tent) and 幡 (long narrow flag).

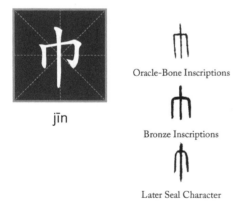

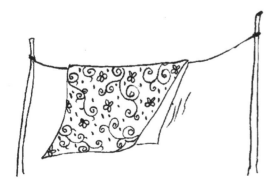

fú

Bronze Inscriptions

Later Seal Character

市 was the original form of 韍, referring to the front lower part of a traditional Chinese gown, worn at sacrifice-offering ceremonies. The character is made up of a stroke standing for the belt and a towel part (巾), signalling it refers to the front part of a gown below the belt.

dài

Chu Character

Later Seal Character

带 means "belt." In the Later Seal Character, the character 带 is made up of two parts: the upper part looks like a belt binding things together and the lower part mainly consists of a towel part (巾), signalling that it is a belt made of cloth. Nowadays, however, it may refer to belts of other material or anything in the shape of a belt as well. Used as a verb, it may mean "to bear," "to carry" and "to lead."

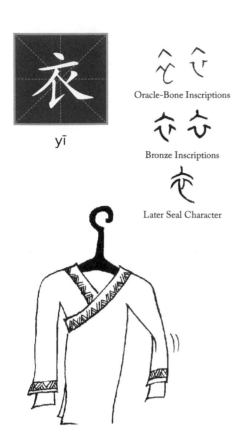

衣
yī

Oracle-Bone Inscriptions

Bronze Inscriptions

Later Seal Character

In ancient writing systems, the character 衣 looks like a sketch of a traditional Chinese upper garment: the upper part is the collar, the lower left and right parts are the sleeves, and the middle part is the front of the garment where the two pieces meet. Hence its primary meaning is "upper garment," whereas the lower garment was known as 裳 in former times. However, the character 衣 may also be used as a general term for clothing. Pronounced as yì, it is used as a verb, meaning "to wear clothes." Characters with 衣 as a component most have to do with cloth and clothing, e.g. 初 (to cut out garments), 衬 (lining), 衫 (unlined upper garment), 裘 (fur coat), 表 (outer garment) and 袂 (mèi, sleeve).

常
cháng

Bronze Inscriptions

Later Seal Character

常 was originally a variant form of 裳. In the Later Seal Character, the character 常 (裳) is a phonetic compound, with 巾 or 衣 as the radical and 尚 as the phonetic, signalling the traditional Chinese lower garment. Nowadays, the two characters 常 and 裳 are different in meaning. 常 is mainly used in the senses of "permanent," "constant," "regulations" and "feudal order of importance," while 裳 retains its original use.

初

chū

Oracle-Bone Inscriptions

Bronze Inscriptions

Later Seal Character

The character 初 consists of a garment part (衣) and a knife part (刀), signalling to cut out garments with scissors. As the cutting up of cloth is the beginning of sewing, the character 初 has taken on the meanings of "beginning" and "original."

表

biǎo

Later Seal Character

In ancient times, people used to wear animal skin. As this type of clothing usually has fur in the outside, the character 表 in the Later Seal Character consists of a garment part (衣) and a fur part (毛), referring to the fur on the outside of the clothing. Hence the primary meaning is "outside" and "surface." As a verb, it may mean "to show" and "to express," from which has derived its use to refer to signs and marks.

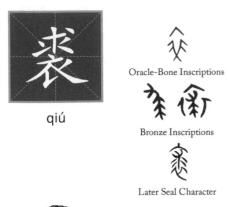

qiú

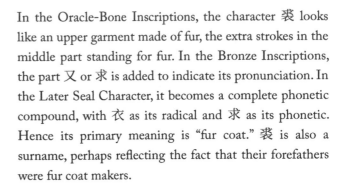

In the Oracle-Bone Inscriptions, the character 裘 looks like an upper garment made of fur, the extra strokes in the middle part standing for fur. In the Bronze Inscriptions, the part 又 or 求 is added to indicate its pronunciation. In the Later Seal Character, it becomes a complete phonetic compound, with 衣 as its radical and 求 as its phonetic. Hence its primary meaning is "fur coat." 裘 is also a surname, perhaps reflecting the fact that their forefathers were fur coat makers.

zú

In ancient writing systems, the character 卒 looks like a garment with a short stroke in the front, signalling that it is a garment with a label attached. This type of clothing was used as a uniform for the rank and file in the army or the government service. Hence its original meaning is "the uniform for the rank and file," but it may also refer to the person who wears it. Used as a verb, it means "to complete," "to end" and "to die."

yì

Oracle-Bone Inscriptions

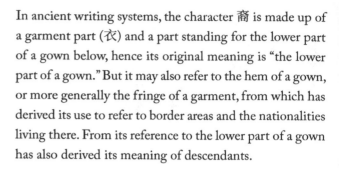

Later Seal Character

In ancient writing systems, the character 裔 is made up of a garment part (衣) and a part standing for the lower part of a gown below, hence its original meaning is "the lower part of a gown." But it may also refer to the hem of a gown, or more generally the fringe of a garment, from which has derived its use to refer to border areas and the nationalities living there. From its reference to the lower part of a gown has also derived its meaning of descendants.

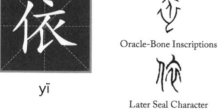

依

yī

Oracle-Bone Inscriptions

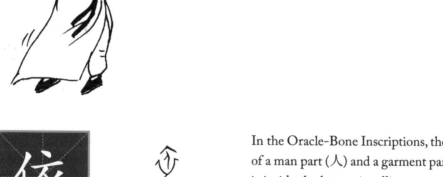

Later Seal Character

In the Oracle-Bone Inscriptions, the character 依 consists of a man part (人) and a garment part (衣), and the former is inside the latter, signalling to put on clothes. From this original meaning have derived its extended meanings "to rely on," "to attach to" and "in accordance with."

shuāi

Later Seal Character

衰 was the original form of 蓑, which refers to a rain cape made of straw or palm-bark. In the Later Seal Character, the character 衰 consists of a garment part (衣) and a part signalling the hanging straw (or palm-bark) threads (冉). Nowadays, however, this character is mainly used in the sense of "declining," opposite to 盛 (thriving), and its original meaning is expressed by 蓑.

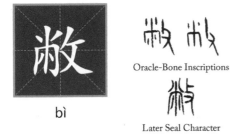

Oracle-Bone Inscriptions

Later Seal Character

bì

敝 is an ideograph. In the Oracle-Bone Inscriptions, the character 敝 has a hand with a stick on the right and a cloth part (巾) with four dots standing for holes on the left. Hence its original meaning is "shabby" and "worn-out," from which have derived the senses of "tired out" and "on the decline."

dōng

Oracle-Bone Inscriptions

Bronze Inscriptions

Later Seal Character

In the Oracle-Bone Inscriptions and Bronze Inscriptions, the character 东 looks like a bag with its two ends tied up. It originally referred to the thing inside the bag, namely, what we now call 东西—thing. But this character is more usually used as a locative, meaning "east," where the sun rises, as against 西 (west).

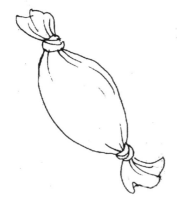

录

lù

Oracle-Bone Inscriptions

Bronze Inscriptions

Later Seal Character

录 was the original form of 渌 or 滤. In the Bronze Inscriptions, the character 录 looks like a bag of wet things hung on a wooden rack dripping water. Hence its original meaning is "to let water go through," i.e. "to filter." However, in the modern simplified form, 录 is used in the senses of the original with 金 as the radical and 录 as the phonetic, such as "recording," "copying," "adopting" and "employing."

gōu/jù

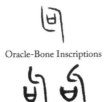

Oracle-Bone Inscriptions

Bronze Inscriptions

Later Seal Character

句 was the original form of 钩 or 勾. In the Oracle-Bone Inscriptions and Bronze Inscriptions, the character 句 looks like two hooks around an eye. Hence it originally meant "to hook," "hook" and "bent." 句 pronounced as jù, means "sentence" or "sense group."

săn

伞 means "umbrella," a circular screen of cloth, oil cloth, plastics, etc., in collapsible form raised on radial ribs attatched to a central stick used for protection against rain or sunshine. This implement was not invented until very late, and there was no character referring to it in early writing systems. In the Regular Script, the character 伞 looks like an open umbrella, with its cover, frame and handle. Hence it is a pictograph.

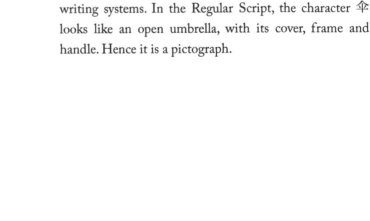

CHAPTER 4

BUILDING

xué

Later Seal Character

The earliest human building was perhaps semi-underground, that is, they would dig a big hole in the ground and build a slant covering of straw or grass on the top, and live in it. In ancient writing systems, the character 穴 looks like a picture of this type of earth house. From this original meaning has derived its use to refer to a hole, cave or anything with an opening. Characters with 穴 as a component most have to do with holes or openings, e.g. 窟 (cave), 窖 (cellar), 窝 (nest; den), 窦 (hole) and 窗 (window).

chuān

Later Seal Character

The character 穿 has a tooth part (牙) under a hole part (穴), signalling that animals like mice make holes with their teeth. Hence its primary meaning is "to make a hole" or "hole," from which have derived the extended meanings "to penetrate," "to break through," "to pass through" and "to wear."

gé/gè

Oracle-Bone Inscriptions

Bronze Inscriptions

Later Seal Character

各 is an ideograph. In the Oracle-Bone Inscriptions and Bronze Inscriptions, the character 各 has a house part (口) under an upside-down foot part (止), signalling to arrive at a house. Hence its original meaning "to reach," "to arrive at," But it is now used as a pronoun, meaning "every" and "each," e.g. 各自 (each side), 各种 (every type).

出

chū

Oracle-Bone Inscriptions

Bronze Inscriptions

Later Seal Character

People began to build houses early in ancient times. But that type of house was very simple, made by digging a hole in the ground and covering the top. As the house was semi-underground, the entrance formed a slope. In the Oracle-Bone Inscriptions and Bronze Inscriptions, the character 出 looks like a foot stepping out of the hole, signalling to go out of the house. Hence its primary meaning is "to go out," from which have derived the extended meanings "to send out," "to produce" and "to appear."

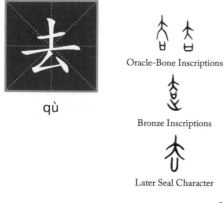

qù

Oracle-Bone Inscriptions

Bronze Inscriptions

Later Seal Character

In the Oracle-Bone Inscriptions and Bronze Inscriptions, the character 去 consists of 大 and 口, the former standing for a man seen from the back and the latter the semiunderground house. Hence its primary meaning is "to leave," e.g. 去国 (to leave one's motherland). It is also used in the sense "to get rid of," e.g. 去伪存真 (to eliminate the false and retain the true). But it is used in a different way nowadays. For example, 去北京 now means "to go to Beijing" rather than "to leave Beijing."

liù

Oracle-Bone Inscriptions

Bronze Inscriptions

Later Seal Character

六 was the original form of 庐. In the Oracle-Bone Inscriptions, the character 六 looks like a house of simple structure, hence its original meaning "hut." Nowadays, however, 六 is used as a numeral, meaning "six," and its original meaning is expressed by a later creation 庐, which has 广 as its radical and 卢 as its phonetic.

yú

Oracle-Bone Inscriptions

Bronze Inscriptions

Later Seal Character

In the Oracle-Bone Inscriptions, the character 余 looks like the framework of a house seen from the side, with its roof, beam and pillar. Hence its original sense "house." But it is used as a first person pronoun now. At present, it is also used as the simplified form of 餘.

jiā

Oracle-Bone Inscriptions

Bronze Inscriptions

Later Seal Character

There was a type of housing in ancient times, in which people themselves lived upstairs, and kept domestic animals downstairs. Reflecting this type of housing, the character 家 consists of a house part (宀) and a pig part (豕), signalling there is a pig in the house. A house with a pig is a symbol of family, hence its primary meaning is "household" and "family."

qǐn

Oracle-Bone Inscriptions

Bronze Inscriptions

Later Seal Character

In all ancient writing systems, the character 寢 looks like a hand with a broom under a roof. In the Regular Script, it even has a bed part (爿), signalling it is a room for sleeping. Hence its primary meaning is "bedroom." But it is also used in the senses "to lie down," "to sleep" and "to rest." It may even mean "to stop." In addition, from its sense of bedroom has derived its reference to a palace or mausoleum.

sù

Oracle-Bone Inscriptions

Bronze Inscriptions

Later Seal Character

In the Oracle-Bone Inscriptions, the character 宿 looks like a man kneeling on a straw cushion, or lying on a cushion under a roof, signalling to rest or sleep. Hence its primary meaning "to rest," "to sleep" and "to stay overnight." As one sleeps at night, the character 宿 also refers to night. And it may also refer the night before, e.g. 宿雨 (the rain last night), 宿醒 (chéng, hangover from drinking too much). From this meaning has derived its sense of "long-standing," e.g. 宿债 (old debt), 宿愿 (long-cherished wish).

ān

Oracle-Bone Inscriptions

Bronze Inscriptions

Later Seal Character

In ancient writing systems, the character 安 looks like a woman sitting peacefully in a house, signalling there is no war or other disaster and life is quiet and comfortable. Hence its meanings is "peaceful," "safe," "easy and comfortable" and "satisfied." Used as a verb, it means "to put" and "to find a place for."

dìng

Oracle-Bone Inscriptions

Bronze Inscriptions

Later Seal Character

In ancient writing systems, the character 定 consists of 宀 and 正, the former standing for a house, and the latter, a destination plus a foot part, signifying the place one has arrived at. In the Oracle-Bone Inscriptions and Bronze Inscriptions, the foot heads toward the house, signalling the man has come back home safely. Hence its primary meaning is "peaceful," "safe" and "to stop." But it may also mean "to decide" and "to fix."

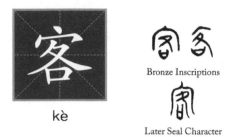

kè

Bronze Inscriptions

Later Seal Character

The character 客 consists of 宀 and 各, the former standing for a house and the latter meaning "to arrive at" and indicating its pronunciation at the same time. Hence its primary meaning is "somebody from another place," i.e. "guest." In addition, it may refer to a person engaged in some particular pursuit, e.g. 侠客 (chivalrous master of martial arts), 剑客 (swordsman) and 墨客 (writers).

bīn

Oracle-Bone Inscriptions

Bronze Inscriptions

Later Seal Character

In the Oracle-Bone Inscriptions, the character 宾 looks like a man coming into a room from outside, signalling the coming of a visitior. In the Bronze Inscriptions, a seashell part (贝) is added to signal the visitor has come with some presents. Hence the primary meaning of 宾 is "visitor," e.g. 来宾 (visitor), 外宾 (foreign visitor). Used as a verb, it means "to submit oneself to."

guǎ

Bronze Inscriptions

Later Seal Character

In the Bronze Inscriptions, the character 寡 consists of 宀 and 頁, the former standing for a house and the latter a person, signalling there is only one person in the house. Hence its primary meaning is "alone." In former times, a woman who lost her husband, and a man who had no wife or lost his wife, were both referred to as 寡. But 寡 also means "few" and "short of," opposite to 多 (many).

kòu

Bronze Inscriptions

Later Seal Character

In the Oracle-Bone Inscriptions, the character 寇 looks like a man hitting someone with a stick inside a house, signalling someone has broken in. Hence its primary meaning is "to rob" and "to invade," and it may also refer to one who robs or invades, i.e. robber or invader.

囚

qiú

Oracle-Bone Inscriptions

Later Seal Character

The character 囚 consists of 囗 (wéi) and 人, signalling a man is in a jail. Its primary meaning is "to imprison," "prisoner" and "prisoner of war."

令

lìng

Oracle-Bone Inscriptions

Bronze Inscriptions

Later Seal Character

In ancient writing systems, the character 令 looks like a man sitting in a room, signalling to issue orders in a room. The primary meaning of 令 is "to order," "to command," or as a noun "order," from which has derived its extended meaning of "good."

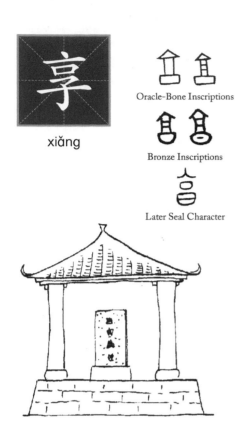

xiǎng

Oracle-Bone Inscriptions

Bronze Inscriptions

Later Seal Character

In the Oracle-Bone Inscriptions and Bronze Inscriptions, the character 享 looks like a simple temple with a high pedestal. The temple is a place for sacrifice-offering ceremonies, hence 享 means "to offer sacrifiecs to gods and the spirits of ancestors." It may also be used in the same sense as 饗, i.e. to entreat gods and spirits to dinner; from which has derived its more general sense "to enjoy."

zōng

Oracle-Bone Inscriptions

Bronze Inscriptions

Later Seal Character

The character 宗 consists of 宀 and 示, the former standing for a house and the latter the stone table used in sacrifice-offering ceremonies. Hence it primarily refers to the place where sacrifice offering ceremonies are held, i.e. the ancestral temple. From this use have derived its extended meanings of "ancestor," "the head god," "patriarchal clan" and "sect." As a verb, it means "to worship."

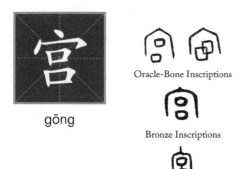

gōng

Oracle-Bone Inscriptions

Bronze Inscriptions

Later Seal Character

The character 宫 consists of 宀 and 吕, the former standing for a house and the latter rooms one after another. Hence its primary meaning is "a complex of buildings," from which has derived its reference to the palace, ancestral temple, Buddhist temple, and Taoist temple. 宫 may of course refer to ordinary houses as well.

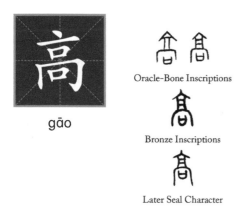

gāo

Oracle-Bone Inscriptions

Bronze Inscriptions

Later Seal Character

In the Oracle-Bone Inscriptions and Bronze Inscriptions, the character 高 looks like a traditional Chinese two-storeyed building with its pitched roof, upstairs and downstairs, and the part 口 standing for the gate. As storeyed buildings are higher than bungalows, the character 高 means "high," opposite to 低 (low). From this primary meaning have derived its senses of "tall and big," "high and far away," "profound," and as a verb, "to heighten" and "to raise." It may also refer to age, e.g. 高龄 (advanced age); or other abstract qualities, e.g. 高尚 (lofty), 高明 (brilliant) and 高洁 (noble and unsullied).

jīng

Oracle-Bone Inscriptions

Bronze Inscriptions

Later Seal Character

In the Oracle-Bone Inscriptions and Bronze Inscriptions, the character 京 looks like a house built on a terrace. Hence its original meaning is "mound," suggesting "high" and "big." As capitals in ancient times were usually built on high places, the character 京 has taken on the meaning of "capital."

liáng

Oracle-Bone Inscriptions

Bronze Inscriptions

Later Seal Character

良 was the original form of 廊. In the Oracle-Bone Inscriptions, the character 良 looks like a house with verandas: the square part in the middle standing for a house and the bent lines on the two sides verandas linking this house to others. Hence its original meaning is "veranda." Nowadays, however, it is used in the senses of "good and kindhearted," and its original meaning is expressed by 廊.

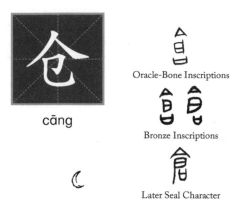

cāng

Oracle-Bone Inscriptions

Bronze Inscriptions

Later Seal Character

In ancient writing systems, the character 仓 looks like a house with its pitched roof, door and window, and terrace. The primary meaning of 仓 is "barn," the building in which one stores grain, though in former times, 仓 only referred to square barns while the circular ones were known as 囷 (qūn). What is more, the character 仓 now may refer to any type of store-house, expressed by the two characters 仓库, which again were strictly distinguished in the past. 仓 referred to places where one stored grain, only buildings for storing other things were called 库.

kù

Bronze Inscriptions

Later Seal Character

The character 库 consists of 广 and 车, the former standing for a house and the latter a vehicle. Hence its original meaning is "a building to keep vehicles," especially "war vehicles." Nowadays, however, it may refer to buildings for storing anything, e.g. 书库 (stack room), 金库 (treasury).

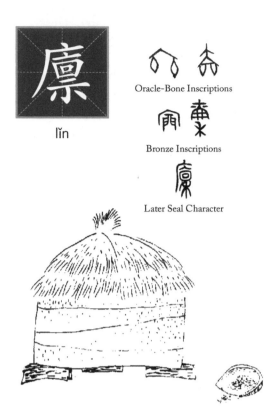

廩

lǐn

Oracle-Bone Inscriptions

Bronze Inscriptions

Later Seal Character

In order to protect the grain against damp, there were usually stones underneath in a barn. In the Oracle-Bone Inscriptions, the character 廩 looks like a grain bin on top of two big stones. In the Bronze Inscriptions, the character looks like a house with a window. And in the Later Seal Character, a house part (广) and a grain part (禾) are added to signal that it is a building for storing grain. Hence its primary meaning is "barn," but it may refer to grain as well. And as a verb, it means "to store."

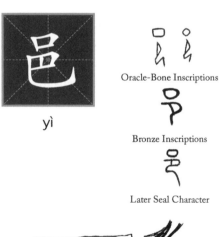

邑

yì

Oracle-Bone Inscriptions

Bronze Inscriptions

Later Seal Character

In the Oracle-Bone Inscriptions and Bronze Inscriptions, the character 邑 has a town part (囗) and a man sitting on the ground, signalling a place to live. Hence the primary meaning of 邑 is "a place where people live in a compact community," such as a town. In former times, big cities were known as 都 and small ones 邑. But it may also refer to the fief of a minister in the feudal society. Characters with 邑 as a component, which is written as 阝 when placed on the right, most have to do with towns or place names, e.g. 都 (capital), 郭 (the outer wall of a city), 邕 (yōng, the alternative name for Nanning, Guangxi), 郊 (suburbs), 郡 (a traditional Chinese administrative area, lagrer than a county), 鄂 (the alternative name for Hubei), 邹 (a county in Shandong) and 邓 (a place name).

guō

Oracle-Bone Inscriptions

Bronze Inscriptions

Later Seal Character

In the early Oracle-Bone Inscriptions, the character 郭 looks like a birds-eye view of a town: the square in the middle standing for the city walls and the parts on the four sides the sentry posts. In the late Oracle-Bone Inscriptions and Bronze Inscriptions, the form is simplified and there are only two sentry posts left. In the Later Seal Character, a town part (邑) is added to emphasize the point that it is a place where people live in compact community. The primary meaning of 郭 is "city wall," especially "the outer wall," but it may also refer to the four sides or outline of something.

bǐ

Oracle-Bone Inscriptions

Bronze Inscriptions

Later Seal Character

In the Oracle-Bone Inscriptions, the character 鄙 is made up of a town part (口) and a barn part (廩). In the Bronze Inscription, the character has either 廩 (barn) or 邑 (town) as the main component, but means the same. Hence 鄙 originally referred to a rural town, especially a remote town, opposite to 都 (capital). As remote rural areas are less developed, the character 鄙 has taken on the senses of "ignorant," "vulgar" and "coarse." Used as a verb, it means "to despise" and "to look down upon."

xiàng

Oracle-Bone Inscriptions

Bronze Inscriptions

Later Seal Character

In the Oracle-Bone Inscriptions, the character 向 looks like a wall of a house with a window in it. It originally referred to a window facing the north. From this use have derived its other senses of "direction," "facing" and "turning towards." Sometimes, 向 be written as "嚮," which is a phonetic compounding with 向 as the radical and 鄉 as the phonetic. In addition, it may mean "in the past" and "all along."

chuāng

Later Seal Character

窗 means "window," a space in a wall of a house to let in light and air. In the Later Seal Character, the character 窗 looks like a traditional Chinese window with lattices on it; sometimes it has 穴 (house) as a component, signalling it is a part of a house.

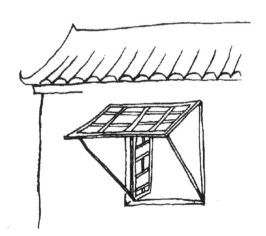

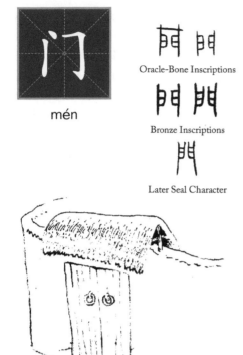

mén

門 門
Oracle-Bone Inscriptions

門 門
Bronze Inscriptions

門
Later Seal Character

門 means "door" or "gate," the entrance to a building. In the Oracle-Bone Inscriptions, the character 門 looks like a complete picture of a traditional Chinese door with its frame, lintel and a pair of leaves. In the Bronze Inscriptions, there are only the parts standing for the two leaves, the lintel is omitted. Characters with 門 as a component most have to do with the entrance, e.g. 闭 (to close [the door]), 间 (gap), 闲 (fence gate), 闸 (floodgate) and 闯 (to break through a gate).

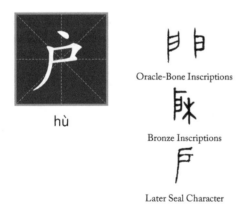

户

hù

户 户
Oracle-Bone Inscriptions

户
Bronze Inscriptions

户
Later Seal Character

户 originally referred to a door with one leaf, and doors with two leaves were known as 门. In the Oracle-Bone inscriptions, the character 户 looks like a picture of such a door. But it is now used in the general senses of "door" or "window," e.g. 门户 (door), 窗户 (window). It is also used in its extended meanings of "household" and "family." Characters with 户 as a component most have to do with the door, window and house, e.g. 启 (to open [the door]), 扉 (door leaf), 扇 (door leaf), 扁 (a horizontal inscribed board), 所 (a classifier used of the house) and 房 (house).

xián

Bronze Inscriptions

Later Seal Character

The character 闲 consists of 木 (wood) and 门 (gate), signalling a gate made of wood sticks, i.e. fence gate. It may also refer to the stable and has an extended meaning of "limit." For example, the *Analects of Confucius* says, "大德不逾闲, 小德出入可也 (In matters of importance one should act in strict accordance with the rules while in trivial matters one may be allowed to act more freely)." Nowadays, however, 闲 is more usually used in the sense of "idle" and "unoccupied."

shuān

In ancient China, one of the ways to keep a door firmly closed was to run a wooden bar across the two leaves. The character 闩 consists of 一 and 门, the former standing for the wooden bar and the latter the door, hence its primary meaning is "the wooden bar for closing a door," i.e. bolt.

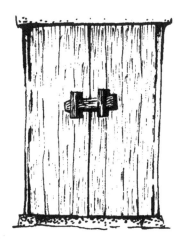

jiān/jiàn

Bronze Inscriptions

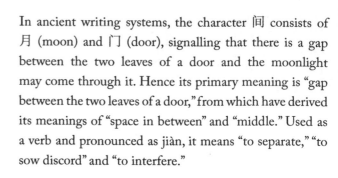

Later Seal Character

In ancient writing systems, the character 间 consists of 月 (moon) and 门 (door), signalling that there is a gap between the two leaves of a door and the moonlight may come through it. Hence its primary meaning is "gap between the two leaves of a door," from which have derived its meanings of "space in between" and "middle." Used as a verb and pronounced as jiàn, it means "to separate," "to sow discord" and "to interfere."

shǎn

Later Seal Character

The character 闪, made up of 人 and 门, looks like a man trying to see the inside through the gap between the two leaves of a door. From this original meaning has derived its use for things which appear suddenly or appear at one moment but disappear at another, e.g. 闪光 (flash of light), 闪电 (lightning) and 闪念 (flash of an idea). It may also refer to actions which last a very short moment, e.g. 躲闪 (to dodge), 闪避 (to sidestep) and 闪击 (to blitz).

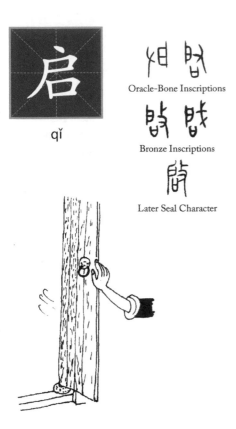

qǐ

Oracle-Bone Inscriptions

Bronze Inscriptions

Later Seal Character

The original complicated form of 启 was an ideograph. In the Oracle-Bone Inscriptions, the character 启 looks like a hand opening a door leaf. Hence it primarily means "to open a door," from which have derived its meanings "to develop," "to open up" and "to enlighten." As to enlighten someone one needs to use speech, the character 启 in the Bronze Inscriptions has a mouth part (口) added. And it has taken on the meaning "to state" as well.

开

kāi

Ancient Script

Later Seal Character

In the Ancient Script, the character 开 looks like two hands opening a door. Hence its primary meaning is "to open a door," from which have derived the extended meanings "to unfold," "to remove obstacles from," "to lift a ban," "to hew out," "to separate," "to start," "to carry out," "to set up" and "to enlighten."

Bronze Inscriptions

Later Seal Character

guān

In ancient China, one of the ways to keep a door firmly closed was to run a wooden bar across the two leaves. In the Bronze Inscriptions, the character 关 looks like a door with a wooden bar, hence its original meaning is "the wooden bar for closing a door," i.e. bolt. As the bolt is used to close a door, the character 关 is also used in the sense "to close." When used as a noun, it means "strategic pass." In addition, it may refer to things which function as linking points, e.g. 机关 (gear), 关节 (joint), 关键 (key point). And it may, as a verb, mean "to link."

Later Seal Character

wǎ

瓦 means "tile," a piece of baked clay for covering roofs. In the Later Seal Character, the character 瓦 looks like one concave tile and one convex tile linked together, hence its meaning is "tile." As tiles are made of baked clay, any object made of baked clay is referred to as 瓦器 (earthenware). Characters with 瓦 as a component most have to do with earthenware, e.g. 瓮 (urn), 瓶 (vase), 瓯 (pot), 甗 (yǎn, steamer), 瓷 (porcelain) and 甄 (potter's wheel).

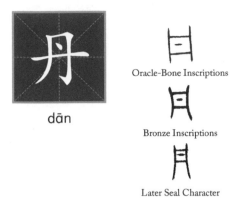

dān

日
Oracle-Bone Inscriptions

日
Bronze Inscriptions

月
Later Seal Character

丹 refers to cinnabar, an element for colouring. In the Oracle-Bone Inscriptions, the character 丹 looks like a well part (井) with a dot in it, the former standing for the mine where the mineral is found and the latter the mineral excavated. As cinnabar is red in colour, it is known as 丹砂, 朱砂 or 朱石, literally "red sand" or "red stone." The character 丹 may also refer to other red things, e.g. 丹唇 (red lips), 丹霞 (rosy clouds).

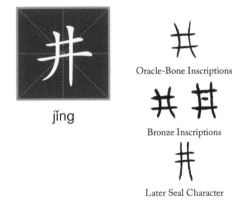

jǐng

井
Oracle-Bone Inscriptions

井 井
Bronze Inscriptions

井
Later Seal Character

In the Oracle-Bone Inscriptions, the character 井 looks like the square railings on top of a well. It primarily refers to a water well, but other enclosed spaces similar to a well may also be referred to by 井, e.g. 天井 (courtyard), 矿井 (mine). In former times, eight households shared a well, and the character 井 has taken on the sense of "neighbour hood," e.g. 市井 (marketplace), 井里 (neighbourhood). 井 may also mean "neat" and "orderly," e.g. 井井有条 (in perfect order), 秩序井然 (in perfect arrangement).

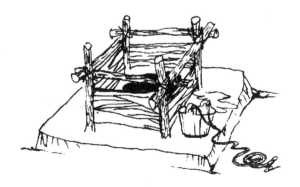

CHAPTER 5

ANIMAL

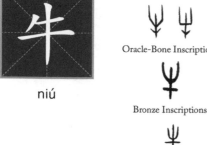

niú

Oracle-Bone Inscriptions

Bronze Inscriptions

Later Seal Character

牛 means "ox," one of the earliest six domestic animals, used for pulling carts or ploughs. In ancient writing systems, the character 牛 looks like the sketch of an ox head, with the horns and ears especially prominent. Characters with 牛 as a component most have to do with oxen and their activities, e.g. 牝 (cow), 牡 (bull), 牟 (the sound made by an ox), 牧 (to herd), 犀 (rhinoceros), 犁 (to plough) and 犊 (calf).

móu

Later Seal Character

In the Later Seal Character, the character 牟 consists of 厶, standing for the breath coming out of an ox's mouth, and 牛 (ox); signalling an ox is making a sound. Hence its original meaning "the sound made by an ox." Xu Shen says in his *Origin of Chinese Characters*, "牟, with its shape of an ox making a sound, refers to the sound made by an ox." Nowadays, however, 牟 is mainly used, the same as 谋, in the sense of "trying to gain," and its original meaning is expressed by 哞.

mǔ

Oracle-Bone Inscriptions

Bronze Inscriptions

Later Seal Character

The character 牡 is an ideograph. In the Oracle-Bone Inscriptions and Broze Inscriptions, it consists of 土 and 牛 (bull) or 羊 (goat) or 鹿 (deer) or 马 (horse). As 土 looks like the image of the masculine genitals, its original meaning is "male animals." After the Later Seal Character, the character 牡 became the only form.

láo

Oracle-Bone Inscriptions

Bronze Inscriptions

Later Seal Character

牢 originally referred to the domestic animals kept in a shed or a stable. In the Oracle-Bone Inscriptions, the character 牢 looks like an ox (or a sheep, a horse) enclosed in a shed. In the later Seal Character, there is a horizontal stroke standing for the gate added at the entrance of the shed. But it may also refer to the place to keep the domestic animals, e.g. 亡羊补牢 (to mend the fold immediately after a sheep is lost); from which has derived its use for the place to lock up prisoners, e.g. 监牢 (prison), 牢狱 (jail). Used as an adjective, it means "firm."

Later Seal Character

qiān

In the Later Seal Character, the character 牵 has three parts: a string part (玄), a horizontal stroke through the middle of the string part standing for the nasal bolt, and an ox part (牛); signalling to lead an ox with a string through the nasal septum of an ox. Xu Shen says in his *Origin of Chinese Characters*, "牵, in the shape of a string to lead an ox, and with 牛 as the radical and 玄 as the phonetic, means to lead along." In this sense, 牵 is both an ideograph and phonetic compound. From its primary meaning is "to lead along," "to pull," have derived the extended senses "to involve," "to implicate" and "to tie up."

mù

Oracle-Bone Inscriptions

Bronze Inscriptions

Later Seal Character

The character 牧 looks like a man driving an ox with a whip in hand, signalling to herd cattle. But it may be used in the general sense of "herding," i.e. the animals looked after may be horses, sheep or pigs as well. As a noun, it refers to the herdsman. In the old days, the rulers saw themselves as herdsmen and the subjects as oxen and horses, so "to rule" was known as 牧民 (to herd people). The rulers of some local areas were known as 牧 or 牧伯 (herdsmen).

wù

Bronze Inscriptions

Later Seal Character

In the Oracle-Bone Inscriptions, the character 物 consists of 刀 (knife) and 牛 (ox), signalling to slaughter an ox with a knife, and the dots on the knife part stand for drops of blood. Hence its original meaning was "to slaughter an ox," from which has derived its reference to oxen of mixed colours, things in general, and content, e.g. 万物 (all things on earth), 言之有物 (having substance in a speech).

mái/mán

Oracle-Bone Inscriptions

Later Seal Character

In the Oracle-Bone Inscriptions, the character 埋 looks like laying an animal sacrifice such as an ox or sheep, a deer or dog into a hole, an important part of a sacrifice-offering ceremony. Hence its original meaning was "to bury an animal," but it may also be used for the covering of anything with earth. In addition, 埋 may also mean "to fill" and "to hide."

gào

Oracle-Bone Inscriptions

Bronze Inscriptions

Later Seal Character

The character 告 consists of 牛 (ox) and 口 (mouth), meaning originally "the sound made by an ox." This character is structured in the same way as 吠 (with a mouth part and a dog part, signalling the sound made by a dog) and 鸣 (with a mouth part and a bird part, signalling the sound made by a bird). But it is now used in the senses of "reporting," "telling," "informing" and "asking for."

bàn

Oracle-Bone Inscriptions

Bronze Inscriptions

Later Seal Character

In ancient writing systems, the character 半 consists of 八 (to separate) and 牛 (ox), signalling to divide an ox into two parts. The primary meaning of 半 is "half," from which have derived its extended meanings: "in the middle of" as in 半夜 (midnight), "very little" as in 一星半点 (a tiny bit), and "semi" as in 半成品 (semi-manufactured goods) and 半透明 (semitransparent).

shěn/chén

Oracle-Bone Inscriptions

Bronze Inscriptions

Later Seal Character

沈 and 沉 were originally variant forms of the same character. In the Oracle-Bone Inscriptions, the character 沈 looks like an ox sinking to the bottom of a river. It was an important part of a sacrifice offering ceremony to offer an animal to the gods and spirits governing mountains and rivers by sinking it. Sometimes, man would be used as a sacrifice as well. In the Bronze Inscriptions, the character 沈 looks like the sinking of a man to a river. The original meaning of 沈 was "to sink," but it may also mean "to indulge" and "deep." Nowadays, 沈 is pronounced as shěn, used as a surname, and its original meaning is expressed by 沉.

quǎn

Oracle-Bone Inscriptions

Bronze Inscriptions

Later Seal Character

犬 refers to the dog, one of the earliest domestic animals kept by man, used mainly for hunting. In the Oracle-Bone Inscriptions and Bronze Inscriptions, the characters 犬 and 豕 (pig) are very similar, except that the character for pig shows that it has a big belly and falling tail while that for dog shows that it has a small belly and rising tail. Characters with 犬 as a component most have to do with dogs and their actions, e.g. 狩 (hunting), 狂 ([a dog] going mad), 莽 ([a dog in] rank grass), 猛 (fierce) and 猎 (to hunt).

Later Seal Character

fèi

The character 吠, consisting of 犬 (dog) and 口 (mouth), is an ideograph, signalling the sound made by a dog, i.e. bark. Xu Shen says in his *Origin of Chinese Characters*, "吠 refers to the sound made by a dog."

xiù/chòu

Oracle-Bone Inscriptions

Later Seal Character

臭 originally meant the same as 嗅, i.e. to smell. The character 臭 consists of 自 (the original form of 鼻, nose) and 犬 (dog), referring to the nose of a dog. As the dog has a very acute sense of smell, the character referring to its nose has come to mean "to smell." The character 臭 may also refer to the quality in substances which the nose senses, i.e. smell, e.g. 无声无臭 ([lit.] without sound or smell; unknown), 其臭如兰 (to have the smell of an orchid). However, the character 臭, pronounced as chòu, now generally refers to foul smell, e.g. 粪臭 (the odour of night soil) and 腐臭 (stinking). And its original meaning, to smell, is expressed by 嗅, with a 口 added.

莽

mǎng

Later Seal Character

In ancient writing systems, the character 莽 looks like a dog running among trees and grass, signalling the dog is chasing a game among plants. The primary meaning of 莽 is "plants growing thickly," but it may also refer to the place where plants grow thickly. And it has an extended meaning of "crude and impetuous."

伏

fú

Bronze Inscriptions

Later Seal Character

In the Bronze Inscriptions, the character 伏 looks like a dog lying on the ground near man's feet. The original meaning is "to bend over," but it may also mean "to hide" or "to vanquish."

tū

Oracle-Bone Inscriptions

Later Seal Character

The character 突 consists of 穴 (hole) and 犬 (dog), signalling a dog rushing out from a hole suddenly. The primary meaning of 突 is "to rush out," and its extended meanings include "to collide" and "to break through." It may also mean "protruding," opposite to 凹 (hollow). From its sense of "rushing out suddenly" have also derived its senses of "suddenly" and "abruptly."

shòu

Oracle-Bone Inscriptions

Bronze Inscriptions

Later Seal Character

兽 was the original form of 狩, meaning "hunting." In the Oracle-Bone Inscriptions, the character 兽 consists of 单 (a forklike hunting weapon) and 犬 (dog), signalling to hunt with a fork and a dog. Nowadays, it refers to the animals captured or killed during hunting, or more generally to any wild animal, opposite to 家畜 (domestic animal). And its original meaning is expressed by 狩 instead.

mǎ

Oracle-Bone Inscriptions

Bronze Inscriptions

Later Seal Character

马 refers to the horse, one of the six earliest animals tamed by man, good at running and carrying things. In the Oracle-Bone Inscriptions, the character 马 looks like a horse seen from the side, with its head, body, feet and tail all represented. In the Bronze Inscriptions, however, only the eye and mane are emphasized. Characters with 马 as a component most have to do with horses, other related animals and their uses, e.g. 驰 (to drive a horse forward), 驼 (camel), 驹 (foal), 骆 (a white horse with black mane), 腾 (to gallop), 骄 ([of horses] tall and strong) and 驴 (donkey).

qí

Oracle-Bone Inscriptions

Ancient Seals

Later Seal Character

奇 was the original form of 骑. In the Oracle-Bone Inscriptions, the character 奇 looks like a man riding on a horse, though the part representing the horse is very simple, and sometimes there is a squrae part (口) underneath. In the Later Seal Character, it consists of 大 and 可 by mistake. The original meaning of 奇 was "to ride a horse," but it is nowadays used mainly in the sense of "strange," and its original meaning is expressed by 骑.

闯

chuàng

Later Seal Character

The character 闯 consists of 马 (horse) and 门 (gate), signalling a horse rushing through a gate. Its primary meaning is "to rush forward fearlessly," suggesting there is nothing to stop it. In addition, it may mean "to experience" and "to go through."

驭

yù

Oracle-Bone Inscriptions

Bronze Inscriptions

Later Seal Character

In the Bronze Inscriptions, the character 驭 consists of 马 (horse) and 鞭 (whip), signalling a man driving a horse forward with a whip. In the Later Seal Character, it consists of 马 (horse) and 又 (hand), but means the same. The primary meaning of 驭 is "to drive a horse or a cart," from which have derived its senses of "controlling," "mastering" and "ruling."

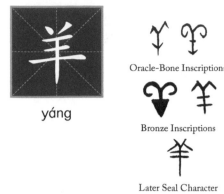

yáng

Oracle-Bone Inscriptions

Bronze Inscriptions

Later Seal Character

羊 refers to one of the six domestic animals, such as goat, sheep and antelope. The character 羊 is a pictograph. But, similar to the character 牛, it depicts only part of the animal, i.e. the head. In the Oracle-Bone Inscriptions and Bronze Inscriptions, it looks like the head of a sheep, and the curving horns are especially prominent so that it will not be mistaken for other animals. It is one of the important ways to create Chinese characters to use the picture of a part for the whole.

shàn

Bronze Inscriptions

Later Seal Character

善 was the original form of 膳. Ancient people thought mutton was the best food, so the character 善 in the Bronze Inscriptions consists of one mutton part (羊) and two speech parts (言), signalling everybody praises mutton. After 善 took on the general sense of "good," another character 膳 was created to express its original meaning. As the sheep is tame and docile, the character 善 can also mean "kindhearted" and "loving," opposite to 恶 (evil). Used as a verb, it means "to love," "to cherish," "to be good to" and "to be good at."

养

yǎng

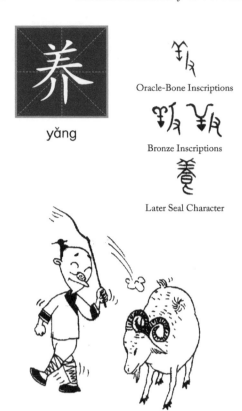

Oracle-Bone Inscriptions

Bronze Inscriptions

Later Seal Character

In the Oracle-Bone Inscriptions and Bronze Inscriptions, the character 养 is an ideograph, looking like a man driving a sheep with a stick in hand. Hence its primary meaning, like that of 牧, is "to herd." In the Later Seal Character, it consists of 羊 (sheep) and 食 (food), signalling to give a sheep its feed. The part 羊 may be seen as a phonetic, in this sense 养 is also a phonetic compound. But the character 养 has also the extended meanings: "to give birth to," "to train," "to recuperate one's health" and "to educate."

羔

gāo

Oracle-Bone Inscriptions

Bronze Inscriptions

Later Seal Character

In the Oracle-Bone Inscriptions, the character 羔 consists of 羊 (sheep) and 火 (fire), signalling to roast a lamb on a fire. As it is usually lambs that are roasted, the character 羔 has come to refer to the lamb as well.

Oracle-Bone Inscriptions

Bronze Inscriptions

Later Seal Character

xiū

In ancient writing systems, the character 羞 consists of 羊 (sheep) and 又 (hand), signalling to present mutton with hands. The original meaning of 羞 was "to present food," but it may also refer to something pleasant to the taste, e.g. 珍羞 (a rare delicacy). However, nowadays 羞 is more usually used in the sense of "shame" or "to feel ashamed," and its original meaning is expressed by 馐.

shǐ

Oracle-Bone Inscriptions

Bronze Inscriptions

Later Seal Character

豕 refers to the pig, now called 猪, one of the earliest domestic animals kept by human beings. In the Oracle Bone Inscriptions, the character 豕 looks like a pig with its long mouth, short legs, round belly and falling tail. In ancient times, however, there was a distinction between 豕 and 猪: the former referring to adult pigs and the latter young ones.

hùn

Oracle-Bone Inscriptions

Bronze Inscriptions

Later Seal Character

The character 圂, consisting of 囗 (wéi, enclosure) and 豕 (pig), is an ideograph. In the Oracle-Bone Inscriptions, the character looks like a pig enclosed in a pigsty, hence its primary meaning is "pigsty." As the pigsty and toilet were usually next to each other, 圂 may refer to the toilet as well.

zhì

Oracle-Bone Inscriptions

Bronze Inscriptions

Later Seal Character

In the Oracle-Bone Inscriptions, the character 彘 consists of 矢 (arrow) and 豕 (pig), signalling an arrow has hit a pig. As it is usually wild boars that are hunted, the character 彘 originally referred to wild boars. But nowadays it may refer to adult pigs in general. For example, the Dialects says, "猪 is known as 彘 in central China."

zhú

Oracle-Bone Inscriptions

Bronze Inscriptions

Later Seal Character

In the Oracle-Bone Inscriptions, the character 逐 consists of 豕 (or 鹿, 兔) and 止 as radicals, looks like a man chasing a pig (or a deer, a rabbit). Hence its primary meaning is "to chase," from which have derived its extended meanings "to drive," "to send into exile," "to compete" and "to seek."

gǎn

Oracle-Bone Inscriptions

Bronze Inscriptions

Later Seal Character

In the Oracle-Bone Inscriptions, the character 敢 looks like a man attacking a wild boar with a hunting fork in hand. In the Bronze inscriptions, the part representing the hunting fork is left out, and the wild boar part is simplified so much that it no longer resembles a boar. To attack a wild boar one must forge ahead. Thus the *Origin of Chinese Characters* says, "敢 means to forge ahead." As wild boars are fierce animals, one fighting with them must be courageous and daring, the character 敢 has also taken on the senses of "courageous" and "daring."

sì

Oracle-Bone Inscriptions

Later Seal Character

兕 refers to a rhinoceroslike animal, which has a horn on its head, also known as single-horned animal. In the Oracle-Bone Inscriptions, the character 兕 looks like such an animal, with its single horn especially prominent. In the Later Seal Character, however, it is the strange shape of its head that is brought into focus.

xiàng

Oracle-Bone Inscriptions

Bronze Inscriptions

Later Seal Character

象 refers to the elephant, a large docile animal, which used to live in central China, a much hotter place then. In the Oracle-Bone Inscriptions and early Bronze Inscriptions, the character 象 is a vivid sketch of an elephant seen from the side, with its long nose and broad trunk especially prominent. However, it is also used in the sense of "likeness," It may also refer to the outside appearance in general, e.g. 形象 (image), 景象 (scene), 星象 (the appearance of stars), 气象 (meteorological phenomena) and 现象 (phenomenon).

为

wéi/wèi

Oracle-Bone Inscriptions

Bronze Inscriptions

Later Seal Character

In the Oracle-Bone Inscriptions, the character 为 looks like a man leading an elephant by the nose, signalling to domesticate an elephant. In ancient times, there were elephants living in central China, a much hotter place then. And people trained elephants to help them with their work. Hence the character 为 has the sense of "working" and "doing things." However, as a result of its evolution from the Oracle-Bone Inscriptions, to the Bronze Inscriptions, Later Seal Character and Regular Script, and especially through the modern simplification, there is no trace whatsoever of the original form left in the present-day 为.

能

néng

Bronze Inscriptions

Later Seal Character

能 was the original form of 熊, referring to the bear. In the Bronze Inscriptions, the character 能 looks like a bear with its big mouth, arched back, strong claws and short tail. As the bear is noted for its strength, the character 能 has taken on the extended senses of "ability" and "talent." Nowadays, 能 is only used in its extended senses, and its original meaning is expressed by a new creation, formed by adding a fire part (火) to 能, i.e. 熊.

虎

hǔ

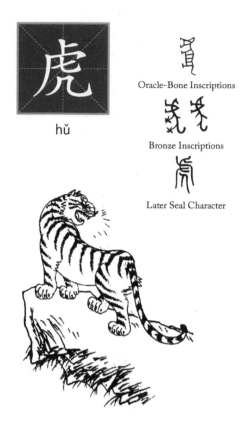

Oracle-Bone Inscriptions

Bronze Inscriptions

Later Seal Character

虎 refers to the tiger, a fierce animal. In the Oracle-Bone Inscriptions, the character 虎 looks like a tiger with its big mouth, sharp teeth, powerful back, strong claws and tail, and colourful fur. In the Bronze Inscriptions and Later Seal Character, its form is simplified and has lost much of its original picturelike flavour. But its meaning has little change throughout the years. As tigers are especially fierce, the character 虎 has also taken on the senses of "brave" and "vigorous," e.g. 虎将 (brave general), 虎威 (tiger's power) and 虎贲 (bēn, warrior).

虐

nüè

Bronze Inscriptions

Later Seal Character

In the Later Seal Inscriptions, the character 虐 looks like a tiger trying to capture a man with its claws. As the tiger is especially cruel and fierce, the character 虐 has taken on the sense of "cruel" and may refer to disasters as well.

鹿

lù

Oracle-Bone Inscriptions

Bronze Inscriptions

Later Seal Character

鹿 refers to the deer, a fast fourfooted animal, of which the males have wide branching horns. In the Oracle-Bone Inscriptions and Bronze Inscriptions, the character 鹿 looks like a male deer with its wide branching horns, long neck and thin legs. Characters with 鹿 as a component most have to do with deers and related animals, e.g. 麟 ([Chinese] unicorn), 麝 (musk deer) and 麋 (elk).

丽

lì

Oracle-Bone Inscriptions

Bronze Inscriptions

Later Seal Character

In the Oracle-Bone Inscriptions and Bronze Inscriptions, the character 丽 looks like a deer, with its beautiful pair of branching horns especially prominent. Hence its original meaning is "a pair" or "a couple." However this meaning is now expressed by 俪, and the character 丽 is used in the sense of "beautiful" and "magnificent."

麓
lù

Oracle-Bone Inscriptions

Bronze Inscriptions

Later Seal Character

麓 is both an ideograph and phonetic compound. In the Oracle-Bone Inscriptions, the character 麓, an ideograph, consists of 林 (forest) and 鹿 (deer), signalling a deer in its favourite living environment, a forest at the foot of a hill. Hence its primary meaning is "the foot of a hill." On the other hand, 鹿 and 麓 sound the same, and the former may be seen as the phonetic of the latter. In this sense, the character 麓 is a phonetic compound with 林 as the radical and 鹿 as the phonetic. In the Bronze Inscriptions, it is a complete phonetic compound, with 林 as the radical and 录 as the phonetic.

尘
chén

Oracle-Bone Inscriptions

Later Seal Character

In ancient writing systems, the character 尘 consists of a soil part (土) and three deer parts (鹿), signalling there is a group of deers running about and clouds of dust flying up. Hence 尘 primarily refers to the dust flying up. But it may also refer to the tiny particles of sandy soil, and that is why later it consists of 小 (small) and 土 (soil).

Oracle-Bone Inscriptions

Stone-Drum Inscriptions

Later Seal Character

tù

兔 refers to a small animal with long ears and a short tail, i.e. a hare or rabbit. In the Oracle-Bone Inscriptions, the character 兔 looks like a sketch of this animal, showing its characteristic ears and tail.

Later Seal Character

shǔ

鼠 refers to the mouse or rat, a small animal with a long tail, whose front teeth are very strong. In the Later Seal Character, the character 鼠 looks like a picture of this animal, showing its characteristic teeth, claws and tail. Characters with 鼠 as a component most refer to animals like the mouse, e.g. 鼹 (mole), 鼬 (weasel) and 鼯 (flying squirrel).

chóng

Oracle-Bone Inscriptions

Bronze Inscriptions

Later Seal Character

虫 is a general term for insects, worms and small creatures like them. In the Oracle-Bone Inscriptions and Bronze Inscriptions, the character 虫 looks like a worm with a pointed head and a curving body, in fact it is the shape of a snake. In the Later Seal Character, the character is made up of three snake parts, perhaps reflecting the fact that there are many different types of insects, worms and the like. Characters with 虫 as a component most have to do with insects, worms and related creatures, e.g. 蛇 (snake), 蜀 (larva), 蚕 (silkworm), 蚊 (mosquito), 蜂 (bee) and 蝉 (cicada).

gǔ

Oracle-Bone Inscriptions

Bronze Inscriptions

Later Seal Character

According to legend there was a venomous worm known as 蛊, which, if eaten, would cause a man to lose consciousness. In the Oracle-Bone Inscriptions, the character 蛊 looks like a vessel with some worms in it. It primarily refers to this venomous worm, but may also refer to parasitic worms living in the human body. And it has the extended meanings: "to entice" and "to confuse."

wàn

Oracle-Bone Inscriptions

Bronze Inscriptions

Later Seal Character

In the Oracle-Bone Inscriptions, the character 万 looks like a scorpion with its big chelae and curving tail, hence its original meaning is "scorpion." Nowadays, however, it is used as a numeral, meaning "ten thousand." But it may also mean "numerous," e.g. 万物 (all the things), 万象 (every phenomenon on earth); and "absolutely," e.g. 万全 (perfectly sound), 万无一失 (no danger of anything going wrong).

zhū

Oracle-Bone Inscriptions

Later Seal Character

蛛 refers to the spider, a small creature with eight legs, which makes webs for catching insects to eat. In the Bronze Inscriptions, the character 蛛 looks like a spider with its long legs, on top of whose head there is a part 朱 representing its pronunciation. In the Later Seal Character, it is a complete phonetic compound with 黾 (frog) or 虫 (insect) as the radical and 朱 as the phonetic.

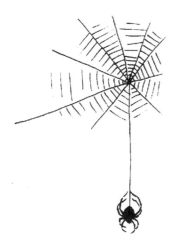

tā

Oracle-Bone Inscriptions

Bronze Inscriptions

Later Seal Character

In the Oracle-Bone Inscriptions, the character 它 looks like a snake with its long winding body and pointed head, hence the original meaning is "snake." As 它 has come to be used as a pronoun for inanimate things, a new character 蛇 was created for the original meaning.

lóng

Oracle-Bone Inscriptions

Bronze Inscriptions

Later Seal Character

龙 refers to a traditional Chinese legendary animal, capable of varying its forms and summoning wind and rain, i.e. dragon. In the Oracle-Bone Inscriptions and Bronze Inscriptions, the character 龙 looks like such a mythical animal with its horns, big mouth and long winding body. In the past, the dragon was a symbol of the emperor and his family, or a person with magical power.

mǐn

Oracle-Bone Inscriptions

Later Seal Character

In the Oracle-Bone Inscriptions, the character 黽 looks like a frog with its big head, round belly and four legs. In the Bronze Inscriptions, the character is simplified in some way and no longer picturelike. 黽 is a general term for frogs but it may refer to a type of frog, known as 金线蛙 or 土鸭, in particular. Characters with 黽 as a component (in their original complicated forms) most refer to creatures like frog in a way, e.g. 鼋 (yuán, [infml.] soft-shelled turtle), 鳖 (biē, soft-shelled turtle) and 鳌 (áo, turtle).

guī

Oracle-Bone Inscriptions

Bronze Inscriptions

Later Seal Character

龟 refers to the tortoise, an amphibian whose body is covered by a hard shell into which the legs, tail and head can be pulled for protection. In the Oracle-Bone Inscriptions, the character 龟 looks like a tortoise seen from the side, while in the Bronze Inscriptions, it looks like a tortoise seen from the top, hence its meaning "tortoise."

yú

Oracle-Bone Inscriptions

Bronze Inscriptions

Later Seal Character

鱼 refers to the fish, an aquatic vertebrate with scales and fins, and breathing through gills. In the Oracle-Bone Inscriptions and Bronze Inscriptions, the character 鱼 looks like a picture of a fish, hence its meaning "fish." Characters with 鱼 as a component all have to do with fish and the like, e.g. 鲤 (carp), 鲨 (shark) and 鲜 (fresh fish).

gòu

Oracle-Bone Inscriptions

Bronze Inscriptions

Later Seal Character

遘 is an ideograph. In the Oracle-Bone Inscriptions, the character 遘 looks like two fishes getting together, mouth to mouth, signalling to meet. In other writing systems, a walk part (止 or 辵) is added, to indicate that it is a human action. Hence 遘 means "to meet" and "to experience."

yú

Oracle-Bone Inscriptions

Bronze Inscriptions

Later Seal Character

There are usually three ways of fishing: with one's hands, a net, or a fishing rod. In the Oracle-Bone Inscriptions, the character 渔 looks like fishing in one of these ways. Hence its primary meaning "fishing," from which have derived its meanings "to plunder" and "to gain by cheating."

chēng/chèn

Oracle-Bone Inscriptions

Bronze Inscriptions

Later Seal Character

In the Oracle-Bone Inscriptions and Bronze Inscriptions, the character 称 looks like a man lifting a fish with his hand. Its original meaning was "to lift," "to raise," from which have derived its extended meanings of "weighing," "recommending," "praising" and "stating." 称 pronounced as chèn means "to be equal to" and "to correspond."

lǔ

Oracle-Bone Inscriptions

Bronze Inscriptions

Later Seal Character

In the Oracle-Bone Inscriptions and Bronze Inscriptions, the character 鲁 consists of 鱼 (fish) and 口 (vessel), signalling that the fish has been cooked and is ready to be served as a delicious dish on a plate. Hence 鲁 meant originally "nice." Nowadays, however, it is mainly used in the senses of "rash" and "stupid," and its original meaning is lost.

niǎo

Oracle-Bone Inscriptions

Bronze Inscriptions

Later Seal Character

鸟 means "bird." In the Oracle-Bone Inscriptions and Bronze Inscriptions, the character 鸟 looks like a bird with its head, tail, legs and feathers all present seen from the side. Characters with 鸟 as a component most have to do with birds and their activities, e.g. 鸡 (chicken), 莺 (oriole), 鸭 (duck), 鹅 (goose) and 鸣 (to chirp).

Oracle-Bone Inscriptions

隹

zhuī

Bronze Inscriptions

Later Seal Character

In the Oracle-Bone Inscriptions and Bronze Inscriptions, the character 隹 looks like a bird with its head, body, wings and legs, but its tail is short. According to Xu Shen's characterization in the *Origin of Chinese Characters*, 隹 refers to birds with short tails while 鸟 birds with long tails. Characters with 隹 as a component all have to do with birds, e.g. 焦 (to roast a bird), 集 (to perch), 雉 (pheasant), 雕 (eagle) and 雀 (sparrow).

乌

wū

Bronze Inscriptions

Later Seal Character

乌 refers to the crow. The crow likes to cry at night, and it is black all over so that the apple is not distinguishable. To reflect these features, the character 乌 in the Bronze Inscriptions looks like a bird with its bill upwards as if crying and there is no apple in the eye. But 乌 may refer to other black things as well.

yàn

Oracle-Bone Inscriptions

Later Seal Character

In the Oracle-Bone Inscriptions, the character 燕 looks like a swallow spreading its wings and flying upwards, hence its primary meaning is "swallow," which is also known as 玄鸟 in Chinese. As the three characters 燕, 宴 and 晏 sound the same, the character 燕 may also be used in the latters' senses of "feast," "easy" and "comfort."

què

Oracle-Bone Inscriptions

Later Seal Character

雀 was originally a pictograph. In the Oracle-Bone Inscriptions, the character 雀 looks like the head of a bird with a crest. It primarily refers to the sparrow or tit. As sparrows and tits are small, the character 雀 may also refer to small birds in general. In the Later Seal Character, however, the character consists of 小 (small) and 隹 (bird), resulting in an ideograph.

fèng

Oracle-Bone Inscriptions

Later Seal Character

凤 refers to the imaginary lucky bird, the king of birds—phoenix. In the Oracle-Bone Inscriptions, the character 凤 looks like a bird with a long tail. This bird has a crest on its head and eyes on its colourful tail feathers, which is in fact an image of a peacock. Sometimes there is a phonetic part 凡 added, so it is also a phonetic compound with 鸟 as its radical and 凡 as its phonetic. As the phoenix is a symbol of good luck, the character 凤 is used to describe anything good and pleasing, e.g. 凤德 (moral integrity), 凤藻 (literary embellishment), 凤穴 (a gathering of talents), 凤车 (the royal carriage) and 凤城 (capital).

jī

Oracle-Bone Inscriptions

Bronze Inscriptions

Later Seal Character

鸡 refers to the chicken. In the Oracle-Bone Inscriptions and Bronze Inscriptions, the character 鸡 is an ideograph, looking like a cock with its crest, bill, eyes, wings, legs and tail all represented. In the Later Seal Character, it becomes a phonetic compound, with 隹 as its radical and 奚 as its phonetic. The modern simplified form is even more remote from its original in that it consists of 又 and 鸟.

Later Seal Character

jù/qú

The character 瞿 consists of a bird part (隹) and two eye parts (目), looking like a bird with its eyes wide open, signalling that fierce birds like the eagle and falcon have big and sharp eyes. Thus the *Origin of Chinese Characters* says, "瞿 refers to the eye of birds like an eagle and falcon." When a man is frightened, he may open his eyes wide, hence the character 瞿 has taken on the sense of "frightened." Used as a surname, it is pronounced as qú.

Bronze Inscriptions

Later Seal Character

dí/zhái

翟 was originally a pictograph. In the Bronze Inscriptions, the character 翟 looks like a bird with a tuft of feathers on its head. In the Later Seal Character, it becomes an ideograph, consisting of 羽 (feather) and 隹 (bird). 翟 primarily refers to pheasants with long tail feathers, and it may, in particular, refer to their tail feathers, used as ornaments by people in former times. 翟, meaning the same as 狄, is also a name of a national minority in the north. And it is a surname, pronounced as zhái.

zhì

Oracle-Bone Inscriptions

Later Seal Character

雉 was originally an ideograph, consisting of 矢 (arrow) and 隹 (bird), signalling to shoot a bird with an arrow. And 雉 referred to the bird captured or killed. As pheasants accounted for a greater part of the birds shot, the character 雉 has come to refer to pheasants in particular. In addition, 雉 may be used as a unit for measuring the area of city walls, and three zhàng (*one zhang* equal to 3.33 metres) in length and one zhàng in height is a zhi (雉). From this sense has derived its use to refer to city walls.

jiù

Oracle-Bone Inscriptions

Bronze Inscriptions

Later Seal Character

旧 was originally a name of a bird, also known as 鸱鸮 (chīxiāo) or 猫头鹰, i.e. owl. This bird is said to be very fierce and often occupies nests of other birds and eats their young. In the Oracle-Bone Inscripitons and Bronze Inscriptions, the character 旧 looks like a bird attacking a nest of other birds, depicting the characteristic behaviour of the owl. Nowadays, however, this character is used in the sense of "old," opposite to 新 (new), and its original meaning is lost.

鸣

míng

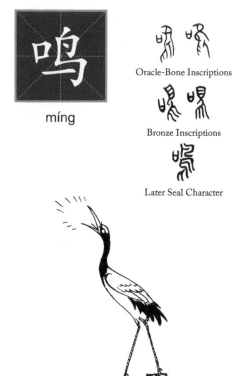

Oracle-Bone Inscriptions

Bronze Inscriptions

Later Seal Character

The character 鸣 consists of 口 (mouth) and 鸟 (bird), referring to the cry of a bird. But its meaning has been extended. It can also refer to the sound made by animals or insects, e.g. 蝉鸣 (the noise made by a cicada), 驴鸣 (a donkey's bray), 鹿鸣 (the sound made by a deer). Used as a verb, it means to make a sound by striking something, e.g. 鸣鼓 (to beat a drum), 鸣钟 (to toll a bell), 鸣枪 (to fire a shot), 鸣炮 (to open fire with artillery) and 孤掌难鸣 (It is impossible to clap with one hand).

习

xí

Oracle-Bone Inscriptions

Later Seal Character

In the Oracle-Bone Inscriptions, the character 习 consists of 羽 (feather) and 日 (sun), signalling that birds are practising flying in the sun. Xu Shen says in his *Origin of Chinese Characters*, "习 means to fly time and again." Hence its primary meaning is "birds' practising flying," from which have derived its more general meanings, "to learn," "to exercise," "to review," "to be familiar with" and "to be used to."

huò

Oracle-Bone Inscriptions

Bronze Inscriptions

Later Seal Character

The character 霍 looks like many birds flying in the rain, referring to the sound made by the birds' fluttering of their wings. It may also be used as an onomatopoeia for sounds similar to it, e.g. 磨刀霍霍 (to sharpen one's swords on a grindstone). As birds fly swiftly and in all directions in the rain, the character 霍 has taken on the senses of "quickly" and "freely," e.g. 霍然而愈 (to recover from an illness quickly), 电光霍霍 (the flashing of lightning) and 挥霍 (to spend freely).

fèn

Bronze Inscriptions

Later Seal Character

In the Bronze Inscriptions, the character 奋 consists of 隹 (bird), 衣 (feather) and 田 (field), signalling that birds are flying across fields with their wings spread. Hence its original meaning is "birds taking wings," from which have derived its senses of "raising," "agitating," "exerting oneself" and "carrying forward."

jìn

Oracle-Bone Inscriptions

Bronze Inscriptions

Later Seal Character

进 is an ideograph. In the Oracle-Bone Inscriptions, the character 进 consists of 隹 (bird) and 止 (foot), signalling that a bird is walking or flying. In the Bronze Inscriptions, a walking part (彳) is added to emphasize its meaning of moving forward. The character 进 primarily means "to move forward," opposite to 退 (to retreat). It may also mean "to enter," opposite to 出 (to exit). In addition, it may mean "to recommend" and "to present."

fēi

Later Seal Character

In the Later Seal Character, the character 飞 looks like a bird flying with its wings spread, hence its primary meaning "to fly." From this meaning has derived its use for anything floating in the air, e.g. 飞蓬 (fleabane), 飞雪 (fluttering snowflakes). 飞 may also be used in the sense of "swift."

fēi

Bronze Inscriptions

Later Seal Character

In the Bronze Inscriptions, the character 非 looks like two wings opposite to each other. The primary meaning of 非 is "to run counter to," from which have derived its meanings "to blame," "to reproach," "wrong" and "not."

jí

Oracle-Bone Inscriptions

Bronze Inscriptions

Later Seal Character

In the Oracle-Bone Inscriptions and Bronze Inscriptions, the character 集 looks like a bird resting on a branch of a tree, hence its original meaning is "to perch." As birds usually perch together, the character 集 in the Later Seal Character consists of three bird parts (隹), and it has taken on the sense of "gathering" and "assembling."

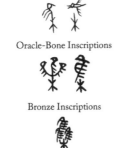

Bronze Inscriptions

Later Seal Character

chóu

The character 雠 is an ideograph. In the Bronze Inscriptions, the character 雠 looks like two birds facing each other, and the speech part (言) in the middle signals that they are talking. The original meaning of 雠 was "to reply" and "to respond," from which have derived its meanings of "corresponding," "equal," "opponent" and "enemy." In addition, 雠 may mean "to come true" and "to proofread."

Oracle-Bone Inscriptions

Bronze Inscriptions

zhī/zhǐ

Later Seal Character

The character 只 in the function of a classifier looks like a bird in the grasp of a hand in all ancient writing systems, the Oracle-Bone Inscriptions, Bronze Inscriptions and Later Seal Character, and its primary meaning is "a single bird." From this sense has derived its meaning of "odd number," opposite to 双 (even number). For example, the *History of the Song Dynasty* records, "肃宗而下, 咸只日临朝, 双日不坐. (After the reign of Suzong, every emperor meets his ministers on odd days only, not on even days.)" But the character 只 in the modern simplified form was originally the form of another character. In addition, 只 also means "only," pronounced as zhǐ, which was originally expressed by 祇.

shuāng

Later Seal Character

In ancient writing systems, the character 双 looks like two birds in the grasp of a hand, hence its primary meaning is "two" and "couple." From this sense has derived the extended meaning of "even number," opposite to 单 (odd number).

jiāo

Bronze Inscriptions

Later Seal Character

In the Bronze Inscriptions, the character 焦 consists of 隹 (bird) and 火 (fire), signalling to roast a bird with fire. In the Later Seal Character, there are three bird parts on a fire, indicating many birds are being roasted. The primary meaning of 焦 is "to roast a bird," from which have derived its use for anything that is dried by fire, the state of being dry and that of being worried.

彝

yí

Oracle-Bone Inscriptions

Bronze Inscriptions

Later Seal Character

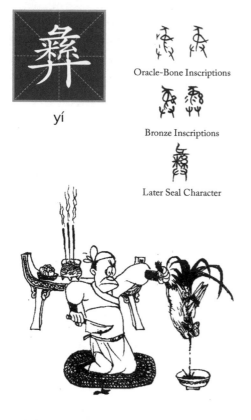

In the Oracle-Bone Inscriptions and Bronze Inscriptions, the character 彝 looks like two hands holding a chicken whose wings are bound at the back, and there are two dots beside the chicken standing for drops of blood, signalling to kill a chicken and use its blood as an offering to spirits. Its original meaning was "to offer a chicken as a sacrifice," from which has derived its reference to any sacrificial objects, a type of wine vessel in particular. In addition, 彝 also means "regulations" and "norms."

羽

yǔ

Oracle-Bone Inscriptions

Later Seal Character

In the Oracle-Bone Inscriptions, the character 羽 looks like feathers, hence its primary meaning is "feather." Characters with 羽 as a component most have to do with feathers and wings, e.g. 习 (習) (to practise flying), 翎 (feather), 翔 (to fly), 翻 (the flying of birds) and 翼 (wing). 羽 may also be used as a substitute for bird, e.g. 奇禽异羽 (rare birds). As arrows usually have feathers at their ends, known as 雕翎箭 (feathered arrow), the character 羽 may also refer to arrows, e.g. 负羽从军 (to join the army with arrows on the back).

番
fān

Bronze Inscriptions

番

Later Seal Character

番 was the original form of 蹯 (fán). In the Bronze Inscriptions, the character 番 has a part like a foot print of beast on top of a field part, signalling the track left by beasts on the field. The original meaning of 番 was "the foot or claw of a beast," from which have derived its meaning "to alternate" and its use as a classifier of actions. In the past, the Han nationality despised the national minorities and foreigners, and referred to them as 番邦, meaning "barbarous peoples."

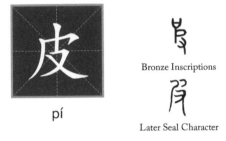

皮
pí

Bronze Inscriptions

Later Seal Character

In the Bronze Inscriptions, the character 皮 looks like a hand removing the skin of a beast. Hence its primary meaning is "hide," or the skin that has been tanned, i.e. leather. But it may also refer to the surface layer of anything, e.g. 人皮 (human skin), 树皮 (bark) and 地皮 (ground), from which has derived the extended meaning "superficial."

肉

ròu

Oracle-Bone Inscriptions

Later Seal Character

In ancient writing systems, the character 肉 looks like a piece of meat with ribs. It primarily refers to the flesh of animals, e.g. 羊肉 (mutton), 猪肉 (pork). From this use has derived its reference to the soft eatable part of a plant, e.g. 枣肉 (jujube), 笋肉 (bamboo shoot) and 龙眼肉 (longan pulp). Characters with 肉 (月) as a component all have to do with the parts of a human being or animal, e.g. 肠 (intestines), 股 (thigh), 脚 (foot), 腰 (waist) and 脸 (face).

有

yǒu

Oracle-Bone Inscriptions

Bronze Inscriptions

Later Seal Character

In ancient writing systems, the character 有 consists of 又 (hand) and 肉 (月) (meat), signalling a man with a piece of meat in hand. Hence its primary meaning is "to possess" and "to obtain," opposite to 无 (not to have); from which have derived its extended meanings "to exist" and "to take place."

zhì

Later Seal Character

In the Later Seal Character, the character 炙 consists of 肉 (meat) and 火 (fire), signalling to roast a piece of meat by fire. Its primary meaning is "to roast," but it may refer to the meat roasted as well.

骨

gǔ

Oracle-Bone Inscriptions

Later Seal Character

骨 refers to the hard parts of body, i.e. bones. In the Oracle-Bone Inscriptions, the character 骨 looks like bones with flesh cut off. In the Later Seal Character, a flesh part (月) is added to signal that flesh and bone are related to each other. Characters with 骨 as a component all have to do with the bones of a human being or animal, e.g. 骷 (kū, skeleton), 骰 (gǔ, bone dice), 骼 (bone), 髀 (bì, thigh bone) and 髓 (marrow).

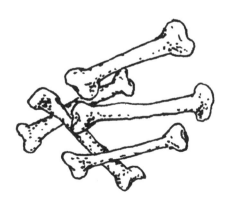

jiǎo/jué

Oracle-Bone Inscriptions

Bronze Inscriptions

Later Seal Character

In both the Oracle-Bone Inscriptions and Bronze Inscriptions, the character 角 looks like the horn of an animal, such as an ox, sheep or deer. The horn in animals like oxen and sheep is a weapon to fight and protect themselves, so the character 角 has taken on the sense of "competition in physical strength" (角力). In former times, the horn was also used as a vessel for drinking, thus the character 角 is used as a unit of volume like 杯 (glass). As a result, characters with 角 as a component most refer to vessels, e.g. 觚 (gū, a wine vessel), 觞 (shāng, a wine glass) and 斛 (hú, a vessel for measuring). In the senses of "contend" and "dramatic role," it is pronounced as jué.

jiě/jiè/xiè

Oracle-Bone Inscriptions

Bronze Inscriptions

Later Seal Character

In the Oracle-Bone Inscriptions, the character 解 looks like two hands opening up an ox horn. Its primary meaning is "to dismember," e.g. 庖丁解牛 (the skillful dismemberment of an ox by a cook). From this meaning have derived its senses "to divide," "to separate," "to untie," "to dispel," "to analyze," "to explain" and "to understand." Pronounced as jiè, it means "to send under guard." And as a surname, it is pronounced as xiè.

máo

Bronze Inscriptions

Later Seal Character

In the Bronze Inscriptions, the character 毛 looks like the hair of a man or animal, hence its primary meaning "hair." But it may also refer to other threadlike growth from the skin of an animal or plant, from which has derived its meaning "rough," "crude." Characters with 毛 as a component most have to do with hair, e.g. 毡 (felt), 毫 (fine long hair) and 毯 (blanket; carpet).

CHAPTER 6

PLANT

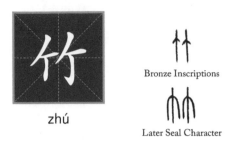

zhú

竹 refers to an evergreen perennial plant of the grass family—bamboo. In the Bronze Inscriptions, the character 竹 looks like two hanging bamboo branches with leaves, signifying "bamboo." But the character 竹 may also refer to bamboo slips on which one writes, or musical instruments made of bamboo, such as flutes and pipes.

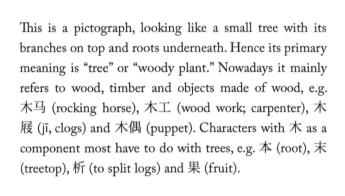

mù

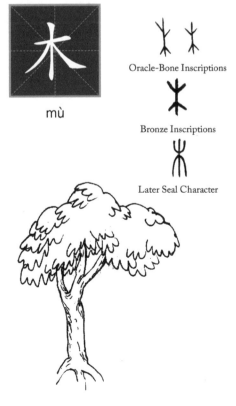

This is a pictograph, looking like a small tree with its branches on top and roots underneath. Hence its primary meaning is "tree" or "woody plant." Nowadays it mainly refers to wood, timber and objects made of wood, e.g. 木马 (rocking horse), 木工 (wood work; carpenter), 木屐 (jī, clogs) and 木偶 (puppet). Characters with 木 as a component most have to do with trees, e.g. 本 (root), 末 (treetop), 析 (to split logs) and 果 (fruit).

lín

Oracle-Bone Inscriptions

Bronze Inscriptions

Later Seal Character

The character 林 consists of two tree parts (木), signalling there are many trees, hence its primary meaning is "forest." But it can also refer to people or things gathered together, e.g. 帆檣林立 (a forest of masts), 儒林 (a society of scholars), 艺林 (art circles), 民族之林 (nationalities in the world) and 书林 (stack room).

sēn

Oracle-Bone Inscriptions

Later Seal Character

The character 森 consists of three tree parts (木), signalling that there is a luxuriant forest. In forests, one often feels something cloudy, gloomy, and solemn, so the character 森 also means "gloomy" and "stern."

yì

Oracle-Bone Inscriptions

Bronze Inscriptions

Later Seal Character

In the Oracle-Bone Inscriptions and Bronze Inscriptions, the character 艺 looks like a man holding a sapling in his two hands, signalling to plant a tree. From this primary meaning has derived its more general sense of cultivation. It was a very important skill to be able to grow things in former times, so the character 艺 has also come to mean "talent" or "skill," e.g. 艺术 (art), 工艺 (craft).

xiū

Oracle-Bone Inscriptions

Bronze Inscriptions

Later Seal Character

The character 休 consists of 人 (man) and 木 (tree), signalling a man is taking a rest against a tree. Hence its primary meaning is "to rest" and "to stop." It is no doubt a great pleasure for a labourer in the sun to take a rest under a tree, so the character 休 also means "good," "lucky" and "happy."

zhī

Later Seal Character

支 was the original form of 枝, meaning "branch." In the Later Seal Character, the character 支 looks like a man with a branch of a tree (or a bamboo) in hand. But it may also refer to other things similar to the branches of a tree, e.g. 分支 (branch), 支派 (a subdivision of a large group), 支流 (the tributary of a river). As a verb, it means "to protrude," "to raise," "to prop up," "to support" and "to order about."

zhū

Bronze Inscriptions

Later Seal Character

In ancient writing systems, the character 朱 looks like a tree with a dot (or a short stroke) in the middle denoting the position of stem. 朱 was the original form of 株, meaning "stem." Nowadays, however, 朱 is used to denote a colour of bright red, and its original meaning is expressed by 株.

běn

Bronze Inscriptions

Later Seal Character

本 originally referred to the root or stem of a tree. The character 本 is made up of a tree part (木) and a dot or short stroke at the bottom denoting the position of root. From this primary meaning have derived its senses of "foundation," "basis," "thing-in-itself" and "main part."

mò

Bronze Inscriptions

Later Seal Character

末 originally referred to the tip of a tree. The character 末 is made up of a tree part (木) and a short stroke on the top denoting the position of the tip of a tree. From this primary meaning have derived its meanings of "top," "end," "last," "incidental," "unimportant," "minor" and "shallow."

wèi

Oracle-Bone Inscriptions

Bronze Inscriptions

Later Seal Character

In ancient writing systems, the character 未 looks like a tree with leaves overlapping one another, signalling it is a luxuriant tree. But this character is now mainly used as a name of the eighth Earthly Branch, a traditional Chinese system of sequence, and its original meaning is lost. In addition 未 is used as a negative adverb, meaning "not."

cì

Oracle-Bone Inscriptions

Bronze Inscriptions

Later Seal Character

朿 was the original form of 刺. In the Oracle-Bone Inscriptions and Bronze Inscriptions, the character looks like a tree with thorns all over it. Hence its original meaning is "thorn." Xu Shen says in his *Origin of Chinese Characters*, "朿 refers to the thorns of a tree." Characters with 朿 as a component most refer to trees with thorns, e.g. 枣 (jujube tree), 棘 (thorn bushes). The character 刺, consisting of 朿, which also serves as the phonetic, and 刀 (knife), is a later development.

zǎo

Bronze Inscriptions

Later Seal Character

枣 refers to the jujube tree, which has thorns when young, produces stoned sweet fruits and supplies timber for furniture. The character 棗 consists of two thorn parts (朿) one on top of the other, signalling it is a tall tree, not a bush.

jí

Bronze Inscriptions

Later Seal Character

棘 refers to a sour jujube tree, short and bushlike. The character 棘 consists of two thorn parts (朿) side by side, signalling it is short and bushlike. But 棘 may also refer to other thorny bushes and herbaceous plants as well.

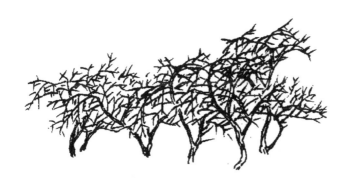

jīng

Bronze Inscriptions

Later Seal Character

荆 refers to a thorny bush, whose branches may be made into baskets. In the early Bronze Inscriptions, the character 荆 is an ideograph, looking like a man whose hands and feet are full of thorns. In the late Bronze Inscriptions, a well part (井) is added to serve as the phonetic, resulting in a phonetic compound. As the man part in it is very similar to a knife part, sometimes the character has a knife part (刀) as the radical by mistake, and 井 as the phonetic, as if it were 刑 (punishment). In the Later Seal Character, a grass part (艹) is added on top of the mistaken variant in the Bronze Inscriptions (刑), resulting in the present form 荆.

束

shù

Oracle-Bone Inscriptions

Bronze Inscriptions

Later Seal Character

In ancient writing systems, the character 束 looks like a bag with its two ends tied up. Sometimes it looks like some firewood bound together. Hence its primary meaning is "to tie," "to bind," from which have derived its senses of "restraining" and "checking."

cháo

Oracle-Bone Inscriptions

Bronze Inscriptions

Later Seal Character

In the Oracle-Bone Inscriptions and Bronze Inscriptions, the character 巢 looks like a bird nest on a tree. In the Later Seal Character, 巢 look like a bird nest on the top of a wood, the three curving strokes on the top standing for the heads of young birds in the nest, signalling that birds are staying in the nest on a tree. Apart from bird nests, 巢 may refer to resting places of other creatures as well, e.g. 蜂窝 (honeycomb), 蚁窝 (ant nest).

xī

Oracle-Bone Inscriptions

Bronze Inscriptions

Later Seal Character

In the Oracle-Bone Inscriptions and Bronze Inscriptions, the character 西 looks like a bird nest. In the Later Seal Character, it has a curving line above the nest, signalling a bird is staying in the nest. Hence the character 西 originally meant "nest" or "to rest." As a bird comes back to its nest for a rest when the sun sets, the character 西 has come to be used as a locative, denoting the direction in which the sun sets, i.e. the west, opposite to 东 (east).

果

guǒ

Oracle-Bone Inscriptions

Bronze Inscriptions

Later Seal Character

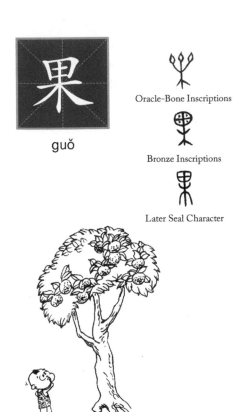

果 is a pictograph. In the Oracle-Bone Inscriptions, the character 果 looks like a tree full of fruits on it. In the Bronze Inscriptions, the number of fruits is reduced to one but the size is increased. In the Later Seal Character, the fruit part becomes a field part (田) by mistake, losing its picturelike image. From its primary meaning is "fruits of a tree" have derived its extended meanings of "outcome," "substantial," "full" and "resolute."

某

mǒu

Bronze Inscriptions

Later Seal Character

某 was the original form of 楳 (梅). The *Origin of Chinese Characters* says, "某 refers to the sour fruit." In ancient writing systems, the character 某 looks like a tree bearing fruits. Some people hold that 某 consists of 木 (tree) and 甘 (sweet), signalling its fruits are sour and sweet. Hence 某 originally referred to the sour fruit, now known as 梅 (plum). But this character is now used as a pronoun, referring to some particular person, place or thing, and its original meaning is expressed by 楳 (梅).

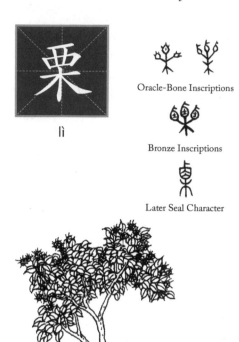

lì

Oracle-Bone Inscriptions

Bronze Inscriptions

Later Seal Character

In the Oracle-Bone Inscriptions, the character 栗 looks like a tree full of prickly fruits—chestnuts, also known as 板栗. The character 栗 may refer to both the fruit and the tree. As the chestnut has a hard cover with dense prickles, the character 栗 has taken on the senses of "hard" and "tight." In addition 栗 may be used in the same sense of 慄, i.e. to tremble with cold or fear.

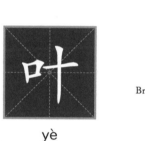

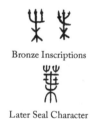

yè

Bronze Inscriptions

Later Seal Character

叶 refers to leaves, the usually flat and green parts of a plant that are joined to its stem or branches. In the Bronze Inscriptions, the character 叶 looks like a tree with three branches on top, on which there are three dots standing for leaves. In the Later Seal Character, a grass part is added on the top to signal that leaves are similar to grass in a way. But the modern simplified form was originally a different character.

sāng

Oracle-Bone Inscriptions

Later Seal Character

桑 refers to the mulberry, a tall tree with broad leaves, which may serve as the food of silkworms. In the Oracle-Bone Inscriptions, the character 桑 is a pictograph, looking like a tree with luxuriant foliage. In the Later Seal Character, its leaf parts are separated from the branch parts and mistakenly changed into hand parts (又), destroying its picturelike image.

cǎi

Oracle-Bone Inscriptions

Bronze Inscriptions

Later Seal Character

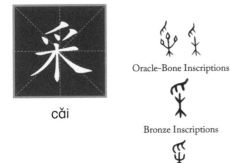

采 is an ideograph. In the Oracle-Bone Inscriptions, the character 采 looks like a hand picking fruits or leaves of a tree. Hence its primary meaning is "to pick" and extended meaning "to gather." In the Bronze Inscriptions and Later Seal Character, the character 采 is somewhat simplified, made up of 爪 and 木. But the original complicated form in the Regular Script goes to the other direction by adding a hand part (扌) to it, which is in fact an unnecessary complication, since the part 爪 has already shown that hand is involved. That is why the modern simplified form does not have it.

huá

Oracle-Bone Inscriptions

Bronze Inscriptions

Later Seal Character

华 was the original form of 花. In the Oracle-Bone Inscriptions, the character 华 looks like a tree in full bloom. In former times, the flowers of a tree were known as 华 while those of a grass 荣. However, nowadays, 花 is used as a general term for any type of flower. As the trees and grasses in bloom look beautiful and luxuriant, the character 华 has also taken on the senses of "beautiful," "magnificent" and "prosperous."

róng

Oracle-Bone Inscriptions

Later Seal Character

In the Bronze Inscriptions, the character 荣 looks like two grasses in blossom crossing each other, the three dots on each of them standing for flowers. Hence its original meaning is "flower of a grass." 荣 consist of 木 and 𤇡 as the radical, and 𤇡 can be the phonetic part either. 𤇡 is the original form of 荧, signaling briliant flowers. As grasses in blossom look prosperous, the character 荣 has also taken on the senses of "prosperous" and "flourishing," from which have derived its senses of "glory" and "honour."

bù

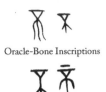

Oracle-Bone Inscriptions

Bronze Inscriptions

Later Seal Character

不 was the original form of 胚. In the Oracle-Bone Inscriptions, the character 不 has a horizontal stroke on top standing for the ground and some curving vertical lines beneath standing for the radicles. Hence its original meaning is "the embryo of a plant." Nowadays, however, it is used as a negative adverb, meaning "no" or "not," and its original meaning is lost.

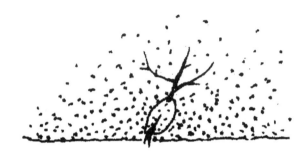

zhūn/tún

Oracle-Bone Inscriptions

Bronze Inscriptions

Later Seal Character

In the Oracle-Bone Inscriptions and Bronze Inscriptions, the character 屯 looks like a young plant newly grown from a seed, the small circle on the top standing for the seedcase that has not been detached yet. Hence its original meaning is "seedling." At the beginning of its life, a seedling will have to break the ground, which is a hard job, so the character 屯 also has the meaning of "hard." In addition, 屯 pronounced as tún, means "to collect" and "to station."

shēng

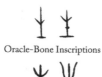

Oracle-Bone Inscriptions

Bronze Inscriptions

Later Seal Character

In the Oracle-Bone Inscriptions, the character 生 looks like a young plant newly raised out of the ground. Hence its primary meaning is "the growth of a plant," from which have derived its more general use for the growth and development of anything, e.g. 出生 (to be born), 生育 (to give birth to), 发生 (to take place). It can also mean "alive," opposite to 死 (dead); and may be used in the senses of "life" and "living years." In short it can be used very extensively in many senses and form many words with other characters.

草

cǎo

Later Seal Character

草 means "grass." In ancient writing systems, the character 草 is an ideograph, looking like two young grasses with their stalks and leaves. The character 草 in the Regular Script is a phonetic compound, which was actually the original form of 皂 (Chinese honey locust). Characters with the top of 草, i.e. ⺿, as a component most have to do with plants, especially herbaceous plants, e.g. 芷 (a fragrant herb, technically known as Dahurian angelica), 苗 (seedling), 荆 (chaste tree) and 薪 (firewood).

Later Seal Character

huì

卉 is a general term for the different kinds of grass. Nowadays, it mainly refers to ornamental grasses, e.g. 花卉 (flowers and plants), 奇花异卉 (rare flowers and grasses). In the Later Seal Character, the character looks like three grasses, signalling there are many grasses.

Oracle-Bone Inscriptions

Later Seal Character

chú

In the Oracle-Bone Inscriptions, the character 刍 looks like a hand taking hold of two grasses, signalling to pull up grasses with a hand. Hence its original meaning is "to pull up grass," "to cut grass." The grass pulled up or cut will serve as food for cattle, so the character 刍 has come to refer to hay in particular, to the feeding of hay to cattle either, and even to the cattle that take the hay. e.g. 牛 (ox), 羊 (sheep).

苗

miáo

Later Seal Character

苗 is an ideograph. In the Later Seal Character, the character 苗 looks like grass growing in the fields. The primary use of 苗 is to refer to crops, especially the young ones, but it may also refer to other plants when they are young, i.e. seedlings. From its use to refer to young plants have derived its meanings of "symptom" and "offspring."

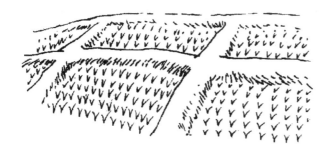

韭

jiǔ

Later Seal Character

韭 refers to the Chinese chive, a vegetable with narrow grasslike leaves. In the Later Seal Character, the character 韭 looks like a Chinese chive with its leaves growing on the two sides orderly, and the horizontal line at the bottom stands for the ground.

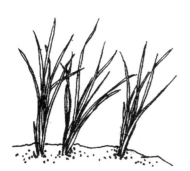

guā

Bronze Inscriptions

Later Seal Character

瓜 refers to the fruit of any creeping or climbing plant with thin twisting stems, such as melon or gourd. In the Bronze Inscriptions, the character 瓜 looks like a large round fruit hanging from a node of two branching vines. Since the shape of the melons is hard to tell, the stems are drawn meantime to indicate the melons.

hé

Oracle-Bone Inscriptions

Bronze Inscriptions

Later Seal Character

Agriculture has been a major industry in China ever since the Shang and Zhou dynasties. In both the Oracle-Bone Inscriptions and Bronze Inscriptions, there are many characters referring to crops, e.g. 禾 (standing grain), 黍 (broomcorn millet), 来 (麥, wheat), 粟 (corn; millet) and 米 (rice). The character 禾 looks like a plant with its roots, leaves and hanging ears. 禾 is a general term for cereal crops. However, it referred, in particular, to millet before the Qin and Han dynasties and to unhusked rice afterwards. Characters with 禾 as a component most have to do with crops or agriculture, e.g. 秉 (a handful of crop), 秋 (the time when crops are ripe, i.e. autumn), 秀 (earing), 种 (seed; to plant) and 租 (land tax).

lái

Oracle-Bone Inscriptions

Bronze Inscriptions

Later Seal Character

In the Oracle-Bone Inscriptions, the character 来 looks like a wheat plant with its roots, leaves, stalk and ears. It originally referred to wheat, but nowadays is more usually used in the sense of "coming," movement towards the speaker, opposite to 去 (go). And its original meaning is expressed by 麦 (麥), a later development.

sù

Oracle-Bone Inscriptions

Later Seal Character

In the Oracle-Bone Inscriptions, the character 粟 looks like a corn plant with its big ears. Hence its primary meaning is "corn or its grains." But the character 粟 could also be used as a cover term in the past for 黍 (broomcorn millet), 稷 (millet) and 秫 (sorghum), and even for all the cereal crops. Nowadays, however, it refers to millet only. Besides, 粟 may refer to particles as small as millet grains.

mù

Bronze Inscriptions

Later Seal Character

In the Bronze Inscriptions, the character 穆 looks like a ripe rice plant with its plump ears hanging down, the three dots below standing for the falling ripe grains. The original meaning of 穆 was "grain," the ripe crop, from which have derived its extended meanings of "mild," "harmonious," "solemn" and "quiet."

qí

Oracle-Bone Inscriptions

Bronze Inscriptions

Later Seal Character

In the Oracle-Bone Inscriptions, the character 齐 looks like a line of earing wheat crops in good order. The primary meaning of 齐 is "level" and "orderly," from which have derived its senses of "equal," "the same as," "in conformity with," "perfect" and "complete."

bǐng

Oracle-Bone Inscriptions

Bronze Inscriptions

Later Seal Character

In ancient writing systems, the character 秉 looks like a hand holding the stalk of a grain plant, signalling to take hold of. From this primary meaning have derived its senses of "handling," "in charge of" and "controlling." Thus the *Classic of Poetry* has the lines, "秉国之钧, 四方是维 (To take hold of the state power and maintain the stability throughout the land)."

jiān

Oracle-Bone Inscriptions

Later Seal Character

In ancient writing systems, the character 兼 looks like a hand holding two grain plants at once. Its primary meaning is "to hold together" and "to combine," and it may also mean "double."

nián

Oracle-Bone Inscriptions

Bronze Inscriptions

Later Seal Character

年 originally meant "the amount of crops gathered." When the crops are ripe, there is 年. Thus we may say 人寿年丰 (people enjoy good health and land yields bumper harvests). In the Oracle-Bone Inscriptions and Bronze Inscriptions, the character 年 looks like a man carrying grain plants on his back, signalling the harvest of crops. As the crops were reaped once a year in former times, the character 年 has come to mean "year," in which there are twelve months, or four seasons of spring, summer, autumn and winter. From this meaning has also derived its use to refer to the age of a person.

shǔ

Oracle-Bone Inscriptions

Bronze Inscriptions

Later Seal Character

黍 refers to broomcorn millet, a glutinous grain used as food or for making Chinese wine. Guan Zi says, "黍 is one of the best grains." In the Oracle-Bone Inscriptions, the character 黍 looks like a grain plant with heavy ears hanging down. Sometimes there is a water part beneath the plant part, signalling that this crop may be used for making wine.

shū

Bronze Inscriptions

Later Seal Character

In the Bronze Inscriptions, the character 叔 consists of 又 (hand) and 尗 (the original form of 菽, bean), signalling to pick up beans with one's hand. Hence its original meaning is "to pick up." Nowadays, however, it is used in the sense of "uncle," referring to the younger brother of one's father in particular, and its original meaning is lost.

mǐ

Oracle-Bone Inscriptions

Later Seal Character

米 refers to the husked seeds of cereal crops, especially those of rice, e.g. 大米 (rice), and 小米 (millet). In the Oracle-Bone Inscriptions, the character 米 looks like scattered grains of rice, and the horizontal stroke in the middle serves to distinguish them from grains of sand or drops of water. Rice is one of the common foods of human beings, so characters with 米 as a component most have to do with food, e.g. 籼 (xiān, long-grained rice), 粒 (a classifier of grains), 粳 (jīng, round-grained rice), 糠 (husk) and 粟 (millet). In addition, 米 is a transliteration of "metre," a measure of length.

xiāng

Oracle-Bone Inscriptions

Later Seal Character

In the Oracle-Bone Inscriptions, the character 香 looks like a high-legged vessel full of food, sending out some fragrance. It primarily refers to the smell of food, from which has derived its use for sweet smell, as against 臭 (foul smell). In the Later Seal Character, the character 香 sometimes consists of 黍 and 甘, signalling that the food is delicious, and this is another sense of 香. In addition, 香 may refer to perfume or spice.

qín

Oracle-Bone Inscriptions

Bronze Inscriptions

Later Seal Character

秦 was originally the name of a state in the Zhou Dynasty, situated in the present-day Shanxi Province, a land well-known for its abundance of grain. In ancient writing systems, the character 秦 consists of two parts: the upper part looks like two hands holding a pestle (for husking rice) and the lower part two grain plants. Hence it originally referred to the harvest of crops. Perhaps because this area was advanced in agriculture, the character 秦 was used as a name of the place and the state. At the end of the Warring States Period, the first emperor of the Qin Dynasty unified China, established the first centralized monarchy and named it Qin. Since then 秦 has also been used as a substitute for the name of China. e.g. In Han Dynasty, states in West Regions called China Qin.

CHAPTER 7

NATURAL

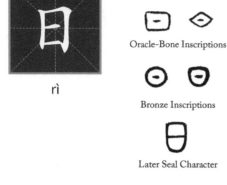

rì

Oracle-Bone Inscriptions

Bronze Inscriptions

Later Seal Character

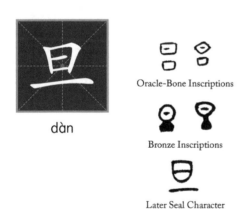

日 refers to the sun. The sun and moon are two of the most common celestial bodies. As the moon sometimes appears to be crescent while the sun is always circular, the characters referring to them are also crescent and circular respectively. The character 日 in the Oracle-Bone Inscirptions and the Bronze Inscriptions, for example, is sometimes circular. For the convenience of printing and writing, however, 日 is more usually square. When the sun rises in the sky it is daytime, so the character 日 also means "daytime," as against 夜 (night). 日 is also used as a unit of time, consisting of twenty four hours, from which has derived its more general meaning of "time."

dàn

Oracle-Bone Inscriptions

Bronze Inscriptions

Later Seal Character

旦 was originally a phonetic compound. In the Oracle-Bone Inscriptions and Bronze Inscriptions, the character 旦 has the radical part 日 (the sun) on the top and the phonetic part, a square or a dot, underneath. In the Later Seal Character, the second part becomes a horizontal line, resulting in an ideograph, signalling that the sun is rising above the horizon, hence its meaning "dawn."

Oracle-Bone Inscriptions

Later Seal Character

yùn/yūn

In the Oracle-Bone Inscriptions, it is an ideograph. The middle part stands for the sun and the four dots around the halo. In the Later Seal Character, the character becomes a phonetic compound, with 日 as the radical and 军 as the phonetic. The character 晕 primarily refers to the halo of the sun or moon, from which has derived its sense "to feel dizzy." Thus we may say 头晕 (to have a dizzy spell), 晕车 (carsickness) and 晕船 (seasickness).

zè

Oracle-Bone Inscriptions

Bronze Inscriptions

Later Seal Character

昃 was originally an ideograph. In the Oracle-Bone Inscriptions, the character 昃 has a sun part on the left and a slant man figure on the right, signalling the shadow of a man when the sun is not directly on his head. In the Bronze Inscriptions, the character 昃 consists of 日 (the sun) and 夨 (zè, a man whose head is tilted to one side), and the latter also serves as the phonetic. But in the Later Seal Character, it becomes a complete phonetic compound with 日 as the radical and 仄 as the phonetic. 昃 primarily refers to the sun approaching the west. Thus the *Book of Changes* says, "日中则昃, 月盈则食 (The sun will approach the west afternoon, and the crescent follows a full moon)." But in the written records of the Shang Dynasty, 昃 was used as a name of time referring to the period equivalent to the present two or three o'clock in the afternoon.

bào

Later Seal Character

暴 was the original form of 曝. In the Later Seal Character, the character 暴 consists of 日, 出, 廾 (gǒng) and 米, signalling to dry grain in the scorching sun for a long time. Hence its primary meaning is "to dry in the sun" and "to expose." As the rays of the scorching sun are strong and forceful, the character 暴 also means "violent," from which have derived its extended meanings of "cruel," "fierce" and "short-tempered."

zhāo/cháo

Bronze Inscriptions

Later Seal Character

朝 was originally an ideograph. In the Bronze Inscriptions, the character 朝 is made up of two parts: the left side looks like a sun in between two plants and the right side a river, signalling the sun is rising from among plants on a riverside in the morning. Hence its primary meaning is "morning." In the Later Seal Character, the character has undergone a series of changes in its form, and its original image is no longer there.

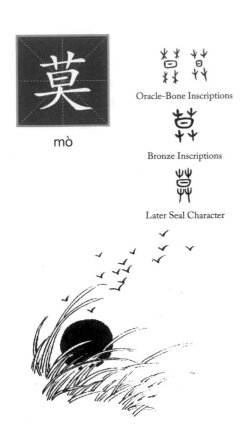

mò

Oracle-Bone Inscriptions

Bronze Inscriptions

Later Seal Character

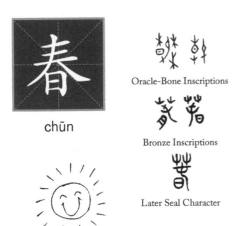

莫 was the original form of 暮. In ancient writing systems, the character 莫 consists of a sun part and four tree (or grass) parts, looking like a sun setting among plants, signalling the sun is setting. Hence its original meaning is "sunset," which is now expressed by 暮. From this original meaning have derived its extended senses of "without," e.g. 溥天之下, 莫非王土 (All the land under heaven belongs to the king without exception), and "no" or "not," e.g. 高深莫测 (too high and deep to be measured) and 莫愁 (not to worry).

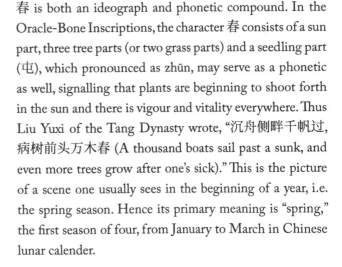

chūn

Oracle-Bone Inscriptions

Bronze Inscriptions

Later Seal Character

春 is both an ideograph and phonetic compound. In the Oracle-Bone Inscriptions, the character 春 consists of a sun part, three tree parts (or two grass parts) and a seedling part (屯), which pronounced as zhūn, may serve as a phonetic as well, signalling that plants are beginning to shoot forth in the sun and there is vigour and vitality everywhere. Thus Liu Yuxi of the Tang Dynasty wrote, "沉舟侧畔千帆过, 病树前头万木春 (A thousand boats sail past a sunk, and even more trees grow after one's sick)." This is the picture of a scene one usually sees in the beginning of a year, i.e. the spring season. Hence its primary meaning is "spring," the first season of four, from January to March in Chinese lunar calender.

jīng

Oracle-Bone Inscriptions

Later Seal Character

In the Oracle-Bone Inscriptions, the character 晶 looks like three stars, sometimes circular, sometimes square (for the convenience of printing), and sometimes with a dot in the centre making it like the character 日. That is why in the Later Seal Character, the star parts are all written like sun parts. The original meaning of 晶 was "a clear night with the stars shining," from which have derived its meanings of "bright" and "clear."

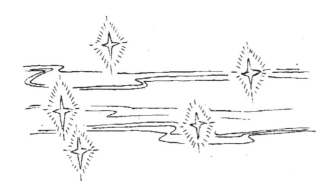

xīng

Oracle-Bone Inscriptions

Bronze Inscriptions

Later Seal Character

星 refers to stars, the shining bodies in the sky at night. In the Oracle-Bone Inscriptions, the character 星 has five little squares standing for stars and the part in the middle, i.e. 生, indicating its pronunciation. As the stars appear to be tiny in the sky, the character 星 can also refer to tiny particles, e.g. 火星儿 (spark), 一星半点 (a tiny bit).

shēn/sān/cān

Bronze Inscriptions

Later Seal Character

参 was originally the name of a constellation, one of the lunar mansions. In the Bronze Inscriptions, the character 参 looks like three stars shining on top of a man, signalling a man is looking at stars. From this meaning has derived its use as a numeral meaning "three," pronounced as sān, and written as 叁. 参, pronounced as cān, also means "to participate in" and "to pay respects to."

yuè

Oracle-Bone Inscriptions

Bronze Inscriptions

Later Seal Character

月 refers to the moon. The moon appears to change its shape all the time, and most of the time it is not completely circular. This phenomenon is reflected in the form of the character. Thus in the Oracle-Bone Inscriptions, the character 月 looks like a crescent moon. As the full moon comes once thirty days on average, the character 月 has come to mean "thirty days," in other words, "a month."

míng

Oracle-Bone Inscriptions

Bronze Inscriptions

Later Seal Character

In the Oracle-Bone Inscriptions, the character 明 has two forms. One consists of 日 and 月, referring to the time when the sun rises and the moon sets, i.e. daybreak. The other consists of a moon part and a window part, signalling that the moonlight has come into a room, and the room is bright. In both the Bronze Inscriptions and the Later Seal Character, the composition of the character 明 follows the second approach, while in the Regular Script the two forms coexist. The modern simplified form, however, consists of 日 and 月 again, but it means "bright" rather than "daybreak."

xī

Oracle-Bone Inscriptions

Bronze Inscriptions

Later Seal Character

夕 refers to night, and dusk in particular. As the moon rises at night, the character 夕 in the Oracle-Bone Inscriptions also looks like a crescent moon. In other words, the moon represents night. In the early Oracle-Bone Inscriptions, the character 夕 has a dot in the middle, to differ from the character 月. In later developments, however, there was confusion between 月 and 夕. As a result, a dot is added to 月, and 夕 becomes 月 without a dot instead.

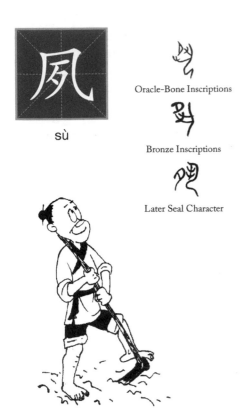

夙

Oracle-Bone Inscriptions

Bronze Inscriptions

Later Seal Character

In the Oracle-Bone Inscriptions and Bronze Inscriptions, the character 夙 looks like a man on his knees working in the moonlight, signalling that the man starts working before dawn. Hence 夙 means "early in the morning." But it may, like 宿, mean "old" and "long-standing" as well.

虹

hóng

Oracle-Bone Inscriptions

Stone-Drum Inscriptions

Later Seal Character

虹 refers to the rainbow, an arch of different colours appearing in the sky opposite the sun after rain. However, ancient people, unable to understand this natural phenomenon, thought it was a mystical animal with a long body, two heads and a big mouth, appearing after rain in the sky to drink water. The character 虹 in the Oracle-Bone Inscriptions looks like a picture of this animal. In the Later Seal Character, the character becomes a phonetic compound with 虫 as the radical and 工 as the phonetic.

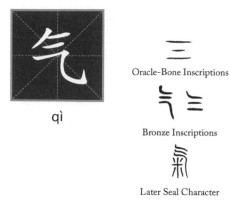

qì

Oracle-Bone Inscriptions

Bronze Inscriptions

Later Seal Character

In the Oracle-Bone Inscriptions, the character 气 looks like three horizontal lines of unequal length, signalling thin clouds floating. In the Bronze Inscriptions and Later Seal Character, the horizontal lines are curved, presenting an even truer description of the floating clouds. From its primary meaning of "thin clouds" has derived its more general use for any gases, e.g. 空气 (air), 气息 (breath). 气 may also refer to the weather conditions of wind, rain, sunshine, snow, etc. e.g. 气候 (climate), 气象 (meteorological phenomena). In addition, 气 is also an abstract concept referring to the mood of a person, e.g. 气质 (temperament) and 气度 (tolerance).

Bronze Inscriptions

Later Seal Character

hán

In the Bronze Inscriptions, the character 寒 looks like a man in a room full of straw (material for warming up), the two dots underneath the man standing for ice blocks, hence the primary meaning is "cold." As cold weather may cause a man to tremble, the character 寒 can also mean "to tremble," even with fear, e.g. 胆寒 (terrified), 心寒 (bitterly disappointed). In addition, 寒 may be used in the sense of "poor," e.g. 贫寒 (poor), 寒酸 (miserable and shabby).

bīng

Oracle-Bone Inscriptions

Bronze Inscriptions

Later Seal Character

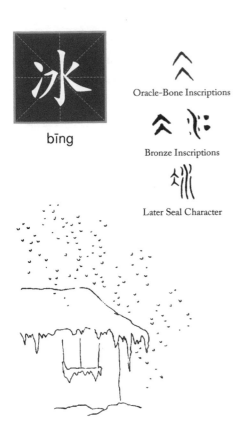

冰 refers to ice, water which has frozen to a solid below zero degree centigrade. In the Oracle-Bone Inscriptions and Bronze Inscriptions, the character 冰 looks like two ridged ice blocks. In the Later Seal Character, a water part (水) is added to indicate that ice is formed from water.

shēn

Oracle-Bone Inscriptions

Bronze Inscriptions

Later Seal Character

申 was the original form of 电. In the Oracle-Bone Inscriptions and Bronze Inscriptions, the character 申 looks like a curving light appearing in the sky when there is lightning. As lightning often occurs during a rain, the character has a rain part (雨) added in its later development, resulting in the original complicated form of 申—電. The character 申 on the other hand is used as a name of the ninth Earthly Branch, a traditional Chinese system of sequence. In addition 申 may mean "to state" and "to express."

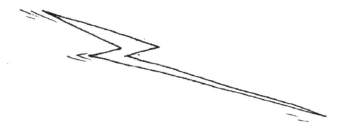

电

diàn

Bronze Inscriptions

Later Seal Character

In ancient writing systems, the character 电 consists of 雨 and 申, referring to the lightning in a rain. From this primary meaning has derived its meaning of "quick." Nowadays, however, it mainly refers to electricity.

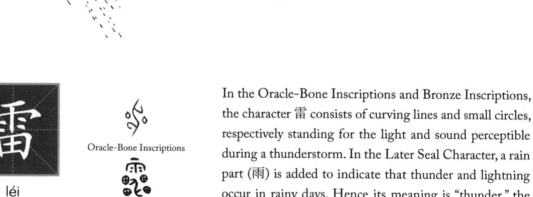

雷

léi

Oracle-Bone Inscriptions

Bronze Inscriptions

Later Seal Character

In the Oracle-Bone Inscriptions and Bronze Inscriptions, the character 雷 consists of curving lines and small circles, respectively standing for the light and sound perceptible during a thunderstorm. In the Later Seal Character, a rain part (雨) is added to indicate that thunder and lightning occur in rainy days. Hence its meaning is "thunder," the loud explosive noise caused by the discharge of electricity in the sky.

yún

Oracle-Bone Inscriptions

Bronze Inscriptions

Later Seal Character

In the Oracle-Bone Inscriptions and Bronze Inscriptions, the character 云 looks like clouds floating about, hence its primary meaning is "cloud." As clouds are in fact light drops of water, which will fall as rain when heavy enough, the character 云 in the Later Seal Character has a rain part (雨) added, to indicate its relation with rain.

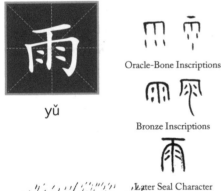

yǔ

Oracle-Bone Inscriptions

Bronze Inscriptions

Later Seal Character

In the Oracle-Bone Inscriptions and Bronze Inscriptions, the character 雨 looks like drops of water falling from the sky, hence its primary meaning is "rain." Used as a verb, it may refer to not only the falling of rain but also the falling of anything from the sky, e.g. 雨雪 (to snow), 雨粟 (to drop millet grains). Characters with 雨 as a component most have to do with weather conditions like clouds and rain, e.g. 雷 (thunder), 雾 (fog), 霜 (frost) and 雪 (snow).

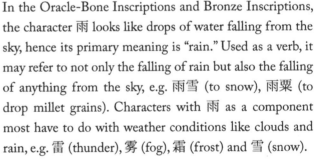

língín

Oracle-Bone Inscriptions

Bronze Inscriptions

Later Seal Character

In the Oracle-Bone Inscriptions, the character 零 consists of a rain part and three big drops of water, hence its original meaning is "to rain continuously" or "rain drop." Sometimes the drops of water are square in shape, but the character is still ideographic. The phonetic compound form with 雨 as the radical and 令 as the phonetic is a later development. From its original meaning have derived its extended meanings of "falling," "withering" and "fragments."

xū

Bronze Inscriptions

Later Seal Character

In the Bronze Inscriptions, the character 需 consists of a part like a man on his feet (天) and a rain part (雨), signalling a man at a standstill waiting for the rain to stop. In the Later Seal Character, the man part (天) changes into 而 by mistake, resulting in a phonetic compound with 雨 as the radical and 而 as the phonetic. The original meaning of 需 was, the same as 鎮 (xū), "to wait," from which has derived its extended meaning of "hesitation." Nowadays, however, it means more usually "to need" and "to require."

shuǐ

Oracle-Bone Inscriptions

Bronze Inscriptions

Later Seal Character

水 refers to water, a transparent liquid without colour, taste or smell. In the Oracle-Bone Inscriptions and Bronze Inscriptions, the character 水 looks like a river turning here and there, the curving line in the middle standing for the main course and the dots on the sides the spray. Hence the character 水 originally referred to the river, or more generally, the water area, including lakes and seas, opposite to 陆 (land). From this meaning has derived its use for liquid in general, e.g. 药水 (medicinal liquid), 泪水 (tears) and 橘子水 (orange juice).

quán

Oracle-Bone Inscriptions

Later Seal Character

In the Oracle-Bone Inscriptions, the character 泉 looks like water trickling from a spring. Hence 泉 primarily refers to spring, water coming up from the ground, or more generally any ground water. In former times, it was also used as a substitute for money.

yuán

Bronze Inscriptions

Later Seal Character

原 was the original form of 源. In the Bronze Inscriptions, the character 原 consists of 厂 (hǎn, rock) and 泉 (spring), signalling there is a spring under the rock. In the Later Seal Character, the character 原 sometimes has three spring parts, signalling many springs are coming together to form a river, The original meaning of 原 is "the source of a river," from which have derived its senses of "earliest," e.g. 原始 (primitive); "original," e.g. 原地 (original place); and "unprocessed," e.g. 原料 (raw material). Used as a verb, it means "to trace to the source." But it may also mean "to forgive."

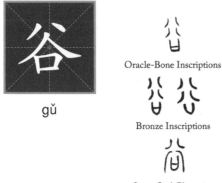

gǔ

Oracle-Bone Inscriptions

Bronze Inscriptions

Later Seal Character

谷 means "valley," the land lying between two lines of mountains, often with a river running through it. In the Oracle-Bone Inscriptions and Bronze Inscriptions, the character 谷 consists of two parts: the upper part looks like streams running out of a valley and the lower part the entrance of a valley. Today, it is also used as the simplified form of 穀.

chuān

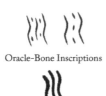

Oracle-Bone Inscriptions

Bronze Inscriptions

Later Seal Character

In the Oracle-Bone Inscriptions, the character looks like a river turning here and there, the two lines on the sides standing for river banks and the three dots in the middle the flowing water. In the Bronze Inscriptions and Later Seal Character, the character simply consists of three curving lines, still signalling a river. The primary meaning of 川 is "river," from which has derived its reference to a large stretch of flat land between mountains, i.e. plain.

pài

Oracle-Bone Inscriptions

Bronze Inscriptions

Later Seal Character

In ancient writing systems, the character 派 looks like a river branching off. Hence its original meaning is "a branch of a river," from which has derived its extended meaning of "division," e.g. 学派 (school of thought), 党派 (political parties and groups) and 宗派 (sect; faction). Used as a verb, it means "to send" and "to appoint."

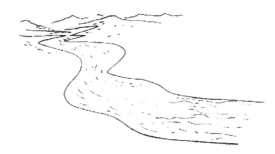

衍

Bronze Inscriptions

Later Seal Character

yǎn

In ancient writing systems, the character 衍 consists of a river part (水 or 川) and a movement part (行 or 彳, chì), signalling water flowing in a river. It originally refers to the flowing of water, from which use has derived its senses "to spread," "to broaden," "to develop," "to evolve" and "to derive."

流

Oracle-Bone Inscriptions

Stone-Drum Inscriptions

Later Seal Character

liú

In the Later Seal Character, the character 流 looks like an upsidedown man whose hair is loose and drifting with the current in between two river parts, signalling a man driven along by currents. The primary meaning of 流 is "to flow," from which have derived its senses "to move," "to spread," "to circulate," "to pass on" and "to send into exile." Used as a noun, it may refer to a river, a branch, a school of thought, or a grade.

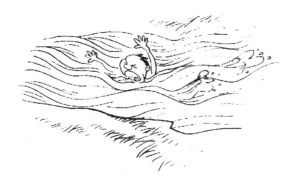

zhōu

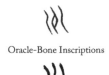
Oracle-Bone Inscriptions

Bronze Inscriptions

Later Seal Character

州 was the original form of 洲. In the Oracle-Bone Inscriptions and Bronze Inscriptions, the character 州 has a river part with a small circle in the middle, signalling there is an islet in the river. Hence its original meaning is "islet," a piece of land in a river rising above the water level. According to legend, when Yu, the last of the three wise leaders in the primitive society of China, conquered the floods, he divided the country into nine administrative areas known as 州. Since then 州 has become a special term for administrative areas, and another character 洲 was created to express its original meaning. Nowadays, as a place name, 洲 is used for continents, such as 亚洲 (Asia), 欧洲 (Europe), while 州 is used for cities, such as 广州 (Guangzhou), 徐州 (Xuzhou). Some exceptions are 株洲 (Zhuzhou, in Hunan), 橘子洲 (Juzizhou, in Hunan), 沙洲 (Shazhou, in Jiangsu), 鹦鹉洲 (Yingwuzhou, in Hubei) and 桂洲 (Guizhou, in Guangdong), which are some famous sand banks of China.

huí

Oracle-Bone Inscriptions

Bronze Inscriptions

Later Seal Character

In ancient writing systems, the character 回 looks like a whirl in a pool. Hence its original meaning is "to whirl" and "to circle," from which have derived its present-day senses "to turn about," "to go back," "to run counter to" and "to be perverse."

yuān

Oracle-Bone Inscriptions

Bronze Inscriptions

Later Seal Character

In the Oracle-Bone Inscriptions and Bronze Inscriptions, the character 渊 looks like a deep pool with whirling water. Sometimes there is a river part added, which is the source of the form in the Later Seal Character. The primary meaning of 渊 is "deep pool," from which have derived its senses of "deep," "profound" and "far-reaching."

miǎo

Later Seal Character

The character 淼, consisting of three river parts, is an ideograph, signalling there is a vast, boundless expanse of water. Xu Shen says in his *Origin of Chinese Characters*, "淼 means a vast area of water." In other words, 淼 means the same as 渺, that is, the space covered by water is so vast that one can hardly see its bounds.

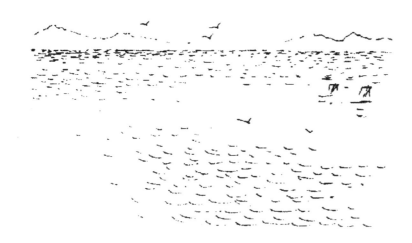

xī

Oracle-Bone Inscriptions

Bronze Inscriptions

Later Seal Character

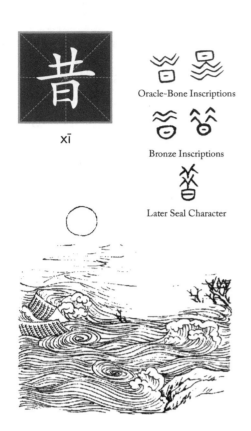

昔 means "former times," "the past," opposite to 今 (the present). In the Oracle-Bone Inscriptions, the character 昔 consists of a wave part and a sun part, sometimes the sun part is above the waves and sometimes the waves are above the sun, signalling that there is water everywhere. According to legend, there were once serious floods in ancient times and people had to stay on top of mountains living on tree barks and edible wild herbs until Yu, one of the three legendary, wise leaders in ancient China, conquered them. After the floods were gone, people would still call to mind those old miserable days, which they invented the character 昔 to refer to.

mò/méi

Bronze Inscriptions

Later Seal Character

In the Bronze Inscriptions, the character 没 consists of 水 and 回, signalling whirling water. In the Later Seal Character, a hand part (又) is added to indicate that a man is sinking into the whirling water. Hence its primary meaning is "to sink," "to submerge," from which have derived its extended meanings "to disappear," "to hide," "to decline," "without" (pronounced as méi) and "till the end (esp. the end of one's life)."

Oracle-Bone Inscriptions

Later Seal Character

yù

In the Oracle-Bone Inscriptions, the character 浴 looks like a man in a bathtub with drops of water around, signalling a man is taking a bath. In the Later Seal Character, the character becomes a phonetic compound with 水 as the radical and 谷 as the phonetic. The primary meaning of 浴 is "to take a bath," but it is also used metaphorically to refer to one's mental hygiene, e.g. 浴德 (to cultivate one's moral character).

Bronze Inscriptions

Later Seal Character

shā

沙 means "sand," extremely small pieces of stone. In the Bronze Inscriptions, the character 沙 consists of 水 and 少, the former looking like a river and the latter particles of sand. Hence it primarily refers to the extremely small pieces of stone on the riverside or riverbed, from which use has derived its reference to loose material of very small fine grains, e.g. 豆沙 (bean paste), 沙糖 (coarse sugar).

xiǎo

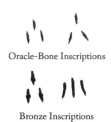

Oracle-Bone Inscriptions

Bronze Inscriptions

Later Seal Character

小 is an abstract concept, meaning "small." In the Oracle-Bone Inscriptions and Bronze Inscriptions, the character 小 consists of three dots, signalling very small fine grains of sand being scattered on the ground. The primary meaning of 小 is "small in size," from which has derived its use for things small in quantity, force, importance, etc., opposite to 大 (big).

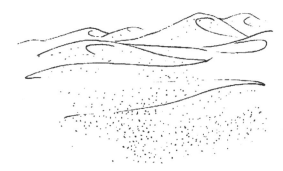

tǔ

In the Oracle-Bone Inscriptions, the character 土 looks like a heap of earth raised above the ground. Its primary meaning is "soil," from which have derived its senses of "field," "land" and "territory." Characters with 土 as a component most have to do with soil and land, e.g. 城 (town), 埋 (to bury), 垣 (yuán, wall) and 塞 (fortress).

qiū

Oracle-Bone Inscriptions

Bronze Inscriptions

Later Seal Character

In the Oracle-Bone Inscriptions, the character 丘 looks very similar to 山, except that the former has two peaks while the latter has three. 丘 primarily refers to hills, not so high as mountains, from which use has derived its reference to any heap of earth raised above the ground, e.g. 坟丘 (grave mound), 丘墓 (grave).

yáo

Oracle-Bone Inscriptions

Later Seal Character

In ancient writing systems, the character 尧 has a soil part (土; sometimes two or three soil parts) above a man part, signalling a heap of earth raised higher than a man. The original meaning of 尧 was "high heaps of earth," or simply "high." Nowadays, however, it is used as a proper name for the first of the three legendary wise leaders of ancient China, or as a surname, and its original meaning is expressed by 峣.

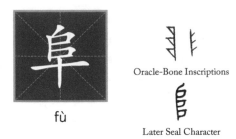

阜

fù

Oracle-Bone Inscriptions

Later Seal Character

阜 means "mound," "hill." In the Oracle-Bone Inscriptions, the character 阜 looks like the steps on a cliff, signalling that the hill is high and one has to climb it through steps. The primary meaning of 阜 is "a high mound," from which have derived its senses of "high," "large" and "many (esp. of treasures)."

阳

yáng

Oracle-Bone Inscriptions

Bronze Inscriptions

Later Seal Character

In ancient writing systems, the character 阳 is a phonetic compound with 阜 as the radical and 昜 as the phonetic. 阳 originally refers to the south of a mountain or the north of a river, i.e. the side sunlight reaches. From this use has derived its reference to the sun, sunlight, or anything standing out, on the surface or in the open, opposite to 阴 (dark; hidden).

shān

Oracle-Bone Inscriptions

Bronze Inscriptions

Later Seal Character

山 means "mountain," the natural elevation of earth's surface. In the Oracle-Bone Inscriptions, the character 山 looks like a mountain range consisting of several peaks. Characters with 山 as a component most have to do with mountains, e.g. 嵩, 崇, 峻 and 巍 used of mountains all mean "high."

dǎo

Later Seal Character

岛 means "island," a piece of land surrounded by water. The character 岛 consisting of 山 and 鸟, is an ideograph, signalling there is a hill in the sea where birds may stay as their resting place. Meanwhile 鸟 may serve to indicate its pronunciation, in this sense, 岛 is a phonetic compound with 山 as the radical and 鸟 as the phonetic.

sōng

Later Seal Character

The character 嵩, consisting of 山 and 高, is an ideograph. It primarily refers to high mountains, and may refer to other high things as well, a use which is often assumed by 崇 now. 嵩 is also a proper name for a mountain in Henan Province, i.e. Mount Song (嵩山 also 嵩岳, 嵩高), also known as 中岳 (the Central Mountain), one of the five famous mountains in China.

shí

Oracle-Bone Inscriptions

Bronze Inscriptions

Later Seal Character

In ancient writing systems, the character 石 looks like a stone underneath a cliff. Hence its primary meaning is "stone" or "rock." Characters with 石 as a component most have to do with stones and their qualities, e.g. 矿 (mineral deposit), 硬 (hard), 研 (to grind), 确 (firm) and 碑 (stele).

Later Seal Character

lěi

The character 磊 consists of three stone parts, looking like many stones piled up. Its primary meaning is "stones piled up," from which has derived its sense of "high."

zhuó

Oracle-Bone Inscriptions

Later Seal Character

The character 斫, consisting of 石 and 斤, is an ideograph. In the Oracle-Bone Inscriptions, the character 斫 looks like a man cutting a rock with an axe in hand. The primary meaning of 斫 is "to cut," "to chop," from which has derived its sense "to attack." Used as a noun, it refers to the axe.

duàn

Bronze Inscriptions

Later Seal Character

In the Bronze Inscriptions, the character 段 looks like a man extracting stones by striking at a cliff, the two dots standing for the broken pieces. Its primary meaning is "to extract stones," from which has derived its sense "to strike." Characters with 段 as a component most have to do with striking, e.g. 锻 (to forge). 段 is also a surname, started perhaps by people who extracted stones or forged iron. But the more usual meaning of 段 now is "section," whether of cloth, time or other things, e.g. 片段 (fragment), 段落 (paragraph) and 分段 (to divide into sections).

tián

Oracle-Bone Inscriptions

Bronze Inscriptions

Later Seal Character

The character 田 has not changed much in its form over the years. It looks like fields with crisscross footpaths in between in any writing systems. Its primary meaning is "farmland," e.g. 稻田 (rice field), 麦田 (wheat field). In some areas, however, only the paddy field is known as 田 while the dry land is referred to as 地. Characters with 田 as a component most have to do with field and cultivation, e.g. 畴 (farmland), 畛 (zhěn, raised paths between fields), 畔 (the border of a field) and 畦 (qí, plot of land).

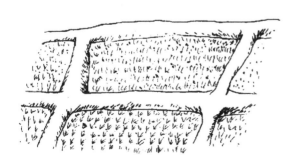

周

zhōu

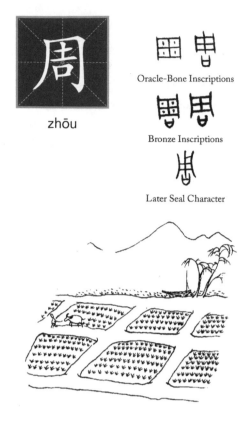

Oracle-Bone Inscriptions

Bronze Inscriptions

Later Seal Character

In the Oracle-Bone Inscriptions, the character 周 has a field part (田) with four dots in each section standing for crops. Hence its original meaning is "farmland." 周 is also the name of a dynasty after Shang. The choice of this name reflects a fact that the Zhou Dynasty started from a place, the present-day Qishan of Shanxi Province, where agriculture was at an advanced stage of development. Nowadays, the character 周 may be used in many senses, but the most important ones are "circumference," "to surround" and "to twist," all deriving from the sense of "border of a field."

行

xíng/háng

Oracle-Bone Inscriptions

Bronze Inscriptions

Later Seal Character

In the Oracle-Bone Inscriptions and Bronze Inscriptions, the character 行 looks like two roads crossing each other. Sometimes there is an additional man part in the middle, signalling that a man is walking on the road. Hence the primary meaning of 行 is "road" and "to walk." From its meaning of "road" have derived its senses of "a row of people" and "a line of business," pronounced as háng. From its sense "to walk" have derived its meanings "to move about," "to circulate," "to perform" and "to experience."

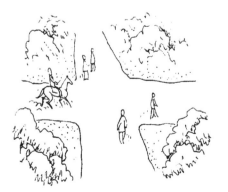

fēng

Oracle-Bone Inscriptions

Bronze Inscriptions

Later Seal Character

In the Oracle-Bone Inscriptions and Bronze Inscriptions, the character 封 looks like (a man) planting a tree or earthing up a tree with his hands. Its original meaning is "to earth up a tree" or "to bank up earth into a grave," from which have derived its senses of "a heap of earth" or "a grave." One of the purposes of planting trees was to draw lines of demarcation between different families or states, so the character 封 has taken on the sense of "boundary." Thus the granting of land or titles of nobility to his ministers by a monarch is known as 封, and the land granted to them 封地. From its sense of boundary have also derived its meanings "to close" and "to limit," e.g. 封闭 (to close), 封锁 (to blockade) and 查封 (to seal off).

jiāng

Oracle-Bone Inscriptions

Bronze Inscriptions

Later Seal Character

In the Oracle-Bone Inscriptions and Bronze Inscriptions, the character 疆 looks like two fields one above the other with a measuring instrument (弓) on the left. Sometimes there is a line between the two fields standing for a boundary. Hence 疆 means "to measure land," "to delimit a boundary," "field boundary" and "national boundaries."

lǐ

Bronze Inscriptions

里

Later Seal Character

里 is an ideograph, consisting of 田 and 土, the former referring to paddy field and the latter dry land. In the agricultural society, one has to have land to produce things and support one's life. The original meaning of 里 was "the place where a community inhabit," i.e. village. Hence it has come to be used as an administrative unit. For example, in the Qin Dynasty, five families formed a neighbourhood (邻) and five neighbourhoods a village (里). In other words, there were twenty-five families in a village. In addition, 里 is a measure of length, equal to 150 zhàng in the Chinese System and 500 metres in the Metric System. In the modern simplified form, 里 is also used in the sense of the original complicated 裏, i.e. inside.

野

yě

Oracle-Bone Inscriptions

Bronze Inscriptions

Later Seal Character

In the Oracle-Bone Inscriptions and Bronze Inscriptions, the character 野 has a soil part (土) in the middle of a forest part (林), signalling the open field and forest. In the Later Seal Character, the character becomes a phonetic compound with 里 as the radical and 予 as the phonetic, but the meaning is not changed. 野 originally refers to the outskirts of a town, or remote areas, from which has derved its sense of "nongovernmental," as against 朝廷 (royal government). 野 may also refer to wild animals or natural plants as against 家养 (domesticated) or 人工种植 (cultivated), from which has derived its sense of "barbarous," as against 文明 (civilized).

yòu

Oracle-Bone Inscriptions

Bronze Inscriptions

Later Seal Character

囿 was originally an ideograph. In the Oracle-Bone Inscriptions, the character 囿 looks like a garden of flowers with walls on the four sides. In the Bronze Inscriptions, however, it becomes a phonetic compound with 囗 (wéi, enclosure) as the radical and 有 as the phonetic, for the convenience of writing. From its original meaning of "walled garden" has derived its use to refer to the royal garden in particular, which is now known as 苑. From this original meaning has also derived its use to refer to a person's knowledge which is limited.

huǒ

Oracle-Bone Inscriptions

Later Seal Character

火 means "fire," the light and flame given out from a burning substance. In the Oracle-Bone Inscriptions, the character 火 looks like the flames of something burning, hence it primarily refers to fire. Characters with 火 as a component most have to do with fire and its uses, e.g. 炎 (a big fire), 炙 (to roast), 焚 (to burn a forest), 然 (to burn), 焦 (burned), 烹 (to cook), and 煮 (to boil).

yán

Oracle-Bone Inscriptions

Bronze Inscriptions

Later Seal Character

In ancient writing systems, the character 炎 has two fire parts one upon the other, signalling there is a big fire. From this primary meaning of "big fire" have derived its senses of "scorching" and "burning hot," used of weather.

liáo

Oracle-Bone Inscriptions

Bronze Inscriptions

Later Seal Character

燎 refers to an ancient sacrificial ceremony in which wood is burned as an offering to Heaven. In the Oracle-Bone Inscriptions and Bronze Inscriptions, the character 燎 looks like pieces of wood crossing each other, with dots around standing for sparks from the fire. Sometimes there is even a fire part beneath. The primary meaning of 燎 is "to burn," from which have derived its meanings of "drying by fire," "torch" and "flammable things."

fén

Oracle-Bone Inscriptions

Later Seal Character

In the primitive society, agriculture was at a low stage of development and people used some primitive methods known as slash-and-burn cultivation, which is to some extent reflected in the form of the character 焚. In the Oracle-Bone Inscriptions, 焚 has a forest part above a fire part, and sometimes the lower part looks like a man holding a torch in hand. Hence 焚 meant originally "to burn a forest," from which have derived its present-day meanings of "burning" and "destruction by fire."

zāi

Oracle-Bone Inscriptions

Bronze Inscriptions

Later Seal Character

The disasters man suffers are known as 灾 in Chinese, e.g. 水灾 (flood), 火灾 (fire), 兵灾 (war), 虫灾 (plague of insects) and 风灾 (disaster caused by windstorm). In ancient times, the character 灾 consists of 宀 (house) and 火 (fire), signalling the house is on fire. Sometimes it has a water part (水) instead of a fire part, signalling there is a flood. And there may also be a weapon part (戈) as a substitute, signalling there is a war. Hence 灾 refers to the different kinds of disaster man suffers, and this meaning has remained unchanged over the years.

shù

Oracle-Bone Inscriptions

Bronze Inscriptions

Later Seal Character

Before the invention of cooking utensils people would burn some stones and then use them to heat food directly or by putting them in a vessel containing water, apart from roasting the food on an open fire. In the Oracle-Bone Inscriptions and Bronze Inscriptions, the character 庶 consists of 石 (stone) and 火 (fire), signalling to burn stones by fire. Hence its original meaning was "to cook." Nowadays, however, 庶 is more usually used in the senses of "the common people" and "numerous," and its original meaning is expressed by 煮.

tàn

Later Seal Character

In the Later Seal Character, the character 炭 has a cliff part above a fire part, signalling to burn wood and make charcoal in the mountains. 炭 primarily refers to charcoal, but in former times it may also refer to coal, known as 石炭, i.e. 煤.

huī

Oracle-Bone Inscriptions

Later Seal Character

灰 means "ash," powder that remains after a substance has been burnt. In the Oracle-Bone Inscriptions, the character 灰 looks like a man stirring ashes with a stick. Its primary meaning is "ash," e.g. 木灰 (plant ash), 石灰 (lime), from which has derived its use to refer to dust. It may also refer to a colour like black mixed with white, namely, grey.

chì

Oracle-Bone Inscriptions

Bronze Inscriptions

Later Seal Character

There was a practice among ancient people to burn a man or animal as an offering to Heaven when they preyed for rain. And this practice is reflected in the form of the character 赤, which in ancient writing systems has a man part (大) on a fire part (火), signalling to burn a man. From this original meaning have derived its meanings of "being redden by fire," "red." According to the five-element theory of ancient China, the South belongs to the element of fire, which is red in colour, so Xu Shen says in his *Origin of Chinese Characters*, "赤 consists of 大 and 火, referring to the colour of the South." In addition, the character 赤 can also mean "pure" and "bare."

Later Seal Character

zhǔ

主 was the original form of 炷 (zhù). In the Later Seal Character, the character 主 looks like an oil lamp, the dot on top standing for the flame of the lampwick. Hence its original meaning is "lampwick." Nowadays, however, 主 is mainly used in the senses of "host," "master," "in charge of" and "to manage," and its original meaning is expressed by 炷.

Oracle-Bone Inscriptions

Bronze Inscriptions

Later Seal Character

guāng

光 means "light," the natural agent that stimulates the sense of sight, e.g. 太阳光 (sunlight), 灯光 (lamplight), from which have derived its senses of "bright" and "smooth." In ancient writing systems, the character 光 looks like a fire on top of a man, signalling that there is kindling material so that it will be bright for ever.

sǒu

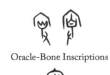

Oracle-Bone Inscriptions

Later Seal Character

叟 was the original form of 搜. In the Oracle-Bone Inscriptions, the character 叟 looks like a man holding a torch in a room, signalling "to search," "to look for." However, it is now used in the sense of "old man," and its original meaning is expressed by 搜.

CHAPTER 8

OTHERS

yī

Oracle-Bone Inscriptions

Bronze Inscriptions

Later Seal Character

一 is a numeral, meaning "one." In Chinese, the simplest numerals are picturelike: one is represented by one horizontal stroke, two by two horizontal strokes, three by three, and four by four. The idea behind it is the same as that behind counting with knots in ropes: one knot represents ten, and two knots twenty. The character 一 may be used in many senses, but the most important two are: as the smallest integer, e.g. 一人 (one man), 一马 (one horse) 一枪 (one gun); and meaning "wholehearted," e.g. 一心一意 (heart and soul).

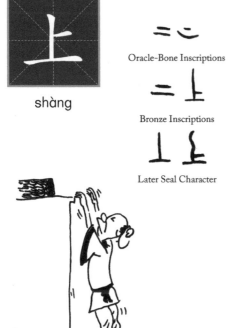

shàng

Oracle-Bone Inscriptions

Bronze Inscriptions

Later Seal Character

The character 上 is an indicative. In the Oracle-Bone Inscriptions and Bronze Inscriptions, it consists of a short horizontal stroke on top of a longer one (or a concave curve), signifying "on top of." Hence its primary meaning is "the higher," "the upper"; from which have derived the meanings of "higher in rank" or "better in quality," e.g. 上级 (higher authorities), 上品 (top grade product); and the meanings of "before in sequence" or "before in time," e.g. 上册 (first volume), 上半年 (the first half of the year). Used as a verb, it means "to ascend," e.g. 上山 (to go up a hill), 上楼 (to go upstairs); from which has further derived its more general sense "to go," e.g. 上街 (to go into the street).

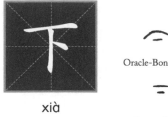

xià

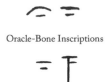

Oracle-Bone Inscriptions

Bronze Inscriptions

Later Seal Character

The character 下, like 上, is also an indicative. In the Oracle-Bone Inscriptions and Bronze Inscriptions, it consists of a short horizontal stroke underneath a longer one (or a convex curve), signifying "underneath." The primary meaning of 下 is, opposite to 上, "the lower," "underneath"; from which has derived its use for things which are lower in rank, worse in quality, or after in sequence or time. Used as a verb, it means "to descend."

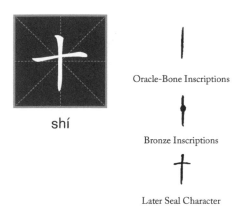

shí

Oracle-Bone Inscriptions

Bronze Inscriptions

Later Seal Character

十 is a numeral, meaning "ten," the unchangeable variant being 拾. In ancient times, people used to calculate through counting objects or tying knots in ropes. When the number was smaller than ten, they would use objects like sticks. For round numbers, they would tie knots in ropes, one knot stood for ten, two for twenty, three for thirty, and so on. In the Bronze Inscriptions, the character 十 consists of a vertical line with a circular dot in the middle (or an enlarged middle part), a vivid description of calculating through knotting.

niàn

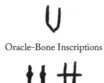

Oracle-Bone Inscriptions

Bronze Inscriptions

Later Seal Character

In the Bronze Inscriptions, the character 廿 looks like a U-shaped rope with two circular dots on the shafts (or two enlarged shafts) standing for knots, signifying "twenty." The *Origin of Chinese Characters* says, "廿 means two tens put together." In the Oracle-Bone Inscriptions, the character has a U-stroke only, there are no circular dots, which are difficult to engrave. In the Later Seal Character, there is a horizontal storke linking the two shafts, which are no longer dotted, losing much of its original picturelike image. In the sense of twenty, 廿 is usually used in classical Chinese, not in the vernacular or the colloquial style. Thus it is used in the lunar calendar, e.g. 廿六年 (the twenty-sixth year), 廿九日 (the twenty-ninth day); but not in the solar calendar, where 二十 would be used in its stead.

sà

Oracle-Bone Inscriptions

Bronze Inscriptions

Later Seal Character

The character 卅 also results from the practice to tie knots in a rope to facilitate counting. In the Bronze Inscriptions, it looks like an almost W-shaped rope with three knots on the shafts, signifying "thirty." For example, the character 卅 in 五卅运动 (the May 30th Movement) refers to the thirtieth day.

ABOUT THE EDITOR

XIE GUANGHUI is a renowned professor in the Fine Arts Department of the Art College of Jinan University. In 1985, he graduated from the Department of Anthropology, Sun Yat-sen University with a Bachelor's Degree in History. In 1988, he graduated from the Chinese Department of Sun Yat-sen University with a Master's Degree in Chinese Language and Literature. He has written many famous monographs, such as *The Great Dictionary of Zhouyi, Illustrations of Commonly Used Chinese Characters, Selected Notes on the Works of China's Top Ten Prose Masters (Volumes 1 and 2), Chinese Character Source Dictionary, Illustrated Chinese Characters, Le Shizhai Book, The Second Edition of Le Shizhai Book and Printing,* and other works.